Finland and National Liberation in Southern Africa

by

Iina Soiri & Pekka Peltola

Nordiska Afrikainstitutet 1999

Indexing terms:
Foreign relations
National liberation movements
Student movements
ANC
SWAPO
Finland
Namibia
South Africa

Cover: Adriaan Honcoop
Language checking: Christine Mann-Löfblom and Elaine Almén

© Iina Soiri, Pekka Peltola and Nordiska Afrikainstitutet 1999

ISBN 91-7106-431-1

Printed in Sweden by Elanders Gotab, Stockholm 1999

Contents

Preface 5

1. **Introduction** 7
1.1. Aims of the study 7
1.2. Finland up until the 1960s 7
1.3. Basic principles in Finnish foreign policy 11
1.4. The role of the civil society 15
1.5. Sources 17

2. **The civil society grows and goes international** 18
2.1. The early birds 18
2.1.1. The Committee of 100 19
2.1.2. Finnish Students' UN Association 23
2.1.3. The South Africa Committee 25
2.2. Students' changing international approach 30
2.2.1. National Union of Students and Students'
       International Assistance 30
2.2.2. Tricont 32
2.3. The first campaign of solidarity with the liberation movement:
     Operation Day's Work, *Taksvärkki* 34
2.4. Travelling solidarity 43
2.4.1. The establishment of the Africa Committee 43
2.5. The "Students and the African Liberation Movement" Conference ... 48
2.6. The visit of Amílcar Cabral 50
2.7. Political parties' international dimension 53

3. **Proclaiming the gospel or politics?** 55
3.1. The Finnish Lutheran Mission in Ovamboland 55
3.2. Taking a stand against racial segregation 60
3.3.. Missionaries face problems in Namibia 61
3.4. Finnchurchaid 64

4. **Finland's foreign policy—do not disturb!** 67
4.1. Finland formulating its position in the world after 1945 69
4.2. A medical doctor, not a judge 71
4.3. The policy change in the UN after 1966 74
4.4. The foreign policy debate in Finland 76
4.5. Support from the official ranks 79
4.5.1. Finland's development aid becomes established 79
4.5.2. Children's parties allow communication with the top 82
4.6. The 'rebel' civil servants 84
4.7. Finland as a member of the UN Security Council 68

4.8.	Outside influence intensifies	87
4.8.1.	The OAU visit to Finland in 1971	87
4.8.2.	Liberation movements approach the Finnish Government	90
4.9.	Winds of change from the field	93
4.9.1.	Chargé d'affaires to Pretoria dismissed	93
4.9.2.	Active Finnish community in Dar es Salaam	95
4.10.	NGO letter to the Foreign Ministry	97
4.11.	Foreign political justifications behind the policy change	99
5.	**Finland supporting liberation struggles**	103
5.1.	The decision of principle in 1973	103
5.2.	The independence of the Portuguese colonies	104
5.3.	NGO aid increases	108
5.4.	Finland's Namibia policy in the UN becomes more active	110
5.5.	The Namibia scholarship programme	113
5.6.	Other cooperation with SWAPO	118
5.7.	Trade unions join in	120
5.8.	Nordic cooperation	122
5.9.	Finnish nationals at the service of Namibia in multinational forums	123
5.10.	SWAPO's internal crisis in 1976	125
5.11.	SWAPO and Finland towards independence	128
5.12.	Zimbabwe/Rhodesia and Finland	134
6.	**South Africa, ANC and the boycott question**	137
6.1.	Joint Nordic programme of action	138
6.2.	Support for ANC and other anti-apartheid organisations	139
6.3.	Pressure for sanctions and the trade ban law	144
6.4.	Towards a democratic South Africa	153
7.	**Conclusion**	155

List of Abbreviations ... 159

Sources and Bibliography ... 171

Appendix 1: Finland's direct support to Namibia and SWAPO ... 177

Appendix 2: Humanitarian assistance to ANC and other anti-apartheid organisations in South Africa ... 178

Appendix 3: Currency conversion table ... 179

Appendix 4: Persons interviewed ... 180

Appendix 5: Interviews ... 181
       Martti Ahtisaari ... 181
       Mikko Juva ... 189
       Janet Mondlane ... 198
       Nickey Iyambo ... 206

Preface

Much has been written on the impact of East-West competition and involvement in Southern Africa. The role of the Nordic countries in shaping recent history in this region has, however, not aroused similar interest—despite the very large contributions made to it both materially and politically by Denmark, Finland, Norway and Sweden. This engagement was not in vain: liberation movements supported by Nordic countries now hold governmental power in their countries.

Finland has figured amongst those nations that supported liberation movements of Southern Africa, because of her role in the Namibian independence process, her contribution to the UN funds for Southern African refugees and victims of apartheid, and—at the end—her direct support to liberation movements, as well as her clearly stated stance against apartheid and colonialism. The part played by Finland and other Nordic countries has, however, scarcely been documented and analysed so far. The end of the era of colonialism and apartheid in Southern Africa now opens up an opportunity to study the subject from different perspectives.

This study is part of a common Nordic research project which documents and analyses the role of the Nordic societies in the struggle against colonialism and apartheid in Southern Africa. This particular study presents Finland's role.

The study is based on extensive archival research as well as interviews in Finland and in the Southern African countries concerned (Angola, Mozambique, Namibia, South Africa and Zimbabwe). Exceptionally, this project has been granted access to the archives of the Foreign Ministry and its department of development cooperation (formerly known as FINNIDA). For this reason, the study has been able to utilise material which has never before been accessible.

The authors are also fortunate to have succeeded in interviewing many of the key persons in this process. We are very grateful to all of them, and we trust that we have used their contributions in an appropriate manner. Our sincere hope is that we have not caused undue offence to any person or cause. This is our interpretation of the processes in Finland and consequently we take full responsibility. In any case, we want to emphasise that all those who have been committed to the struggle against colonialism and apartheid deserve our sincerest appreciation. Particular thanks are due to the President of the Republic of Finland, Mr Martti Ahtisaari, who generously gave of his time and efforts for this study.

This study has been financed from different sources. Special thanks go to the Foreign Ministry of Finland, which, in addition to financial assistance, provided an office and communication facilities for the study. We are also grateful to the University of Lapland and the University of Helsinki for providing employment for Iina Soiri as a postgraduate student in order that she could concentrate on research work. The Nordic Africa Institute assisted with travelling expenses to make it possible to also conduct interviews and archival research in Southern Africa.

Finally, we also wish to express our gratitude to all the archival personnel—especially in the Foreign Ministry's Research Service and at the People's Archives—who, with their professionalism and true interest were able to dig into an endless amount of material to find relevant documents. Without them, we would have been completely lost in the information jungle. Furthermore, we are grateful to Ms Pirjo Virtaintorppa, who transcribed the interviews that we conducted.

The study is written for an international audience and may therefore include some elements and information which are in fact common knowledge to Finnish readers. Conversely, being written by two Finns, it might have taken something for granted without clarification, and we apologise for that, too. Thinking of our audience, we have conducted the interviews in English, with the exception of the one with Mr Risto Kuisma. The language checking of the interviews was kept to an absolute minimum, so as not to harm their authenticity.

The archival research was done by Iina Soiri, who also wrote the first drafts of the manuscript, with Pekka Peltola in a supervisory role. Subsequent writing has been done collectively and both authors are equally responsible for the text. In this connection, we are especially indebted to Raimo Lintonen's detailed criticism and comments.

Helsinki, 4 May, 1998
Pekka Peltola and *Iina Soiri*

Chapter 1
Introduction

1.1. Aims of the study

Africa is very far from Finland. It becomes even more distant when we place ourselves in the reality of Finland in the 1960s. In order to understand the nature of the interaction between Africa and Finland, we must clarify some of the basic conditions and political processes in our own country.

This study covers a period when the cold war dominated international politics. Finland's freedom of movement was influenced and restricted in many ways, not least by the proximity of one of the two major power centres of the world: the Soviet Union. The dynamics of this relationship, which had an impact in Finland's policy towards Southern Africa, must be discussed in this connection, too.

Another relationship, at least of equal importance, is Finland's traditional and cultural closeness to Sweden, Norway and Denmark. This is also an important connection with the West. It was through this connection that Southern Africa rose to the political agenda in Finland, whenever political and economic circumstances allowed it, in the 1960s.

This is a study on how and why Finland supported the Southern African liberation struggle in various ways. The core question is why Finland, together with the other Nordic countries, came to play such an important role—as will be shown later—in legitimising the liberation movements, in looking for solutions to the colonial situation and, finally, in channelling financial and material aid to the movements directly as well as to the victims of colonialism and apartheid via multilateral channels. We are looking at the roles played by successive Finnish governments, established organisations of the civil society such as churches and trade unions, and more ad hoc and loose non-governmental organisations and groups. The objectives of these actors were partly different and did conflict. We have tried to describe and analyse this conflict by simplifying it into two approaches: "realist" and "idealist".

The liberation struggle, in this study, is defined as the popular uprising against colonialism, minority regimes and racism that intensified in Southern African countries from the beginning of the 1960s. We concentrate on those Southern African countries where people formed national liberation movements which, as their major strategy, took up arms against the colonial masters of the day. Those countries are Mozambique, Angola and Guinea-Bissau[1] (Portuguese colonies), Rhodesia/Zimbabwe (a British colony), South Africa and South West Africa/Namibia (controlled by a South African minority regime). The struggle to abolish racial segregation practised by the South African apartheid regime is also included in this study. In each of the countries, nationalist liberation movements[2] were established, which, due to repression at home, had to look for support beyond their own territories. The liberation movements brought their struggle to the knowledge of the international community, and the struggle against the last remnants of colonialism as well as apartheid soon became an internationally recognised issue, especially in the context of the United Nations. This study also tries to touch on the regional context of the struggle, that is, how the other Southern African countries—such as Tanzania and Zambia—had an impact on the regional political setting.

1.2. Finland up until the 1960s

Finland has been an independent country for only 80 years. It achieved its independence in 1917, after centuries of foreign rule. After first being a province of the Swedish Kingdom, Finland's territory was occupied by Russia in the war between these two countries in 1809. Finland became an autonomous province of the Great Russian Empire. It was linguistically and culturally different from Russia, and towards the end of the century this fact contributed to growing nationalist tendencies. Finland was an agrarian country, and the industrial revolution that was developing elsewhere in Europe had not yet started on a larger scale. The country's independence was achieved during a period when Russia was undergoing a socialist revolution. There was a conflict between strongly anti-communist bourgeois political forces and a relatively strong labour movement. After a civil war between these forces—"Whites" and "Reds"—Finland became a Western-style republic, but the polarisation of Finnish society persisted for decades. Until the Second World War, the organisational freedom of the labour movement was limited, and this left traits which persisted well after

---

1. A Portuguese colony in Western Africa. Although not geographically situated in Southern Africa, the struggle in Guinea-Bissau became an important factor in mobilising support against the Portuguese colonial system and popularising the African liberation movements.

2. The following movements were the key organisations: ANC (African National Congress, South Africa), FNLA (*Frente Nacional de Libertação de Angola*, Angolan National Liberation Front), FRELIMO (*Frente de Libertação de Moçambique*, Liberation Front of Mozambique), MPLA (*Movimento Popular de Libertação de Angola*, Angolan Popular Liberation Movement), PAC (Pan-African Congress of South Africa), PAIGC (*Partido Africano de Independência da Guine e Cabo Verde*, African Party of Guine and Cabo Verde), SWANU (South West African National Union), SWAPO (South West African People's Organisation), UNITA (*União National para a Independência Total de Angola*, Union for a Total Independence of Angola), ZANU (Zimbabwe National Union) and ZAPU (Zimbabwe People's Union). There were others, too, but they did not get substantial support.

that. Growing fears in connection with the powerful and socialist Soviet Union, especially among the right-wing groups, brought Finland closer to Germany, to which it has culturally and politically been rather near. Germany had also supported the bourgeois side militarily in the civil war. There was, however, a powerful Social Democratic Party as well as a Communist Party in Finland, and these organised the increasing numbers of the working class, a product of the rapidly advancing industrial development. Fear of the Soviet Union, coupled with the sentiments towards Germany, resulted in Finland allying itself with Nazi Germany during the Second World War.

This alliance almost became fatal to Finland's survival as an independent country. Finland not only lost the war, but also had to give up large areas of its territory to the Soviet Union. Nearly half a million people ended up as internal refugees. War-torn Finland had to look for ways to recover from the damage. Furthermore, it was obliged to pay the war reparations demanded from it by the victorious powers. As a result, Finland recognised her geopolitical realities and started to pursue a policy of good neighbourly relations. The Treaty of Friendship, Cooperation and Assistance between Finland and the Soviet Union (YYA) was made in 1948. The relations between the two countries were characterised as peaceful coexistence. Finland maintained a liberal democracy and mixed economy, and benefited from this, but also became initially more dependent on its economic relations with the Soviet Union. The demand for industrial goods from the huge Soviet market, supplied mainly in return for oil and raw materials brought a welcome boost to the rapidly growing Finnish economy and helped to build a basis for a diversified and more self-reliant economy later on.

If we think of post-war Finland from the 1940s onward, the country and its people had very limited international contacts. The still suspicious Soviet Union did not allow Finland to receive Marshall aid or to join the United Nations. Nordic cooperation was, however, possible, as was membership in the IMF and World Bank. Being a relatively poor country after the war, Finland was still in the 1950s at the receiving end of international development efforts like World Bank loans, UNICEF programmes etc. Its geographical position meant not only that it had a powerful neighbour, which was busy building its socialist camp around Finland; but also that Finland was far away from the European powers, not to mention other continents like Africa. Having been a colony itself until 1917, Finland has not had colonial ambitions; and it has not been a maritime nation like Norway, for example. Direct links with Africa were few. Finland did not necessarily come into political contact with many international questions before she became a member of the UN in 1955.

An attentive public gained its experience of other countries and nations mainly through emigration to Sweden and to the United States, a phenomenon which had already started in the 19th century.[3] Tourism, mass media and inter-

---

3. Although the great majority of the emigrants made their way to North America, South Africa was also one destination. However, as the emigration was very modest at the turn

national trade had not yet reached the scope that they have today, and daily contacts with the outside world were not that common. After the First World War, and especially during the Great Depression in the 1930s, Finnish paper companies had started to look for markets in Africa. This trade—mainly with South Africa—increased after the Second World War, but it never became a significant factor.

There were, however, exceptions. The labour movement in Finland had close international connections almost from the start, albeit mainly with industrial countries. The Red Cross was well organised in Finland early in the 20th century. For this study it is of particular importance that the Lutheran Church of Finland, the country's main religious institution, to which about 90 per cent of the population belongs, had started its missionary activities in the remote area called Ovamboland—or *Ambomaa* as it was known in Finnish—in 1870. That activity, which was extended over the years, became familiar to many Finnish citizens through fund-raising and information activities. Many congregations made donations in kind, and elderly citizens in particular used to take part in those collections. In the schools, *Ambomaa* was a standard example of a colony or an "uncivilised, backward" country, to which the missionaries had been sent to preach the gospel and bring the light of God and civilisation to the heathen. The Finnish Missionary Society (FMS) acted under the regime of the day, with its acceptance, but kept at a distance from the political matters of the colony. It was not until the 1960s that Ambomaa became a foreign policy issue in Finland,[4] because of the organising of people's resistance which was growing rapidly in the area. All in all, the missionary activities have had an important socialising effect in Finnish society, an effect which will be further described in the course of this study.

It was only in the 1960s that Finland started to open its windows to the world at large. The Anglo-Saxon world began to replace Finland's formerly German-dominated contacts in culture, science and education. The new generation, which was not carrying the memories of the Winter War[5] in its collective memory, was freer to adopt new ideas of internationalism, cooperation and solidarity, which were starting to circulate in the world community. In general,

---

of the century (approximately 1000 Finns—depending on the method of calculation—in 1815–1914) and also temporary, it did not contribute a lot to Finns' knowledge of the African continent. See Kuparinen, 1991.

[4]. In the early 1920s, however, a group of individuals proposed that Finland should take Ovamboland under its protection, i.e. as a colony. A representative of the Foreign Ministry took a negative attitude toward the request of that small delegation, and the matter was buried. One has to bear in mind, though, that this system of forming a delegation to demand action from the government is commonly used in connection with all kinds of matters in a democratic country like Finland. A delegation to approach an authority does not in itself indicate that the issue in question is of high priority in Finnish society.

5. Finland's solitary war against Russia, which took place in the winter months of 1939–40. It was followed by another, called the Continuation War, when Finland allied with Germany in trying to reoccupy the territories lost in the Winter War.

the world became smaller, and mass media were reaching more distant corners of the world. The birth of that new political generation in Finland was made possible by the rapid economic development, migration to towns, and the Finnish Government's commitment to opening up formerly elitist institutions such as high schools and universities to lower social strata. In 1966, the leftist political parties had gained a majority in Parliament, thus boosting the building of a society which has become known collectively as the Nordic welfare state.

1.3. Basic principles in Finnish foreign policy

The traditional concept of foreign policy refers to the activities of a state which are directed outside its territory, toward other countries or toward international organisations. In short, it means governments' actions in the international system. It consists of various diplomatic, military, and economic activities, agreements, statements, plans and thoughts.[6] Traditionally, foreign policy is practised by states or their governments, and relies on different premises than domestic policy. In many cases it is, however, very difficult to make a clear distinction between foreign and domestic policy. Especially in Finland, the distinction between the two is often described as a 'line drawn in the water', because they are interlinked political sectors.[7]

In this study, we are interested in the contribution of internal social forces to foreign policy. The different social actors like NGOs, churches and political groups also practise international activities and create their own international relations. This shapes the country's position in the international arena. They, too, are likely to have a say in the official foreign policy decision-making process through different channels, and not without a certain friction. In the case of Finland, we adopt the idea that domestic and foreign policy are heavily interlinked. For the purpose of clarity, when we talk about the foreign policy practised solely by the Finnish state (diplomacy, state visits etc.), it is called official foreign policy. This does not, however, entail the assumption that the decisions on these activities have been made in isolation from the social forces active in the country.

Initially, the Finnish Government's policy towards the national liberation struggle was a side issue and thus not a problem. Later on, in the early 1970s, it became a difficult question internally as well as internationally, because the struggle against colonialism represented conflicting interests of East and West, becoming part of the ideological competition between communism and capitalism. When Finland became a member of United Nations in 1955, international constraints to her policy were relaxed. In keeping with the situation, Finland adopted a policy of non-interference in issues where the interests of major

---

6. Forsberg, 1993:11.
7. Ibid., p. 12.

powers may have conflicted. Another policy line was non-use of force in international matters. This doctrine also emphasised the desire of Finland to take into account the legitimate security interests of the Soviet Union. Finland had good and important relations with the colonial powers of the day and with the Soviet Union, and did not want to interfere with any country's internal affairs. Yet the Finns held a basic sentiment in favour of civil rights. This—in time—supported the growth of public opinion in favour of liberation from racism and colonialism.

In order to understand Finland's position, one must go deeper into the country's foreign policy thinking. Finland wanted to retain her independence and traditional societal order, trying to limit the potentially negative impact of international conflicts and interference in her internal affairs by her great neighbour. The special position of the Soviet Union was instituted by the Pact of Friendship, Cooperation and Mutual Assistance (YYA), concluded in April 1948 between the two countries.

Commonly known as the 'Paasikivi-Kekkonen line'[8] after the Second World War, Finland's foreign policy was described as a policy of neutrality. This policy doctrine was formed after the Second World War by agreeing that relations with the Soviet Union would be handled on a bilateral basis. The Finnish brand of neutrality was of a particular kind, diverging from the classical model of Switzerland. It was a policy, not based on legal instruments, of building relations of trust with members of rival blocs. It was also a cautious and bridge-building model of neutrality. Finland's neutrality was constrained when defined in a traditional legal or political manner. But for Finland, active participation in economic and political East-West cooperation was a means toward strengthening her position. Initially, the Finnish doctrine entailed a rather passive, even isolationist trait, which implied a desire to keep a distance to risky conflicts and—indeed—the Soviet Union. An important interest was also to maintain Finland's traditional relations with the West.

Initially, the first years of independence—when the so-called "White side" gained a victory over the "Reds" in the civil war fought immediately after the independence declaration—left the country polarised according to political and class divisions. As a result of the "White" victory, the constitution accorded a powerful role to the president. Thus, the president is the constitutional leader as regards foreign policy and until Finland joined the European Union the government had a secondary role. Moreover, unlike in many other Western democracies, the role of the parliament in foreign policy decision-making has remained modest. In foreign policy, the decision-making rests with the president, who is also the supreme commander of the Finnish army. There is, however, variation in the presidential uses of prerogatives. Some presidents have wanted and needed more support from the government than others.

---

8. Named after those two presidents of Finland, Juho Kusti Paasikivi (1948–1955) and Urho Kaleva Kekkonen (1956–1981), who created the foundations of Finnish foreign policy after the Second World War.

The role of the president has naturally varied during Finland's history, according to the president in question. Traditionally, in the spirit of *Realpolitik*[9]—political realism—the foreign policy administration has also possessed a high degree of authority in the decision-making process. There has been reliance on decision-making whose main purpose is to maintain the national sovereignty. The Foreign Ministry's authority has been strengthened by the centralised bureaucracy. Foreign policy officials have been chosen from among those most trusted by the president and the government of the day. After the Second World War, Finland's foreign policy became a subject of extreme concern due to its importance to the neighbour who was the other party in the Cold War. The foreign policy was considered so important for the nation that daily domestic policies were not allowed to have a direct influence on it. This placed it as much behind closed doors as it ever has been. The maintenance of a consistent foreign policy line demanded abstention from critical discussion.

In 1956, Dr Urho Kekkonen was elected President of Finland. His strong personality, growing public support and working methods kept the foreign policy decision-making strictly under his control. After his illness, 26 years later in 1982, a new president was chosen from the Social Democratic party, Dr Mauno Koivisto. Despite his very different style compared with his predecessor, Dr Koivisto continued along the lines drawn by those preceding him. He was committed to the line determined by President Kekkonen, although the rapidly changing international situation had a major impact on Finland's foreign policy thinking and reality. Economic alignment with Western Europe was accelerated when the country joined OECD and EFTA as a full member. Major changes were made when the Soviet Union began to disintegrate in the late 1980s. The peace treaty ending the Second World War for Finland's part was unilaterally limited, the YYA-pact was redrawn, and the process towards the European Union began.

The time frame of this study falls mainly within the years of the foreign policy practised by President Kekkonen, who led Finland between 1956–1981. A great deal of research is presently being done on those years in order to reveal the real processes and developments in Finland's relationships with the Soviet Union, and in the President's real intentions, activities and motivations. In fact, the very foundation of Finnish foreign policy is currently under active reassessment. The findings of those studies cannot yet, however, be fully utilised by this study.

The foreign policy during the years under study can be divided according to the following periods: first, the period of confirmation of Finland's neutrality, after she had joined the UN in 1955 and also the Nordic Council in the same year. The Porkkala military base near Helsinki, occupied by the Soviet Union since the war, was also returned to Finland. During this period, in 1961, Dr

---

9. A decision-making tradition which advocates the idea of centralisation in foreign policy decision-making on the grounds of efficiency in diplomacy.

Kekkonen made a significant speech in the UN, where he presented Finland as being rather a medical doctor than a judge, emphasising Finland's neutrality and commitment to negotiated settlements of international disputes. Second, a period of active neutrality started in the mid-1960s, when the warming-up period in international relations allowed a small neutral country to play a more active role in making international initiatives in the UN, in the German question and the CSCE[10] in the early 1970s.

This period of active foreign policy coincided with the time when African questions gained more attention in the international community. The wave of independence of African states brought dozens of new actors to the international scene, especially to the UN. After the CSCE conference, Finland felt more secure in pursuing the policy of active neutrality, looking for ways to carry out a foreign policy which was more independent of the shadow of the Soviet Union, as the situation between the superpowers allowed.

What is important to note is that during the years of the events analysed in this study, there was a general consensus on the main foreign policy principles of Finland, which was shared both by the policy-makers and the general public. That was mainly due to President Kekkonen, who powerfully pursued acceptance for his foreign policy line from all sectors of the society. This support was given.

During the 1950s and the early 1960s there was some debate about the policy line, but it was strictly limited to small leftist or ultra-rightist periodicals.[11] The main newspapers and magazines avoided this debate, often actually discouraging it. Support for research on foreign policy or its alternatives was mainly reserved for those scholars expected to support the existing doctrine. One can speak of some kind of internal censorship, which in some aspects grew stricter during the 1970s. Those who wanted to argue for a policy change were ignored or accused of rocking the boat. It was thus made to appear as if the policy consensus was shared by practically everybody. The 'Paasikivi-Kekkonen' line always formed the basic starting-point for any decision-making in matters concerning both external and internal affairs of the country. The policy implications concerning cooperation with the Soviet Union were not shared by everybody, but the necessity of agreeing with the basic assumption (that is, the geopolitical

---

10. The Conference for Security and Co-operation in Europe, the final communiqué of which was signed in Helsinki by most of the industrialised world leaders, including the presidents of the USA and the Soviet Union, in 1975

11. Social democratically oriented discussion was published in magazines like *Ulkopolitiikka* (Foreign Policy), *Ydin*, some student papers, in the Huutomerkki series of pocket books, and occasionally also in the party paper *Suomen Sosialidemokraatti*. The journals *Tilanne* and *Aikalainen* represented more leftist thinking. Serious efforts to influence Finnish policy towards the Soviet Union, like *Kaksiteräinen miekka* (Two-edged Sword) by Jaakko Blomberg and Pertti Joenniemi, published in 1972, met with official silence. On the far right, Kauko Kare edited the *Nootti* magazine, which specialised in criticising the Soviet Union and President Kekkonen. He also published a number of books on the subject. Kare was kept completely out of the limelight, apart from the fact that some of his books sold very well.

reality) was shared quite widely. This resulted in public consensus. On the sidelines of publicity there was, however, continuing interplay between the sympathetic approach (upheld by the greater part of the leftist groupings) and the critical approach supported by independent leftist groups not fond of the Soviet model of socialism and its superpower attitudes.[12] The greater part of the right wing did not really participate in this discussion, having doubts of their own. The attitude of right-wing Centre party politicians was commonly described as 'friendship with the Soviet Union with one's fist in one's pocket'.

Another common saying was that 'foreign policy is a matter too difficult for the common man to understand and decide about'. The president, the government and the foreign ministry had held a certain authority in the eyes of the general public. This affected even the most critical groups in the society. The officials in the Foreign Ministry, who traditionally came from the wealthy, predominantly conservative stratum, had a strong prerogative to act, because only they were expected to know about the issues. The centralised state administration in Finland has further concentrated the decision-making and excluded the general public from knowing the real intentions and justifications of certain policies.

As we see now, with the perspective of time, the relationship with the Soviet Union has been a kind of a paradox in Finland's foreign policy. Although Soviet influence was not something which could be brought to an end, to minimise this influence had been a major aim of Finland's foreign policy throughout the years.

In addition to the relationship with the Soviet Union, Nordic cooperation has always played a role in Finnish foreign policy. The five Nordic countries, with their national particularities, have pursued similar kinds of policies during recent decades and formed a commonly identifiable group. Due to its neutrality during the Second World War and its consequent uninterrupted industrial and social development, Sweden has in many cases assumed a leading role in the Nordic group. As a former regional power, Sweden has always played a special role in relationship to Finland, her former province. They share the same idea of a mixed economy, as well as a strong commitment to the welfare state. For Finland she has been a role model, a competitor or just a good neighbour, depending on the issue at stake.

However, in foreign policy decision-making, it has always been the case that Finland's policy has relied on different foundations than Sweden's, especially in security policy. Sweden has been the most able to act in international questions, due to her more traditional brand of neutrality. Norway and Denmark have been restricted by their allies, and Finland had its special relationship with the Soviet Union. This has not prevented all these countries from co-operating in

---

12. These included Sadankomitea (the Committee of 100) which conducted a non-aligned campaign against nuclear and other weapons. But among them were also emerging Maoist groups, which later lost membership and support to Stalinist political organisations.

other areas. The common Nordic framework has also proved to be useful in pursuing policies which need more weight behind them, e.g. in the larger international forums like the UN. In the particular question under study, that of liberation movements, the Nordic cooperation and exchange of views proved to be very important.

1.4. The role of the civil society

Keeping this in mind, the study will argue that Finnish involvement in the African liberation struggle was not only a question of the relationship between Finland and Africa. It was an issue which had to be evaluated in the light of the general foreign political framework of Finland. The fact that from the 1970s Finland became one of the main supporters of the liberation cause was a result of particular developments, as well as certain changes in the international community, which allowed the decision-makers to support the liberation movements under the newly formulated line of *active neutral* foreign policy. Supporting the liberation movements and taking a stand for their cause definitely demanded this new formulation. Despite being a relatively small part of Finland's foreign relations, it became an important issue in her foreign policy decision-making with consequences beyond its original magnitude.

The liberation struggle was brought onto the Finnish foreign policy agenda by forces outside the traditional foreign political setting. Popular movements born in the 1960s drew attention to the African situation and demanded that their governments support the poor and oppressed people under colonial rule. The youth and student movements adopted ideas of common solidarity and anti-colonialism. This happened in Finland, too, where the growing NGO sector made the liberation struggle known and mobilised substantial support.

Attention to global affairs coincided with important changes in Finnish society, when the leftist forces gained a greater share of the political power. Their questions concerning foreign policy principles emerged on the scene, with the young and predominantly leftist activists arguing for a more idealistic foreign policy to replace the narrow realist line. The East-West conflict was, however, reflected in the Finnish social movements. A relatively non-aligned student and youth movement was party-politicised throughout by the 1970s. International questions were promoted from the ideological points of view that were also entering domestic policy. The conservative fortresses of the society, the church above all, had to reconsider their international policy. In the end, parts of two generations—divided by the Second World War—found each other, surprisingly, on the same side defending the rights of the oppressed in Africa.

This study will show that there developed a special alliance never seen before in Finnish society, which was able to mobilise a cross-section of the public behind its main ideas regarding Southern Africa and liberation movements. Although individual groups and movements were important in their respective contexts in popularising and mobilising for the liberation struggle, the crucial strength of this cause in the strictly divided world of the 1970s and 1980s depended on the fact that the alliance gathered forces from all walks of life in Finnish society. This alliance—which consisted of groups from right to left, people from all generations, political and unpolitical, educated and working class people—was a reality that the foreign policy decision-makers could not leave unnoticed. The official foreign policy, which originally tended to ignore and even oppose the liberation movements, changed direction. Therefore, the commitment that Finland made towards the liberation struggle was a result of important changes in Finland's foreign policy thinking.

1.5. Sources

The potential research material for this study is very extensive. The time frame covers more than three decades. Dozens of organisations, groups and institutions have been involved, as well as hundreds of individuals. Thus, this is not a comprehensive study on 'everything' in connection with Finland and the liberation movements. This report aims to cover the most important processes and episodes and to identify the main causes and consequences.

This study is based on comprehensive archive research complemented by interviews with 28 persons[13] who have been closely connected with the liberation struggle in one way or another. We are most grateful to have been able to use the archives of Finland's Foreign Ministry. An exceptional research permit has allowed us to study the documents right up to the present. In addition, we have used the People's Archives, where most of the important NGO collections are situated (Tricont, Africa Committee, South Africa Committee, EELAK). The Finnish Missionary Society's Archives in the National Archives, as well as the Secondary Students' School Union's Archives (STL) in the same location, have been studied. A list of the archive material made available for this study—including many personal collections—is included in the last section (Sources).

---

13. See Appendix 3.

Chapter 2
The Civil Society Grows and Goes International

2.1. The early birds

The first Finnish societal activities focusing on the Southern African countries occurred in the 1960s, when growing radicalism appeared among the Finnish youth. Many of the NGOs and informal groupings were set up on the pattern of examples from abroad.

Reflecting their family backgrounds, students represented liberal or conservative tendencies in their activities. Democratisation of education brought pressures against traditionally authoritarian and conservative university structures and the bourgeois hegemony in the flow of information.[14] First, these pressures led to the setting up of the student press at the beginning of the 1960s. *Ylioppilaslehti* (The Student Paper) of Helsinki got a new editor-in-chief Arvo Salo[15], and a cultural and political discussion began on its pages the likes of which had never been seen there before. Ylioppilaslehti was joined by its Swedish language counterpart *Studentbladet*. Soon the discussion included Finland's relationship with the outside world and criticism and demands concerning Finland's position in the international community. Swedish speaking students[16] were first in setting up a short-lived independent peace movement. *Kampanjen för nukleär nedrustning* (Campaign against Nuclear Weapons) was founded in January 1963. It published a book written by Johan von Bonsdorff, Claes Feiring and Pär Stenbäck[17], auguring a new era in Finnish student politics.

---

14. Educational possibilities increased in Finland with the introduction of the unitary comprehensive school system at the end of the 1960s which replaced the former two-tier primary and secondary schools. More young people were also admitted to study at tertiary institutions after completing the matriculation examination. In 1960 there were 25,042 students studying at universities and other tertiary institutions (including universities of technology) out of Finland's population of 4.4 million. By 1974 the number of students had increased to 66,690 (out of the total Finnish population of 4.6 million). *Suomen tilastollinen vuosikirja* (Finland's statistical yearbook), 1973 and 1974.
15. A writer, later a Social Democratic MP and a Minister of Culture.
16. Erik Pakarinen, Lars D. Eriksson, Carl Arne Hartman, Henrik Westman.
17. *Front mot kärnvapen* (Front against Nuclear Weapons), 1963.

2.1.1. The Committee of 100[18]

Soon after both student papers began their new line of approach, another student peace organisation was founded on 6 August 1963 in Helsinki. It was called the Committee of 100, to correspond to the direct action peace movement in Britain, which was supported by Bertrand Russell. In fact, the Finnish version was more like the British Campaign for Nuclear Disarmament, CND, with some moderation and leaning towards peace research and other means to enhance credibility. The Finnish Committee of 100 never restricted itself to opposing nuclear weapons, which Finland did not have and did not imagine that it would get, but engaged itself straightaway in Third World questions. The logic was that injustice anywhere is a threat to world peace.

Led by leftist students,[19] the Committee soon spread to all the university towns. In its heyday 1964–70, it had only a couple of thousand members in Helsinki and a few hundred more in other (university) towns, but its influence on its generation was significant.[20] One must bear in mind, that in spite of the increasing number of university students, they were still a minority amongst the Finnish youth. And the majority of the students were, after all, comfortable with their conservative views. Moreover, in spite of some efforts, this movement could never establish links with working-class people and trade unions, only with their political parties. The closest organisation to the Committee of 100 was the Finnish Students' United Nations Association (UNSA), actually established at a meeting originally called to establish the former. Many of the activists served both organisations at the same time, or alternated in leading positions.

The atmosphere during the early 1960s in Finland can be described as one that broke the ice of a long intellectually stagnant period. After the election of Urho Kekkonen to the presidency of the Republic in 1956, the political hegemony began slowly to shift from conservative, partly far-right forces. These forces, however, still dominated political, scientific and cultural discussion in the press, on radio and television, and in publications. An example of the pre-

---

18. The following account and analysis is based on the reminiscences and archives of Dr Pekka Peltola, who served as the first secretary of the Committee of 100, and later on in the 1960s as its chairman and the editor of *Ydin*. He now serves the Ministry of Labour. A history of the Committee of 100 has been written by Kristiina Hallman: *Tottelisinko?* Vaasa 1983.

19. Persons involved included Kalevi and Helena Suomela, Pekka and Kati Peltola, Ilkka and Vappu Taipale, Pentti Halme, Jaakko Blomberg, Erkki Tuomioja, I.-C. Björklund, Otso Appelqvist, Pentti Järvinen, Johan von Bonsdorff, Marja Kurenniemi, Johannes Pakaslahti and Paavo Lipponen, to mention just a few.

20. Almost all the persons mentioned have later served as MPs (Kati Peltola, Ilkka Taipale, Erkki Tuomioja, I.-C. Björklund, Paavo Lipponen, who is now the Prime Minister of Finland), civil servants (Vappu Taipale former minister, now Director General of a central social institution STAKES; Jaakko Blomberg ,Under Secretary of State leading the political department of the Foreign Ministry; Pakaslahti, former Secretary General of the World Peace Council, now researcher for the European Commission); and in other influential positions.

vailing information culture is the story of the press conference of a representative of the National Liberation Front of Vietnam, Nguyen van Dong, in Helsinki at the end of October 1965. Despite having sent reporters to the occasion, the main Finnish newspapers did not report Dong's visit or his message, which was that the 'viet cong' did not insist on the departure of US-troops from Vietnam as a precondition to negotiations to end the conflict. "We are not interested", commented e.g. *Helsingin Sanomat*, when asked. Through a radio interview, done by Paavo Lipponen, the news spread, however, around the world through *Stockholms-Tidningen*, The Guardian and the press in continental Europe. Still, the Finnish press kept up their silence, commenting the news only through their correspondents abroad and headlining it: "the newsworthiness of Dong's statement is refuted by Washington". [21]

Students opposed all this censorship. It was against the interests of their families as well as their own.

Despite its radical demands (unilateral disarmament, for one), the Committee of 100 was never far from the holders of political power. Non-aligned, quality-conscious analysis and some moderation in action paved the way to contacts. The obvious sympathy shown by President Kekkonen—who desperately needed popular support for his foreign policy—certainly helped, too.

The activists and their periodical *Ydin* (Nucleus), the mouthpiece of the Committee of 100, probably constituted the strongest progressive influence in the minds of students during the years 1963-1968. Established by Ilkka Taipale in 1966, the periodical started to write about Southern Africa from its very first issue onwards. It also started to publish series of analyses produced by the Committee of 100. In 1967, development aid was discussed, and the policies of successive Finnish governments criticised.

> Finland has taken part in international development aid for about six years. Our input, however, is still infinitesimally small both absolutely (FIM 13.4 million) and relatively (0.04 per cent of GNP). Most worrying is, however, that the leaders of foreign policies seem not to have any insight on why we take part in development work. They also lack any vision about developing countries, not to speak of having a plan for action. Fundamentally, the problem of developing countries is both political and economic.[22]

In the statement, a more active policy on Vietnam and against White power in Southern Africa was demanded. A volunteer workers' programme for developing countries was proposed; the Peace Corps of the USA and the Swedish Volunteer Services were mentioned as examples. It was demanded that volun-

---

21. Pekka Peltola: *Mitä meille kerrotaan* (What we are told). *Ylioppilaslehti*, 5 November 1965.
22. "*Kehitysmaat ja kehitysapu/Sadankomitean puheenvuoro*" (Developing Countries and Development Aid/Standpoint of the Committee of 100), by Ilkka Taipale et al. *Ydin* 4/1967.

teer service in the developing countries should be created as an alternative to the compulsory military service. [23]

At the time, solidarity with poor countries was not a popular theme. Not even many young people were in favour of it in 1967–68. According to a poll, among 15–40 year olds 23 per cent were in favour of increasing Finland's minuscule development aid effort, 32 per cent did not know and 45 per cent were against. There was no difference between right and left.[24]

In 1965, the campaign to stop the war in Vietnam was initiated by the Committee of 100. The first demonstration on 16 March 1965, with the moderate slogan "USA to the negotiation table !" only drew 130 placard bearers to the US embassy. There were more police around.

The intellectual nature of the movement is evident. One of the most discussed and influential actions at the time was the publication of another collective article by the Committee of 100, discussing liberation wars.[25] It produced a wave of comments in the media. A teach-in type discussion at the Old Student House drew an audience of a thousand in the hall designed for 500. The idea of the article was to give all-out support to national liberation struggles; and to differentiate between the methods available to people in developing countries for struggling against oppression and those in, for instance, Finland who desire to support them.

> Although we see that in some developing countries violence is often the only alternative to the continuation of oppression, we are faced with the same options. Our task is to support the social and political goals of national liberation struggles: freedom of the people, development of democratic institutions and economic progress. We are most effective by not furthering violence but non-violent means of struggle.[26]

The statement called all NGOs, first of all, to engage in information activities in their own countries, thus creating a public opinion which understood the social and political nature of the situation in the developing countries, and their international connections.

> After having won over the enlightened support of the public, we can expect the political parties and the state to become interested in development questions and to act accordingly.[27]

---

23. Finland started a volunteer programme at the end of the 1960s but it only survived a few years. A new volunteer programme was started by *Kepa* (Service Centre for Development Cooperation), financed one hundred per cent by Finnida in the mid-1980s. It is presently undergoing reassessment.
24. Eino Hosia: "*Maailma vuonna 2000*" (The World in the Year 2000). *Ydin* 4/1968.
25. "*Kansalliset vapaussodat/Sadankomitean puheenvuoro*". (National Liberation Wars/Standpoint of the Committee of 100), by Pekka Peltola and Kalevi Suomela. *Ydin* 7/1967.
26. Ibid.
27. Ibid.

The emphasis was on education and other humanitarian assistance, demanding an immediate government programme to support the NGOs' involvement in development aid.

The statement warned about the probability that an armed struggle would create a model for behaviour after the liberation. Any war itself not only produces a great deal of suffering, but a victory through violence leaves a tendency for violence to remain an everyday tool for new governments, disturbing democratic developments.

Later, in another more concrete article, the development aid budget of the government for the year 1970 was discussed by a young student Paavo Lipponen.[28] He compared the allocations to development aid by Sweden and Finland, and noticed the millions of crowns Sweden gave to FNL of Vietnam, PAIGC, ZANU, ZAPU and the Mozambique Institute, and the probability of support to ANC and MPLA. Finland gave little to the victims of apartheid, and only 62,900 FIM to the UN Fund for Namibia. Having shown the discrepancy, Lipponen demanded a programme for supporting liberation movements in Africa.

> No policy of neutrality can prevent Finland [from giving aid], because this is a question of following the consistent anti-colonial line adopted by the United Nations. Portugal, South Africa and Rhodesia have systematically said no to all compromises and to the help of the UN. A political solution can only be achieved by strengthening African liberation movements in order to create enough pressure on those intransigent governments. In regard to the future of these countries, it is also necessary that after independence and the abolishing of apartheid, they are able to take care of their own affairs. Liberation movements represent wide movements among the people. Future political life can be organised on that basis. The alternative is powerlessness of the people and chaos.[29]

The discussion on Finland's foreign policy continued in other forums throughout the years at the turn of the decade. As we will see later, the credo of the Committee of 100's statement was to become the essence of Finland's development aid policies, especially in relation to liberation movements, albeit that parts of it only became reality much later. Volunteer service to Africa only started for real in the 1980s. The same can be said of Lipponen's analysis. From the perspective of the 1990s, even the warning against militarism after liberation has been shown to be quite realistic, when thinking of Vietnam, among others.

In its heyday, the Committee of 100 was thus only partly a pacifist organisation, but also consciously a political movement that could unite students from the left to the liberals. This was possible, because of the non-aligned credo of the movement, which criticised the security policies both of East and West. This was cemented as a result of an internal struggle between ultra-leftist (later Stalinist) and more moderate views in 1969–70. In a rapidly escalating

---

28. Paavo Lipponen: *"Ulkopolitiikan kukoistus ja koetus"* (The Flourishing and Testing of Foreign Policy). *Ydin* 5/1970.
29. Ibid.

ideological conflict between East and West, Finnish NGOs took sides, mostly Soviet, the Committee of 100 being an exception.

That was something neither the Soviets nor the Americans ever forgave. Neither did those political forces in Finland most closely allied to the two superpowers, the Conservatives and the Stalinist minority fraction of the Communist Party. Consequently, the Committee of 100 was never invited to join any of the innumerable peace delegations to the Soviet Union, nor approached by any other means. Americans made contact in order to get information, especially during the early Vietnam war period, but were apparently frustrated in their efforts to gain influence. The Soviet Union operated through the Finnish branch of the World Peace Council, the Finnish Peace Committee, with which the Committee of 100 could not establish effective cooperation, exactly because of WPC's unquestioning support of Soviet policies. In the African questions, too, differences were experienced, as we will see later.

The leaders of the Committee of 100 wrote the first Finnish articles and books which discussed development aid and apartheid, and also organised the first demonstrations against the Vietnam war. The same people took initiatives to establish other social movements like Women's Liberation (*Society 9*, by Kati Peltola), Homeless Alcoholics (*November Movement*, by Ilkka Taipale), and Third World (*Tricont*, by Johan von Bonsdorff). The activities of Tricont will be presented later in this chapter. The 1960s were a productive era, when various "one-issue movements", as they were known in accordance with their deliberately limited scope of interest, were started and run. Later on, the demonstrations against the Vietnam war grew, children's day care centres freed women to take full-time jobs, and social security covered ever larger sectors of society. The Third World and its liberation appeared on the agenda, too.

2.1.2. Finnish Students' United Nations Association (UNSA)

Suomen Opiskelijoiden YK-liike (UNSA as an English acronym) was established in the spring of 1963 mainly by social democratic students,[30] for supporting the United Nations and for activating Finland's policy in the world organisation. The idea came straight from Sweden. From the very beginning, UNSA took up the problem of apartheid and organised well-attended meetings to find ways of opposing it. UNSA popularised the UN policy and reflected the points of view of the Southern world in Finland. It may be said that UNSA brought the North-South global conflict to Finnish attention. UNSA kept abreast of Finnish UN policy and monitored the country's commitment to UN declarations and decisions. The special campaigns of the UN were celebrated. The working style of UNSA was during its first years rather factual and reformist, and relied on

---

30. Pekka Autti, J.v. Bonsdorff, Jorma Kalela, Jaakko Kalela, Paavo Lipponen, Klaus Mäkelä and Pekka Korvenheimo, the first chairman. Other activists were Lauri Hannikainen, Aira Kalela, Ilkka Ristimäki, Juha Kuusi, Mai Palmberg and Pentti Halme.

using established paths of influence.[31] In this it differed from its more popular sister organisation, the Committee of 100, which was more idealist and radical in its activities.

In 1965 UNSA had spread to several towns and formed a national union. Under its chairman Paavo Lipponen and general secretary Jaakko Kalela,[32] UNSA began to really pressurise the government into adopting a more active policy against apartheid. Osmo Apunen, Pekka Autti and Kari Möttölä wrote in favour of the Third World in general.[33] An important argument was the fact that Finland's reserved policy in the UN diverged from that of other Nordic countries. This was the message that UNSA delivered to foreign minister Ahti Karjalainen in December 1965. The following year, UNSA was the breeding ground for an initiative called New Foreign Policy. In essence, the New Foreign Policy demanded a more active foreign policy not only against apartheid but also for peace, conflict resolution and disarmament. It was widely discussed in the student press, and some inroads to the wider public were opened. A large teach-in on New Foreign Policy took place at the University of Helsinki, and a radio programme on it reached a wide audience. Apparently this publicity went too far, however. Paavo Lipponen comments: "Kekkonen saw the discussion as a threat. It went to the area of the YYA pact."[34]

During 1967 and 1968 UNSA became more and more radical. It began to participate in demonstrations, for instance against the war in Vietnam. In October 1968, UNSA organised a march to Parliament under the slogan: 'Support to liberation movements of Southern Africa'. Under the leadership of Nils Torvalds and Liisa Manninen,[35] the society took the step from supporting national liberation movements toward a more general anti-imperialist policy line.

In 1969 the new chairman Börje Mattsson and vice-chairman Mikko Lohikoski were elected to lead the organisation. For them it was especially important that UNSA had financial means, being supported by the Ministry of Education.

> We had this UN Student Association. And that one was a real student organisation, which worked among the students and had a very established position among the students in Finland. It was very accepted because in these first days and first months the only one that had any money was the UN Student Organisation,

---

31. The account of UNSA is largely based on Hurskainen, 1988.

32. Jaakko Kalela has served presidents Kekkonen and Koivisto as a foreign policy adviser. He is now the general secretary at the office of president Martti Ahtisaari. His brother Jorma is now a professor of political history. Klaus Mäkelä is a well-known sociologist, Pekka Korvenheimo an ambassador. Johan von Bonsdorff, like Mai Palmberg, is a writer. Osmo Apunen is a professor of international politics.

33. Pekka Autti & Osmo Apunen, 1965. Interestingly, the publisher was Suomen Teiniliitto (Finland's Teen Union, STL).

34. Hurskainen, ibid., interview with Paavo Lipponen, 30.3.1988.

35. Both are now TV journalists working for the Finnish Broadcasting Company, Liisa Liimatainen (Manninen) based in Italy and Nils Torvalds in Moscow.

because we got money directly from the Ministry of Education. And that was the first student body that took really radical standpoints and that was a nation-wide organisation. We had groups at least in all university towns.[36]

But Mattsson and Lohikoski led the organisation into an impasse. In a seminar in November 1969 the Finnish Students' United Nations Association accepted a proclamation stating 'The United Nations does not represent the world's people and there is no reason to have faith in it'. Having thus turned against its own premises, the organisation began to fade away, having already lost half of its 2,000 members in 1969.

2.1.3. The South Africa Committee

The first NGO concentrating fully on the Southern African question was one of the new 'one-issue movements', namely the South Africa Committee. Because it was the first one with this purpose, even though small, quite a number of pages will be devoted to it here.

In Spring 1965, some students and representatives of various youth and students' organisations came together to discuss forming a special committee to deal with the questions concerning South Africa. It was decided that a South Africa Committee would be established on 29 April 1965. Although the Committee survived only three years, it set up a basis for other organisations to come.

The Committee was formed following the examples of other countries, where there were already organised activities against South Africa and apartheid—among others, the big British Anti-Apartheid Movement (AAM). It aimed at bringing together those opinions which the youth in the country had formed on the question of South Africa.

In the process of forming the Committee, there were two competing ideas, mainly whether to form a South Africa Committee or an anti-apartheid movement. In the first year of the Committee's existence the discussion was still centring around this question. In any case, the committee decided in the first place to concentrate geographically on the Republic of South Africa, because there the violations of human rights were most severe.[37]

The Committee took the form of an alliance, which was joined by several already existing political and non-political youth and student organisations. Individuals were also allowed to join as members. The committee was politically very representative, because it drew members from the whole political spectrum. The chairman was a well-known journalist, Erkki Hatakka,[38] the

---

36. Interview with Börje Mattsson, 29.2.1996.
37. Report of the South Africa Committee, date unknown. Foreign Ministry's Archives.
38. He worked on current affairs programmes of the Finnish Broadcasting Company, later becoming a head of department. He is also an active Social Democratic politician at municipal level.

secretary a young student, Kati Peltola.[39] The Committee first decided to concentrate on information and aid work. Boycott questions were also on the agenda.[40]

The Committee's first encounter with the authorities involved in Finnish foreign policy happened when it applied for registration to the Ministry of Justice, which keeps the register of associations in Finland. The Ministry of Justice referred the matter to the Foreign Ministry, because it was unclear whether the Committee's constitution was in accordance with Finnish foreign policy. After a consultation with the Ministry, it recommended that the Committee reformulate some of its aims, namely those which favoured resorting to actions to weaken the apartheid regime in South Africa. Otherwise, there was a danger that the Committee might violate the principle of non-interference. Finland had, after all, recognised the South African government and could not allow its citizens to violate diplomatic relations.[41] Ironically, the violation of diplomatic relations was the very intention of the Committee. It is unclear whether there was a reformulation, and if so, what kind; but in any case the Committee could continue its activities according to its original objectives.

In its report on information work, the preparatory group suggested among other things that materials and films etc. should be ordered from ANC. But ANC was not the primary reference group. A more important partner, at least in the beginning, seems to have been IDAF, the International Defence and Aid Fund—based in Great Britain—as well as Nordic anti-apartheid organisations. Accordingly, the Committee was humanitarian in its approach. It was mainly concerned about the victims of apartheid, their legal aid, and support to their families, which were precisely the tasks IDAF was fulfilling.[42]

International contacts provided more information and a power base for the Committee's activities. Its representatives Pär Stenbäck[43] and Niilo Wälläri (chairperson and a powerful figure in the Seamen's Union) participated in the South West Africa Conference on 1 April 1966. The Committee also received guests from South Africa and IDAF.

It also relied on the idea of a consumer boycott. It decided to contact wholesale dealers as well as the trade union movement concerning the boycott question. According to the Committee's report, the trade union movement in

---

39. An activist who later became an MP for the leftist Finnish People's Democratic League, a city councillor and the head of social services for the city of Helsinki.

40. Report of the preparatory group 21.4.1965. People's Archives.

41. Letter 12/3676 K 1965 from the Foreign Ministry to the Registration Office in the Ministry of Justice, 1.12.1965. Foreign Ministry's Archives.

42. Report on activities 1965–66. South Africa Committee. People's Archives.

43. His humanitarian activities continued when he joined the Red Cross, first as the Secretary General of the Finnish Red Cross in 1985–88, whereafter he served the International Federation of the Red Cross and Red Crescent Societies in 1988–1992, before returning to the Finnish Red Cross of which he is currently the President. He was the Chairman of the Swedish People's Party and also an MP during 1970–1985, the Minister of Foreign Affairs in 1980–81 and later Minister of Education.

Finland was very sympathetic to the boycott idea.[44] Especially the Seamen's Union, which had already started its unilateral boycott action against South African shipments in 1963, co-operated closely with the Committee. Its chairperson, Niilo Wälläri, took the initiative to establish a separate boycott body among the individual trade unions. The Boycott Committee was established in spring 1966, after which the South Africa Committee decided to concentrate on information, lobbying and fund-raising work.

The Committee organised several meetings and events where South African issues were discussed, often together with representatives from South Africa or South West Africa/Namibia. For example, the SWAPO representative Nickey Iyambo (who had studied in Finland since 1964) and SWAPO's information secretary Andreas Shipanga gave a lecture on the situation in South West Africa/Namibia. The biggest event was organised at the end of 1966, when a special Anti-apartheid Week was held, with eight different activities.

In 1966, the advocacy work became more important. The Finnish Government had already voted in favour of many UN Resolutions to condemn apartheid. The Security Council had terminated the South African mandate in Namibia in 1966. In line with the criticism of the time carried on by the active discussants of foreign policy (e.g. in *Ydin* and *Ylioppilaslehti*), the South Africa Committee used those international agreements as a basis for pressuring the Finnish Government into practising a more active foreign policy in regard to the South African question. At its annual meeting in May 1966 the Committee decided to send a petition to the newly formed Finnish Government urging it to adopt a more active policy toward South Africa. The petition called on the Finnish Government, together with the other Nordic countries, to promote the cause more actively in the UN as well as to support the legal defence and families of those who were accused under the apartheid laws. In addition, the Government was urged to organise scholarships for the young people from South West Africa.[45]

This petition was soon followed by another letter which, in addition, called on the Finnish Government to decrease its trade with South Africa.[46] The letter was a result of a meeting with the SWAPO representatives Nickey Iyambo, Andreas Shipanga and Emil Appolus. The representatives of the Committee also organised a meeting with interested parliamentarians to raise more interest toward the Southern African question.

The South Africa Committee had also initially planned to start supporting the South African and Namibian peoples' organisations financially. The Committee was approached by the SWANU representatives in Stockholm requesting financial support for their participation in the UN General

---

44. Report of the South Africa Committee, date unknown. People's Archives.

45. Statement of the Annual Meeting of the South Africa Committee 27.5.1966. People's Archives.

46. Press release by the South Africa Committee 18.8.1966. People's Archives.

Assembly's Special Session on South West Africa in 1966. The Committee promised to donate 1000 FIM. In order to raise the money, the Committee invited all the Finnish political parties to give donations for that purpose. This first-ever fund raising campaign was not a great success. Only the Communist Party (SKP), the Democratic League (SKDL) and the Swedish People's Party (RKP) contributed, the rest had to be collected from individuals.[47]

This did not, however, discourage the Committee, which in autumn 1967 opened a special 'Solidarity Account' to raise funds for the national liberation movements. The main recipient was SWAPO, but it was planned that FRELIMO would also get funds at later stage. SWAPO was supported because it had an immediate need of funds to defend the 37 accused, led by Herman Toivo ya Toivo, who were arrested on charges of terrorism. SWAPO's armed struggle had begun the previous year. An important reason for choosing SWAPO as a recipient was the fact that Finland had a student from SWAPO, Nickey Iyambo, who was an active promoter of his cause.

In its annual report of 1967–68, the Committee could happily note that the Finnish Government had for the first time reserved funds in the budget to support the UN Funds for victims of apartheid. The Government had also, on its own initiative, criticised the illegal trial of South West African citizens in Pretoria. The Committee's cooperation with the liberation movements had increased during the year, when ANC representatives Joe Matthews and Robert Resha led a public discussion evening organised by the Committee.[48] In that connection, for the first time, ANC also applied for financial assistance from the Finnish Government. The Foreign Ministry did not react to the application in any way.[49]

The Committee reorganised its work by establishing a separate national branch of IDAF in Finland. The creation of this brought together many prominent members of society from the older generation, such as Prof. Kustaa Wilkuna, Mr Niilo Hämäläinen (the president of the Central Union of the Finnish Trade Unions, SAK), Rev. Juhani Simojoki, Prof. Mikko Juva (chairperson of the Finnish Missionary Society), Ms Hilkka Pietilä (UN Association) and Mr Jörn Donner (a well-known cultural figure).[50] It was a clear sign that the South African apartheid question was attracting wider concern and was no longer purely an object of youth interest.

The work of the Boycott Committee, on the other hand, did not proceed after the death of its founder, Niilo Wälläri. The Solidarity Account had received donations to a total value of 1250 FIM, which was sent to SWAPO in Dar es Salaam.

---

47. Annual Report 1966. South Africa Committee. People's Archives.
48. Annual Report 1967–68. South Africa Committee. People's Archives.
49. Foreign Ministry's Archives.
50. Donner has been a politician and parliamentarian in several parties, and is now a social democratic Member of the European Parliament.

Despite the South Africa Committee's achievements, some weaknesses in organisation and overworking on the part of some Committee activists started to take its toll. From the beginning, the Committee had suffered from the fact that all its activists were representatives of other active organisations, who could not fully concentrate on the Committee's work. The Committee was continuously aware of this and several times urged its member organisations to resolve the matter, which reflected the still rather narrow basis of this kind of activism in Finland. In spring 1968, the Committee attempted to organise a special meeting to change its constitution.[51] But as a final sign of the loss of interest and change of priorities in the member organisations, that special meeting never took place. The Committee's work died a natural death. As a result, the newly started IDAF never really got off the ground before the late 1980s, when it was re-established by some newer anti-apartheid activists.

To sum up, the South Africa Committee was the first attempt to form an organisation concentrating particularly on questions concerning South (and Southern) Africa, including apartheid and colonialism in the area. Its short but intense history shows that there was a need for it. And its death did not mean that those questions were no longer of interest in Finland. Similar activities were continued in other forums.

The Committee's death and the birth of others was merely a sign of the times. During the 1960s, Finnish society saw a rise in activism never experienced before. While this had not yet spread very widely, the same few persons were active in various issues. Solidarity and peace were on the agenda of many groups and organisations.

In the history of these movements, the year 1968 was crucial. Culminating in the spectacular occupation of the Old Student House, a new era began.[52] Party politics took over the hearts of students and new divisions emerged, especially within the Left. Briefly Maoist, but soon Stalinist ideologies were to overrun universities and cultural societies in the early 1970s. These were linked with the Soviet-supported minority faction of the Finnish Communist Party, but the influence of these ideologies was also strongly felt within Social Democratic youth organisations, and even in the young political Centre. Internationally, the occupation of Czechoslovakia in that same year divided the youth and solidarity movement into those who condemned the occupation (e.g. the Committee of 100) and those who supported the Soviet Union's policy (e.g. the Finnish Peace Committee).

Movements concentrating on one issue fell into the background as the much more popular radical political movements stepped in. But these hardly lasted a decade. In the latter half of the 1970s students began to turn green. The 1980s were already the decade of the Greens. Now, lively discussion on social

---

51. Letter from the board of the South Africa Committee to the member organisations, 2.3.1968. People's Archives.
52. See e.g. Bonsdorff (1986), where the event is more profoundly described.

questions was carried on throughout society, also in the mainstream media, and included the question of who ultimately decides about Finland's foreign policy and, more fundamentally, on what grounds. The activity against apartheid and on behalf of the national liberation continued within the new organisational frameworks.

2.2. Students' changing international approach

2.2.1. National Union of Students (SYL) and Students' International Assistance (YKA)

Historically, students in Finland have been well organised in their own educational institutions. Membership of a local students' union has been obligatory for them by statute, and the unions have a varying capacity for organising socio-economic benefits (housing, cheap meals, health care etc.) for their members, as well as political activities. The biggest and wealthiest of the students' unions is Helsinki University Students' Union, HYY, which has often played a leading role in introducing the political ideas of the time. [53]

Since the 1940s, the students of the tertiary educational institutions in Finland had organised themselves in the individual students' unions, under the common umbrella of the National Union of Students (SYL). The Union had always been very international in its approach, international cooperation being one of the very reasons for its establishment. Many of the individual student unions (with the exception of HYY) did not have resources to practise international activities and thus delegated them to SYL. SYL participated in the formation of the International Union of Students (IUS) after the Second World War. The aims of the IUS included action for peace, democracy and anti-fascism, but it could be considered a Soviet front organisation. Thus, the Cold War brought division into student circles, too. The IUS belonged to the Socialist camp, and the Western Unions established another short-lived international organisation called the International Students' Conference (ISC). Soon SYL resigned from both organisations.

Thereafter, at the end of the 1960s, SYL was actively looking for other ways of international cooperation. Nordic cooperation was one channel. Joint meetings were held, and areas of interest identified. Another international activity was to take part in the scholarship programmes for students from the developing countries. SYL also developed its bilateral relations with the foreign student organisations. Visiting delegations were received, e.g. from South West Africa and Zimbabwe in 1969. In the bilateral negotiations, humanitarian and solidarity questions were discussed and statements drawn up.[54]

---

53. For a more detailed history of the Finnish students' organisations see Laura Kolbe's studies on HYY, 1993 and 1996.
54. See the history of SYL in Sundbäck, 1991:91–93.

In the framework of SYL, but as an independent organisation, the Finnish students had formed a branch of the World University Service (WUS) called Students' International Assistance (YKA) in 1961. Its main activity was to provide scholarships to students from the poorer countries. Voluntary contributions were collected from the students for development cooperation. For historical reasons, YKA was formed as a separate body alongside SYL, individual student organisations and some other smaller student associations. YKA had, for a time, its office in the same premises as SYL. Its activities were transferred to SYL in 1968, because it was at that time actually run mainly by SYL activists. So YKA, too, was short-lived but had a marked effect on Finnish support to the liberation movements as well as development cooperation as a whole. Activists and later development aid officials such as Jaakko Iloniemi, Martti Ahtisaari, and Kari Karanko[55] started their international career in YKA.

It was YKA that received Nickey Iyambo from South West Africa/ Namibia as a scholarship student. This first representative of the Southern African national liberation movements to reside in Finland was an active member of SWAPO, and he came to the country in autumn 1964.

> My reason for going to Finland was actually to study. That was reason number one. Two, I also had a responsibility given to me by SWAPO of Namibia to mobilise and inform the people in the Nordic countries in general and Finland in particular about life in Namibia, particularly the political life when it comes to the position of the black majority in this country.[56]

Nickey Iyambo's role in preparing the ground for Finnish attitudes towards liberation movements and especially SWAPO cannot be overestimated. But Mr Iyambo did much more than that: he was instrumental in starting many concrete programmes and projects on behalf of Namibia and SWAPO, as well as bringing more organisations to join the solidarity front for the liberation struggle. He took first a Master of Political Science degree in three years, and thereafter became a Doctor of Medicine. He also turned around many Finns' attitudes concerning Africans and served as an example for inviting other students to the country.

For Nickey Iyambo, a natural way to start the mobilisation work was among the students. Furthermore, the 1960s proved a specially active decade among Finnish youth, and many were willing to take an active part in the foreign activities formerly considered the work of diplomats only. Finland's relationship with South West Africa/Namibia already existed thanks to missionary work, but Nickey Iyambo was the first to spread the message of SWAPO. His arrival in Finland also signalled a change in the policy of SYL, which wanted to gear its international activity more toward solidarity and political involvement.

---

55. They will all be introduced in the course of the study.
56. Interview with Dr Nickey Iyambo, presently the Minister of Local Government and Housing of Namibia, 20.8.1996.

The new generation of students became active in matters concerning solidarity and international affairs. During the 1960s, the international work of SYL increased considerably. Organisations concentrating particularly on questions of solidarity with areas outside Europe were established, such as the South Africa Committee. The next step was Tricont, an organisation to disseminate information about Third World countries, in 1968.

2.2.2. Tricont

A special association called Tricont (= Tricontinental) discussing colonialism and the national liberation movements in territories outside Europe had been established in 1968. It grew from the study group of the Committee of 100 and was organised into an independent association because of the huge interest that the questions generated within the Committee. In the backgrounds of its activists one could see the influence of Swedish discussion as represented for instance in the writings of *Häften för kritiska studier* and *Kommentar*. Tricont cooperated with the other organisations interested in the same matters, but concentrated mainly on publishing and information work. Many of the classic Finnish publications concerning the national liberation movements and the struggle against colonialism were initiated by Tricont.[57] Tricont was more an intellectual organisation than a popular mass-based movement for practical solidarity work. With the benefit of hindsight we may say that it was crucial in preparing public opinion on the support campaigns to come.

Tricont was also an important breeding ground for development studies, which began to attract more, albeit quite modest, interest among the students. Dependency theory, theories of underdevelopment, Andre Gunder Frank, Franz Fanon, and other new directions in Third World studies gave new understanding of the structural problems in the developing countries. Another organisation, called Intercont, was established among students of geography, and study groups were set up. By the early 1970s, development studies had been introduced to the University of Helsinki, with the help of some established academics. Persons who had acquired theoretical education in development studies abroad and practical experience in developing countries joined in. The Institute of Development Studies at the University of Helsinki, established in 1969, grew on that foundation, hosting many radicals from the 1960s.

Activists in Tricont operated inside SYL as well. SYL's own development policy had until then consisted mainly of giving support to students from developing countries. In 1969 the old so-called 'deacon approach' (i.e. relief aid

---

57. Tricont published e.g. the following reports and publications: *Sosialismi Tansaniassa* 1, 2 (Socialism in Tanzania); Mattsson: *Opinto-ohjelma eteläisestä Afrikasta* (Study material on Southern Africa); Mondlane, Eduardo: *Mosambikin taistelu* (The Struggle of Mozambique). It also published a periodical called *Tricont Journal*. Many Tricont activists had their studies and pamhplets included in a new publication series produced by the publisher Tammi, called *Huutomerkki* (Exclamation Mark). Its editorial board comprised many activists of the time.

with no political aims attached or structural changes demanded) was reformed and SYL approved a new programme of development policy, which pursued a more politically active policy toward colonialism and the national liberation struggle. This so-called *Riistoraportti* ('Oppression Report') was for a long time considered to be the first Finnish presentation of modern thinking on development cooperation.[58]

In 1969, SYL took a decision to establish a system of collecting voluntary donations from its donors. '*Vapaaehtoinen Kehitysyhteistyömaksu*' ('the Voluntary Development Cooperation fee') modelled on YKA's fee, formed a basis for SYL's development cooperation. Lobbying, fund-raising and material assistance were defined as main activities in its development cooperation. Many events were organised together with other like-minded organisations.[59]

The standpoints of the different political youth and student organisations were, of course, reflected in the framework of SYL. The Students' Union board members are elected annually, and different groupings can nominate their candidates. The youth organisations of the different political parties in Finland have played a varying role in the process down the years. During the 1960s, the student movement was not necessarily attached to any political party as such, but it was a movement inspired by international ideas urging more active participation in political and social affairs.

At the end of the decade, the political parties of the left attracted young people to their ranks by allowing them to bring their radical ideas inside the party structures. The relatively independent student radicalism, or its spearhead, was co-opted into the parties' decision-making structures. The new ideas were channelled through the parties, and global solidarity became part of their programmes and policy, especially on the leftist side of the party structure. In the 1970s elections, many young radicals entered Parliament from the Social Democratic Party's list, becoming actual practisers of power. Fewer managed to do the same from the lists of the Finnish Peoples' Democratic League and the Swedish Peoples' Party.[60]

This was naturally reflected in the student organisations, where the leftist parties attained an ideological hegemony. It has been said that what students are today, society will be tomorrow. In that respect, SYL was a discussion forum where political ideas were debated and tested among the leaders of youth organisations of different parties.

---

58. Sundbäck, 1991:93–94.

59. Ibid.

60. One who did was Pär Stenbäck who also became Chairman of the party, and later Minister of Foreign Affairs.

2.3. The first campaign of solidarity with the liberation movement: Operation Day's Work, *Taksvärkki*

Another important student organisation in Finland was *Suomen Teiniliitto*, STL (Finland's Teen Union) along with its Swedish equivalent FSS (*Finlands svenska skolungdomsförbund*; Finnish Swedish Pupils' Union). They organised students at the secondary level of the comprehensive school and in the upper secondary schools.[61] The organisations focused their attention on the quality of education, on students' social questions as well as the school and learning environment. STL worked in close cooperation with its Nordic sister organisations.

The students' interests brought forward were not limited to those concerned with school. Many social questions arose. In the active 1960s, younger students were also imbued with the new social and international ideas that were emerging. In 1967, STL and FSS organised their first ever solidarity campaign. The idea was that the pupils of different schools could by their own work, help people in the developing countries. The *Taksvärkki* (Operation Day's Work) Campaign was started.

The origin of the idea, like the word *Taksvärkki* itself, came from Sweden, were '*Operation Dagsverk*' had already been organised before. Finnish students joined the Nordic campaign and adopted the same kind of fund-raising methods, as well as the target group for the fund-raising: the Inca Indians in Peru. The aim was to collect money to develop social and educational work among the Inca people in Peru.[62] The method of collecting money was simple: students were granted a general day off from school, during which they worked in any private or public institution, or a company, for a fixed salary (10 FIM). That money was then deposited in the fund-raising account.

The first *Taksvärkki* in 1967 was a success. The money collected amounted to nearly 600,000 FIM. Most schools and students participated. Encouraged by the first campaign, STL decided to organise another one soon afterwards in 1969. The decision was made by the Autumn Federal Assembly of STL in 1968, which at the same time approved its programme for international cooperation. In line with SYL, there was a need to renew the international thinking of the STL. The new *Taksvärkki* was to be held in the spirit of the new programme, which emphasised support for people still under colonial rule. Their struggle to change social structures on the way to development towards social and economic equality was to be supported in accordance with the Resolutions of

---

61. School attendance is compulsory in Finland up to the age of 16. During this time pupils go to primary schools and secondary schools. In the early 1970s a new comprehensive school system was gradually introduced in Finland. After the comprehensive school pupils can continue in different vocational schools or upper secondary schools, the latter culminating in the matriculation examination. STL mobilised pupils in all schools and at all levels.

62. The campaign newsletter, *Taksvärkki* 1967. Archives of the STL.

the UN. The other objective of the new policy was to provide opportunities for the members to take part in international development cooperation.[63]

The secretariat of STL started to prepare suitable projects for *Taksvärkki*. The project was to contain educational elements. In addition, its administration would not have to be too difficult for an organisation which was not primarily a development organisation, but a student body with limited capacity and experience. Two projects were identified: a literacy campaign in Tanzania run by UNESCO, and the Mozambique Institute in Dar es Salaam.

The idea of supporting the Mozambique Institute (MI) emerged in late 1968 during the visit of its director, Ms Janet Mondlane, to Sweden, where some of the STL activists met her. The Institute, which was founded in 1963 in Dar es Salaam to support the growing number of refugees fleeing Mozambique, was actively looking for funds overseas. The Swedish International Development Authority, SIDA, was financing some of its activities, and the Swedish Secondary School Students' Organisation (SECO) was also planning to adopt the MI as a campaign target.

> Anyway, the first real contact in Sweden was with the Secondary Students' Union, the School Union.[64] They were going to have a work day as they always did. And marvel of marvels, they adopted the Mozambique Institute. And I think probably that's how Finland began to get involved in this, as there was an alliance among those Secondary School students. It turned out that all the Secondary School Unions finally adopted the Mozambique Institute as their Day of Work.[65]

Supporting the Mozambique Institute was not a clear-cut decision, either within STL or in society at large. In 1966 Finland had voted in favour of UN Resolutions condemning the colonial policy and supporting the right to independence, but prior to the 1970s the Government had made it clear that Finland's role was not to support the liberation movements. Neither had any other organisation in Finland supported the liberation movements on such a large scale. But the activists of *Taksvärkki*'s international section were more in favour of supporting the MI than the conservative and secure UNESCO campaign. The decision as to the target group was to be made at the Spring Federal Assembly, but the preparations for the MI campaign were well on the way earlier.

> We have been discussing a lot about our plan to collect money among the secondary school students and our possibilities to send it to you to the Mozambique Institute. But the problem is that the public opinion wants a concrete project, where our possibilities to control how the money is used come through. We plan that we (the union for Finnish Secondary School Students and the Union for Swedish Secondary School Students and then the union from Sweden SECO) have a chance to get in about 500,000 FIM from Finland and about 800,000 SEK from

---

63. The Programme for International Action 1968. Archives of the STL.
64. Ms Mondlane is referring to Finland's Teen Union. It was occasionally called Secondary Schools' Students' Union or Secondary School Union in English translation. We use the abbreviation STL for clarity.
65. Interview with Janet Mondlane, 18.7.1996

Sweden. These sums are of course only calculations, so it would be good if Mozambique Institute could put up some plans from which it would be possible to take off about 200,000 FIM or to which we would be able to add an equal sum. Waiting for a quick answer.[66]

The main concern of the STL—in respect to Finnish public opinion—was about the legal status of the MI and its ability to secure the use of funds for those activities that were agreed on together. In the background, of course, there was its relationship to FRELIMO, which was waging an armed struggle against Portugal in Mozambique. The opinion of the public was quite clearly against supporting any violent activities, even though they could sympathise with the refugee problem. That was also in line with the official foreign policy. Also in the youth movement itself, there was a lively debate centring on the question of whether armed struggle and other violent means were justified methods. As the matter was so delicate, would it not be better to go around it, if possible? In that respect, the MI seemed to provide a secure option for Finnish students to support.

> The MI was founded separately from FRELIMO. It was not legally a part of FRELIMO. We had our own legal constitution. We had our own Board of Trustees. I was the Director. And we can say yes, the MI served FRELIMO as much that it helped to educate refugees. Also the fact that the director of the MI was the wife of the president of FRELIMO always counts for something. But if one really tracks down to see how it developed, one could see that of course there was a very strong link with FRELIMO, but really we developed separately. That was the excuse the Nordic countries used to say that they were not involved with a terrorist organisation. They were involved with a refugee school, people who were working with refugees and then later on with the social services because MI didn't stay as a school, it expanded tremendously and even went to the liberated areas of Mozambique. And we were organising the social services of FRELIMO without saying we were FRELIMO. So when the MI went to Sweden and Norway and Finland and Denmark, it was going as a separate branch of FRELIMO.[67]

Naturally, there were groups in Finland, as well as in STL itself, that did not support the African issue at all, or did not believe in its importance in relation to the other aims STL was to pursue. They said that STL should rather help the suffering people in their own country, e.g. the war veterans. Both groups, the radicals and the conservatives, were working to persuade more followers to support their standpoints while the Spring Assembly was approaching. To justify the project, some of the activists asked for advice and public support from Finnchurchaid, which had already donated 99,000 FIM to the Mozambique Institute via the Lutheran World Federation.[68] This was to prove

---

66. A letter to Janet Mondlane on April 1, 1969 from Camilla von Bonsdorff of STL. Archives of the STL.
67. Interview with Janet Mondlane, 18.7.1996.
68. Interview with Yrjö Höysniemi, 11.10.1995.

that a traditional institution like the church was also able to support the Institute.

The Assembly in May solved the question by voting: 121 representatives voted for the MI, against 108 in favour of the UNESCO project. As a result of their defeat, 60 representatives left the meeting hall in protest.[69] The Assembly set up the National Committee for *Taksvärkki-69*, which was the highest organ administering the campaign. The secretary for the Committee was Ms Camilla von Bonsdorff. Among the most active members was Mr Erkki Liikanen,[70] who later that year became the campaign secretary.

When the Committee was busy setting up the campaign, more problems soon arose. The president of FRELIMO, Eduardo Mondlane, was assassinated. The international propaganda war broke out again, also reaching Finland. The STL became more aware of the risks of the project. The leadership of FRELIMO and of the MI was under speculation. The students got a glimpse of the reality of the colonial war.

Fortunately, the personal loss and increased work load of Ms Janet Mondlane did not, however, cause her to be ousted from her position and prevent her from continuing the preparations for *Taksvärkki-69*. In the negotiations with Janet Mondlane, STL decided to raise funds for a printing press, its setting-up costs and running expenses for one year (approximately 100,000 FIM), hospital equipment and medicines and a library.[71] The MI was in great need of a printing press to produce material for its educational programmes.

> The evolution of that printing press, the justification I made, was to make textbooks. And we made the first textbooks of FRELIMO really, for FRELIMO schools. So those Finnish students were really involved in the first educational programmes of an independent Mozambique.[72]

The *Taksvärkki* Campaign had two different but interlinked aims: to disseminate information in order to create and deepen discussion on the Third World, and to collect money to assist people in the Third World. In this particular campaign, the first aim became ever more important. There was a severe lack of awareness of the situation in the colonies and the nature of the liberation struggle.

For that reason, special attention was given to the information work. There were training courses for representatives of different schools, and films and booklets were produced. Before *Taksvärkki-69* there were three specific press

---

69. *Ylä-Vuoksi* (local press), 10.5.1969.
70. Mr Erkki Liikanen was a student of political science, active in the Social Democratic Party. He was elected as an MP in 1972 and served in Parliament until 1990. He was also the party secretary of the SDP as well as Minister for Finance. Presently he is the first Finnish Commissioner in the European Union.
71. Minutes of the meeting 6.7.1969, *Taksvärkki-69* Committee. Archives of the STL.
72. Interview with Janet Mondlane, 18.7.1996.

conferences. Radio and TV were regularly informed too. In addition to the church, different Finnish organisations in favour of the liberation struggle were mobilised to support the campaign. The UN Association of Finland expressed its opinion that while the Government did not support the liberation movements, private individuals and organisations should.[73] It urged its member organisations to donate money to *Taksvärkki*, to arrange work for pupils, and to encourage young members to participate. The UN Association was instrumental in disseminating information on the UN policies concerning the Mozambican issue.

The most important work was naturally done in the schools.

> I remember I had to go speak to schools, representatives of schools, I had to go to public meetings organised by them. The idea of these students was that this is what we are doing today, but it will have a very long term effect not only on the attitudes of the students as they grow, but on their parents, because the students and their parents are so linked with ideas. If students are working hard on a project, of course their parents are going to get involved. If not physically involved, at least they are going to get intellectually involved. So I think it made a big impact on the Finnish political and social scene.[74]

Discussions on the campaign's legitimacy in respect of the Finnish foreign policy continued all the time. By then even though Finland supported the African peoples' right to self-determination, she had stated over and over again that it was not her policy to support liberation movements. But under pressure from the radical NGOs, a policy was beginning to emerge, whereby the free citizens' groups could support the victims of colonialism and apartheid, as long as it did not require any government involvement.

But to silence the heavy criticism coming from the right of the political spectrum,[75] general statements and Janet Mondlane's persuasion seemed not to be enough. In consequence, STL asked the opinion of the Foreign Ministry as to whether the Campaign violated the main principles of the Finnish foreign policy. After a careful assessment, the Foreign Ministry responded that the campaign was not in contradiction with the policy of neutrality. The fund-raising was in line with the policy of Finland, which aimed to relieve conflicts in the Third World.[76]

This *Taksvärkki* aroused a lot of discussion. Unfortunately, the discussion did not develop into a very deep one. However, hopefully the discussion during the

---

73. UN Association, Circular Letter 6/1969, signed by Ms Hilkka Pietilä, a long standing Secretary General of the UN Association. Archives of the STL.

74. Interview with Ms Janet Mondlane 18.7.1996.

75. A group of school unions, led mainly by the Conservative Party youth activists, planned to resign from STL, though this was also due to other political reasons. *Taksvärkki-69* was an example of the radical leftist policy of STL and was thus opposed. Newspapers close to the Conservative Party—*Uusi Suomi* and *Aamulehti*—were very vocal in criticising STL. Archives of the STL and University Library, press microfilms.

76. *Uusi Suomi*, daily newspaper, 10.10.1969.

fund-raising could lessen the emotional attitudes of the Finnish people towards underdeveloped countries and their problems. The result of the fund-raising was satisfactory—in fact more than satisfactory, taking into account the exceptionality of the target group. It was, after all, the first large-scale fund-raising campaign for people who were still fighting for their independence.[77]

The Committee worked hard on the organisational and practical arrangements. A special sponsorship agreement was made with the Post Bank of Finland, which paid for all the administrative costs. The *Taksvärkki* Day was on 15th October.

The official result of the fund-raising was 449,630.95 FIM. 434 Finnish schools and 44 Swedish schools with altogether 75,000 pupils participated in the campaign.[78] The money was a little less than expected. Therefore the *Taksvärkki-69* Committee decided to donate all the funds for the printing press, or more ambitiously, for setting up a publishing house.

The use of the money collected was another impressive story indeed. The *Taksvärkki-69* Committee had received a plan for the publishing house from Jorge Rebelo, the information secretary of FRELIMO, whose office was situated in the MI. After consulting some of the local Finns in Dar es Salaam[79] about the plan, one participant in Finland's newly started volunteer programme, Kid Ahlfors, a professional publisher, came to help. He designed another, more realistic plan for a publishing house together with Erkki Liikanen, who visited Dar es Salaam and the MI in January 1970. Later that spring Ahlfors was appointed as a technical assistant by STL to establish the printing press at the MI.

The process was slow and difficult, because most of the materials were not available in Tanzania and a lot of technical decisions and arrangements had to be made.[80] The publishing house was finally set up by the end of 1970, and the first books to be produced were 'The History of Mozambique' for the primary and secondary schools. After STL's funds were consumed, a Norwegian agency decided to continue to finance the publishing work.

Taksvärkki-69 was a unique story. It was the first project of its kind unifying large sectors of Finnish society behind a project supporting the not so well known liberation struggle. Furthermore, the practical arrangements—the campaign itself, the information work, the setting up of the publishing house, etc.—

---

77. Internal evaluation report of *Taksvärkki-69*, 25.2.1970. Archives of the STL.

78. In 1969 the population of compulsory school age was 729,046 (out of which 686,932 received education). There were 5,221 primary schools and 661 secondary schools in Finland. (*Suomen tilastollinen vuosikirja* (Finland's statistical yearbook) 1973 and 1974.)

79. Finland had a volunteer programme in Tanzania during those years, and it had an Embassy in Dar es Salaam. Persons like Kirsti Anttila, Henrik Westman and his wife Johanna were consulted. Archives of the STL.

80. Situation Reports by Kid Ahlfors, correspondence between Ms Janet Mondlane and Mr Erkki Liikanen 1970–1971. Archives of the STL.

constituted an enormous task for a small, non-professional student organisation.

Finland's contribution was noted with gratitude by FRELIMO. In 1971 Kid Ahlfors visited the province of Cabo Delgado. His visit was reported, with a photo, in FRELIMO's publication *A Voz da Revolucão*. In the text, it was mentioned that he was working in Dar es Salaam to install the printing press which was donated by the Finnish students.[81] Interestingly, the publication itself had improved considerably the same year, from a type-written leaflet to a printed publication made in Dar es Salaam, thanks to the *Taksvärkki* printing press.

> The most important thing that Finland did was to give the printing press to the MI. ... That printing press did a lot of things. ... And certainly we were the first liberation movement with a printing press, if we can say it was a liberation movement's printing press. In fact, it put out a lot more than just MI text books. It was the printing press that printed the magazine "Moçambique Revolution", which was an international magazine. FRELIMO really did very well on the international arena. I hope that the Nordic countries today realise what a contribution they made in that sense. It was a tremendous contribution. And they [the students] were the only ones that made it.[82]

In the late 1960s, Finland's *Taksvärkki* was of great value as an attitude forming campaign. There was an idea of backward countries and an image of simple and violent people, in whose wars Finns did not want to get involved. Then came a white, American lady, the widow of the president of FRELIMO, who talked about the injustices and inhuman conditions people had to suffer in the colonies. And promoted the idea of a just and free society, that the liberation movement was pursuing.

> One had to talk about the situation as I used to do. The situation in Mozambique, the situation in the struggle. What we were trying to do to solve it. Of course it appeals to the emotions of the people even if they hadn't thought of it before. But for one to get over the emotional effect, you have to appeal to them also intellectually, otherwise it doesn't stick. That's where the secondary school students were good, because although they were caught up in a sense of an emotional side, they were also very intelligent. Those that I dealt with. And I admired them a lot.[83]

Precisely because of the attitude campaign *Taksvärkki-69* did not stop at that, at the schools. *Taksvärkki-69* was an example for many other social groups to follow. It prepared the ground. The International Solidarity Foundation, for example, a Third World arm of the Social Democratic Party, was established the following year, in 1970.

> [I remember] Finland with Erkki Liikanen, and his group. He was very active. ... He certainly was very influential, had many inroads in government. And I remember

---

81. *A Voz da Revolucão*, No 4, Setembro de 1971, Arquivo Histórico de Moçambique, Maputo.
82. Interview with Janet Mondlane, 18.7.1996.
83. Ibid.

he was the one that organised the appointments for me in the government with parliamentarians and so on. And I suspect that's where all this began. And the secondary school students were very active. I was so impressed with the students, how mature they were.[84]

In those years, strong winds of change were blowing in Finnish political life. The left was gaining considerable victories in politics and Erkki Liikanen and his colleagues—Erkki Tuomioja[85] among others—were elected to Parliament, becoming vocal advocates of the liberation movements. There were visits to and from the Mozambique Institute and a lot of information work was carried out. The success of these—and some other—radicals of the SDP, the biggest parliamentary group, was remarkable, especially because Dr Mauno Koivisto formed another social democratically led government.[86] Encouraged, the students decided to arrange another *Taksvärkki* in 1971.

For the above reasons—changing public attitudes and growing influence of the leftist parties in politics—*Taksvärkki-71* was politically and practically much easier to organise. STL was keen to adopt a target group from another Portuguese colony. But the preconditions—strict control of the money and complete financial reports on the funds donated—acted in favour of the MI.

Once again Erkki Liikanen travelled to Dar es Salaam, in May 1971, and another project was outlined together with Janet Mondlane: to support schools in the liberated areas, in the 'interior', as it was called, in Mozambique. The MI was running about a hundred village schools in the regions of Cabo Delgado, Niassa and Tete, which were under FRELIMO's control. *Taksvärkki-71* was to collect money to equip the schools with educational and other materials and to assist with the running costs of the 10 schools for one year.[87] The *Taksvärkki -71* Committee was established, and its key activists were the chairperson Satu Hassi[88] and the secretary Folke Sundman.[89] This time the Nordic students' organisations had different target groups, but the common campaign theme was people in the Portuguese colonies. The students of the vocational schools in Finland joined *Taksvärkki* for the first time.

---

84. Ibid.

85. Dr Erkki Tuomioja, an activist, who as early as 1969 edited a book on South Africa, served in Parliament during the period 1970–1979 before becoming the Deputy Mayor of Helsinki. He was the chief editor of *Ydin* for many years in the 1970s and 1980s. He made a comeback to Parliament in 1991 and is presently the leader of the Social Democratic group in Parliament.

86. Letters to Jorge Rebello 6.4.1970 and Janet Mondlane 22.7.1970 from Erkki Liikanen. Archives of the STL.

87. Minutes of the meeting 23.6.1971, *Taksvärkki-71* Committee. Archives of the STL.

88. Later a civil engineer and an MP, and chairperson of the Green Union, a party in the Government of Finland since 1995.

89. A young activist of the Social Democratic Party. At present the director of the Service Centre for Development Co-operation in Finland (KEPA), an umbrella organisation for NGOs in development and solidarity work.

In the information work, several organisations joined forces. The Africa Committee (see below) had been established by Börje Mattsson and Mikko Lohikoski at the beginning of the year, and planned to organise an Africa Week in the autumn. Training seminars were organised together. The FRELIMO representative in Cairo (who was contact person for Europe), Armando Panguene, stayed in Finland from 26 September to 20 October 1971 together with Kid Ahlfors to help with the fund-raising. They toured schools and other institutions to spread information about Mozambique. This time there was a successful project to present, the functioning printing press, to prove that the money collected would be used for the right purpose.

The day of work was again 10 October, and fund-raising continued until the end of the year. *Taksvärkki-71* was expected to collect more funds than the earlier one, and it succeeded. Around 100,000 pupils participated, collecting 775,000 FIM.[90] Janet Mondlane visited Finland in March 1972 to negotiate about the use of the money raised. Her programme was busy and full of meetings with new organisations who had joined the front supporting the liberation struggle. This time she could also urge support from the Finnish Government. Negotiations on direct aid were well on the way.[91] She was very pleased with her visit.

After these two *Taksvärkki* Campaigns, the idea spread to other organisations as well. The interest was directed elsewhere in the world, because there were other burning issues emerging. Vietnam and Chile were supported in 1972 and 1974. The Southern African question gained attention again in 1978, when a wide ranging *Taksvärkki-78* Committee was established, with 23 member organisations.[92]

> Not many countries had done an operation *Taksvärkki* for a liberation movement before Finland did in 1969 for the MI and 1978 for ANC and SWAPO. That to me was very important, because it was saying: let us organise and mobilise our national will to assist these people, who were supposed to be "terrorists" and "communists". For the country to take that decision was phenomenal at the time. And Finland did it again, for the second time, together with all the Nordic countries in 1985. Altogether around $2.5 million was raised for the ANC school in Tanzania. That was significant.[93]

The *Taksvärkki* Campaign succeeded in acquiring not only materials and long-lasting machinery (the printing press is still functioning in Maputo,

---

90. In 1971 the population of compulsory school age was 709,609. There were 331,946 students in general secondary schools. Those were the schools were STL was most active in campaigning for Taksvärkki. *Suomen tilastollinen vuosikirja* (Finland's statistical yearbook) 1973 and 1974.
91. *Kansan Uutiset*, daily newspaper, 23.3.1972.
92. Archives of the STL 1972–78.
93. Interview with Lindiwe Mabuza 14.10.1996. She was the ANC representative in the Nordic Countries, based in Stockholm 1978–1987. Presently South African Ambassador to Bonn, Germany.

Mozambique) but also human friendship. The letters from Janet Mondlane show the warm relationship between the key activists in STL and the MI and the irony with which the common enemy was often referred to:

> The enemy is always throwing me out of my position. They want to eliminate me like my husband Eduardo Mondlane. According to the Western press, I should have been killed so many times. But here I am until defeated. This time (however worried by the reports of the press) you did not send a cable, but a normal letter. You are learning. Yours, Janet. [94]

2.4. Travelling solidarity

Teiniliitto and SYL were very important bodies of growing Southern Africa support. There were however many others: long-established ones that became interested in the struggle and joined the ranks or newcomers that were particularly devoted to the liberation cause.

Although we in this study have chosen to present the activities mainly in the organisational context, this is done only for the purpose of facilitating understanding and clarity. Once and for all, most importantly, one should keep in mind that however important the organisational context is, more important still is the general atmosphere of the time. People and organisations were very flexible at that time: the ideas and tasks even when similar were always implemented in the particular context which proved to be the most expedient and efficient for the issue in question. The same people were co-operating freely with many bodies, joining hands, helping each other and airing ideas. The idea of supporting the liberation struggle was a common cause which unified many, even surprisingly different, social groups. Despite the ideological struggle which entered into the spirit of the Cold War, the support for the liberation struggle did not suffer from that detrimentally. Instead, the overpoliticisation of some youth organisations, notably *Teiniliitto*, led to their demise only a few years later.

The 1960s and 1970s were a period of generation change. For many, the struggle became a very personal experience. Many of the key activists will appear in the following pages as interviewees, telling their very personal motivation for joining the struggle, and thus complementing the extensive archival material.

2.4.1. *The establishment of the Africa Committee*

Through the Finnish Students' UN Association (UNSA), many student leaders had another horizon to the events in the South. It offered opportunities to travel and meet activists from other countries. Members of UNSA participated in

---

94. Letter to Erkki Liikanen from Janet Mondlane 11.3.1970. Archives of the STL.

international meetings, where they met leaders of the liberation movements. In 1969 the chairperson of the UN Association, Börje Mattsson,[95] went to Uganda to attend the first ISMUN (International Students' Movement for UN) international conference in Africa with another board member, Mikko Lohikoski.[96] In Uganda, Mattsson and Lohikoski met—among others—Agostinho Neto of MPLA, who invited them to visit the Angolan war front. They also visited Tanzania and Zambia and met e.g. Samora Machel and Sam Nujoma, leaders of FRELIMO and SWAPO respectively.

At a time when Southern Africa was not high on the agenda in Finnish foreign policy, the press was not overly interested in reporting on the local events there. Reports reflected mainly the viewpoints of the colonialists. And, as is commonly said, a Finn must always see with his own eyes before he believes. Mattsson relates:

> When I worked in Tricont with these Africa questions and in the UN Student Association, I just felt that there is so much going wrong in the world, something very wrong between the rich countries and the poor countries. And on a more intellectual basis and on an emotional basis we took a standpoint for the liberation movements. But we had no facts really at all. Only facts that you could read in some books or the liberation movements' own publications. But again, to be honest, it was clear that when the liberation movements publish some material, it is their material and still we did not know for sure.
>
> So it came to me at least, very powerfully; I have to see it myself. I have to go there myself to really know am I right or wrong? Is this a right struggle or not? And then when I went there, I could feel that any ideas I had, I could see I was right, I was even more right than I had even thought myself. That the liberation struggle was really a right struggle, it was a human struggle. So that's why it also made a very deep impression, because you had thought about the things yourself and now you went there to see if you were right or not, and you could see it was OK.[97]

Consequently, Mattsson and Lohikoski continued their travels in June 1970 to Rome, where a solidarity conference on behalf of the Portuguese colonies was held. With limited resources and by hitch-hiking, they travelled further to Addis Abeba, Ethiopia, in September and participated in the OAU conference, and went again to Lusaka to observe a conference of the Non-Aligned Countries in September. The two friends returned to Dar es Salaam in October, where they got the idea of establishing a special political organisation to support the liberation struggle, which had made such a big impression on these

---

95. A student of journalism and the founder of the Africa Committee, who worked for more than two decades in the Africa campaigns and other peace and solidarity action for the Finnish Peace Committee. He is presently a refugee counsellor.

96. A student and freelance journalist, who worked for the Finnish Peace Committee until he became the first information secretary for the Service Centre for Development Co-operation (KEPA) in 1985. After KEPA he worked for a few years in the European Council's Programme against Racism as a media officer in Strasbourg.

97. Interview with Börje Mattsson, 29.2.1996.

two travellers. Their personal and political motivation was later a driving force behind many campaigns on behalf of liberation movements.[98]

A cable message from Mattsson and Lohikoski about the idea of a new organisation received a positive response in Finland. As a result of the campaigns and information work so far, the time was ripe to establish a new organisation to specifically support the liberation struggle in Africa. The Africa Committee was founded on December 11, 1970. The main focus of the Committee was to awaken public opinion to oppose colonialism, and also through practical support to promote the end of colonial rule. Timo Ristimäki[99] was elected as chairperson; the other candidate was Erkki Liikanen. Many activists of Tricont and STL were present at the meeting: Camilla von Bonsdorff, Mikko Pyhälä, Johannes Pakaslahti, Kristina Vanajas, to mention just a few.[100] Marja-Liisa Kiljunen served as secretary for a while, before departing to England, where she and her husband Kimmo Kiljunen went to take a course in development studies.[101]

Ironically, neither one of the 'founding fathers' was present at the first meeting, as they were still on the road. Or rather, in the bush, because they had finally had a chance to visit the liberated areas of Angola with MPLA:

> It may be too strong to say that this [the visit to the liberated areas] changed my life, but it in any case influenced me very strongly, because until then we had been in Africa before and we had met the guerrillas and so on. But on that trip, we got the concrete experience of what this struggle was. And we could see that indeed the guerrillas were the nicest men you could think of. On our trip there were real hardships. The circumstances were extremely difficult. I learned that, let's say, the normal picture of an African and especially a wild African terrorist was so completely untrue. Instead, you could find the nicest men, but still having to wage a bloody struggle. And the other thing was to see the situation of the civilian population. The situation in the whole of Eastern Angola was extremely difficult, and none of the propaganda from the Portuguese had any facts in it. You could see that the only one that kept up even some type of normal civilian life was MPLA. So it made a very strong impression that you could see the complete difference between

---

98. Later—in the 1980s—they wanted to close UNSA and concentrate all activities to the Finnish Peace Council.

99. He left the Committee soon afterwards. He was succeeded by Eino S. Repo, a well-known journalist and a former Chief of Radio at the Finnish Broadcasting Company.

100. Minutes of the founding meeting of the Africa Committee 11.12.1970. Camilla von Bonsdorff was secretary of *Taksvärkki*. Kristina Vanajas was translator. For Mikko Pyhälä, see note 104 below. SRP Collection. People's Archives.

101. They later directed their attention particularly to Namibia, and published one of the first studies in Finnish (an English edition followed soon afterwards) on the Namibian question, based on their field work on Namibian territory: *Namibia—the Last Colony*, 1980/1981. Kimmo Kiljunen continued his work as a researcher later becoming Director of the Institute of Development Studies. He was also one of the leading members of EELAK (see Chapter 6). He is presently a Social Democrat MP. Marja-Liisa joined the Department for Development Co-operation, where she returned after serving the Finnish UN Association and UNDP.

the normal Western propaganda in the newspapers and the actual life of the real people and how they behaved and how they spoke and so on.[102]

The Africa Committee was a political advocacy organisation. It was set up as an independent body, but was affiliated to the Finnish Peace Committee (SRP). SRP had already been established in 1949 as a national organisation of the World Peace Council. The reason for joining under the umbrella of SRP was, according to Mattsson, the fact that SRP was not a pacifist organisation like the other Finnish peace organisations, the Committee of 100 or the Finnish Peace Union. The Committee of 100 had included Tricont under its wing, but an organisation accepting the idea of a just war, the liberation struggle, could not fit in there.[103]

The Committee of 100 did, though, adopt another viewpoint. By then, after a long debate, it had accepted and politically supported the liberation struggle just as Mattsson and Lohikoski did. However, the Committee of 100 did not want to align itself with the Soviet Union, or any other power, in its activities. SRP was also clearly a front organisation not only of the Soviet Union, but also of the Stalinist minority faction of the Finnish Communist Party, in this area allying itself mainly with the Centre Party. Thus the Committee of 100 kept at a distance from SRP. Furthermore, the Committee of 100 was locked in conflict over Finland's defence policy and conscientious objection, which consumed its energies but did not produce any noticeable immediate success. This led to a demise of the organisation for the next decade, although it never faded out completely like UNSA, but recovered in the 1980s.

Here, at the birth of the Africa Committee, the first signs of ideological divisions among the Africa activists can be found. By joining the Peace Committee the Africa Committee became inextricably locked in the arms of the minority faction of the Communist Party of Finland. It gradually came to be run almost completely by interests directed from party politics, of the Centre and the far left. Not that the socialist ideology in its Soviet version was not accepted by many of its activists, on the contrary. In any case, their foremost interest was in the struggle for African independence. In that respect, the socialist ideas seemed more productive and formed the principal guidelines of many liberation movements themselves. In a world divided by the Cold War it was quite a challenge to pursue any political aims without allying with either one of the camps, as the Committee of 100 did. Consequently, the Finnish left split into fractions, which had its impact on everybody who was involved in it.

The Africa Committee was in full action soon after its establishment. It started to edit a newsletter, which was published inside the SRP publication *Rauhan Puolesta* (For Peace). It approached all the liberation movements to establish official contacts with them, acquired information material, and informed them of its existence as their support organisation. It organised

---

102. Interview with Börje Mattsson, 29.2.1996.
103. Ibid.

several visits to Finland by representatives of the liberation movements during which public meetings and seminars were held. Representatives of AAPSO, OAU, MPLA (Antonio Neto), ANC (Alex La Guma), PAIGC (Onesimo Silveira), and FRELIMO (Armando Panguene, Oscar Monteiro) were hosted during the initial years. However, the most important event to be organised was the official visit of the president of PAIGC, Amílcar Cabral. Before we come to that we will present another important event, which took place a little earlier.

The above-mentioned activists of the Africa Committee (Mattsson, Lohikoski, Vanajas) together with Mikko Pyhälä were also the architects behind the new policy line of SYL, the National Union of Students. Mikko Pyhälä[104] was the secretary for higher education of SYL and had been specially interested in the developments in Guinea-Bissau and Cap Verde, where the PAIGC was waging a war against the Portuguese regime. He had a chance to visit the liberated areas of Guinea-Bissau in December 1970 in the delegation of IUS.

Guinea-Bissau was geographically and culturally, if possible, even more distant from Finland than any Southern African country. It was a small Portuguese colony and not near to any areas formerly known to be of interest to anybody in Finland. But because of its liberation struggle, which was personified in its talented leader, Amílcar Cabral, it had already attracted a lot of attention. It was believed that Portuguese rule was at its weakest in Guinea-Bissau, where the liberation movement had occupied large territories and gained a substantial following. PAIGC had also started to develop the areas under its control.

For that reason, Mikko Pyhälä's trip to Guinea-Bissau generated a lot of interest in Finland. He gave interviews, and his film material was used to make a documentary, which was broadcast on Finnish TV. He wrote an exciting travel report for one of the popular family magazines, *Apu*.[105] His travel reports from Africa were supplemented by Mattsson and Lohikoski. The leading national daily newspaper, *Helsingin Sanomat*, reported on their visit to Angola in a detailed article on the war situation.[106]

Without this information activity the public opinion would hardly have been prepared for the shift in foreign policy that was to come.

---

104. A young student, who soon afterwards became an official in the Foreign Ministry, as one of the radicals in the ranks. He is now Finnish ambassador to Lima, Peru.
105. Foreign Ministry's Archives and personal archives of Mikko Pyhälä.
106. *Helsingin Sanomat* 21.1.1971. Travel reports were also published by student papers, e.g. *Teinilehti* 3/71 (Teen Magazine), *Studentbladet* 2/71, *Ylioppilaslehti* 5/71 (Student News) and another daily, *Päivän Sanomat* 12.3.1971 (Daily News). SRP Collection. People's Archives.

2.5. The "Students and the African Liberation Movement" Conference

Although SYL (The National Union of Students) had resigned from membership of IUS (the international student body), it had developed a relationship with the organisation on a project basis, especially concerning Third World questions. SYL and IUS decided to organise a conference on liberation movements in 1971. The general framework for all of them was the announcement of the UN to dedicate the year 1971 to the struggle against racial discrimination.[107] The experiences and contacts of Mattsson, Lohikoski and Pyhälä were efficiently exploited, contributing to existing IUS links with the liberation movements. SYL and IUS, which were the main organisers, joined hands with other student and youth bodies and held a five-day seminar on 14–18 February 1971 attended in by the representatives of the student movements of 60 countries, as well as six liberation movements (ANC, FRELIMO, MPLA, PAIGC, SWAPO and ZAPU). In addition to this "Students and Liberation Movements" conference, there was another open event, organised in the Old Student House on 15 February, which attracted a large audience. All the liberation movement representatives were present to introduce the situation in Africa and to promote their causes.[108]

> And there was another seminar also, that was organised together with Helsinki University Students in the Old Student House that got much more publicity than SYL's one; because SYL's conference was more a closed seminar for student politicians, but this other seminar was an open one for people from all walks of life. And the main hall in Vanha was full of people, and it was a big event. I feel that one had great importance: because that meeting made a very public decision that our aim is to see that Finland will support the liberation movement. So that was more of a public start.[109]

In addition simultaneously all over the country, during the whole of February, several events were arranged to draw attention to the problems in colonial Africa. Furthermore, SYL published a special booklet with travel reports by Mattsson, Lohikoski and Pyhälä which was distributed widely.[110] Encouraged by the positive response to its activities SYL decided to start fund-raising for PAIGC in the academic year 1971–72.[111]

---

107. Press release of SYL 14.1.1971, and the Final Communiqué of the Conference 22.2.1971. Foreign Ministry's Archives.

108. Full presentations of the liberation movement representatives were published by, for example, *Kansan Uutiset* 21.2.1971. Personal collections of Kimmo Pulkkinen.

109. Interview with Börje Mattsson, 29.2.1996.

110. Lohikoski, Mikko and Mattsson, Börje: "*Raportti Afrikan vapautusliikkeistä*" (Report on the African Liberation Movements) 3.11.1970. Unpublished report. SYL published an edited version of the report in its conference papers with many photographs, as well as Mikko Pyhälä's report. SRP Collection. People's Archives.

111. SYL Archives.

The publicity already generated by the travel reports and the visits of the liberation movement leaders further increased when SYL came into an open conflict with the Foreign Ministry. One of the background factors to holding the conference in Finland, was to produce increasing pressure against the Finnish Government to change its policy towards liberation movements. As emphasised at the conference that policy was considered old-fashioned and thus ought to be changed.

Concrete proof of that policy was given when the government decided not to fund the conference arrangements. SYL had decided to ask for financial support from the state for organising the conference. The system of co-financing the NGOs' development activities did not yet exist, but financial support had been granted for some organisations' information and campaign work on an ad hoc basis. That is why SYL also believed that it would qualify for assistance. In SYL's case, the response from the ministry was very surprising:

> When SYL asked for financial support for the conference, the Foreign Ministry sent a very surprising note saying that violent activities of organisations should not be supported with taxpayers' money. When you read the letter, it gave the impression that SYL would have been involved in violent activities. It was drafted in such a funny way.[112]

According to the statement, Finland, bound by the principles of international law and the Charter of the UN, could not support groupings which used violent means. Their information and conference activity were not to be financed by state funds.[113]

The hard-line decision of the Foreign Ministry was an obvious mistake. It gave the conference organisers an additional weapon against the conservative policy of the Government, which was fully exploited. The statement was badly drafted, its political support was weak. It soon became known that the Foreign Minister of the day, Social Democrat Väinö Leskinen, had declined to sign the statement. It was then issued by the Secretary of State Richard Tötterman.

The activists criticised the Government openly and accused it of having spoilt Finland's reputation. The news of the negative response was reported in the international press, showing Finland's foreign policy in a strange light. The decision to intensify the pressure against the Government to change its policy was received with enthusiasm at the conference.[114]

The young MPs and their sympathisers brought the discussion inside Parliament. MP Erkki Tuomioja asked an oral parliamentary question, on how the Government saw its attitude to be in harmony with the UN Declaration against colonialism, which had been unanimously accepted. A similar question

---

112. Interview with Mikko Lohikoski, 22.12.1995.
113. Foreign Ministry, letter No. 42352, 10.2.1971. Foreign Ministry's Archives.
114. Editorial, *Ylioppilaslehti* (Student News) 19.2.1971. Personal collection of Kimmo Pulkkinen.

was also asked by MP Mirjam Vire-Tuominen (SKP).[115] The Government's policy was also strongly criticised in public by SDP's Secretary General Kalevi Sorsa.[116] The criticism was answered by his party colleague, Foreign Minister Väinö Leskinen (SDP), who said that Finland supported the struggle for freedom, but only a struggle by non-violent means. He himself had given the impression that he supported the liberation movements, but was restricted by the official policy line. The discussion on the foreign policy line had begun to enter the official ranks. The conservative line was firmly held by the Foreign Ministry, by its top officials, although the political leadership itself was turning towards a more radical standpoint.

2.6. The visit of Amílcar Cabral

As a result of all this, the NGOs continued to put more pressure on the Government. During his visit to Guinea-Bissau, Mikko Pyhälä had met the President of PAIGC, Amílcar Cabral. At its special session on 13 April 1971, the International Solidarity Foundation had decided to grant a special donation to PAIGC. For that reason, they were interested in inviting the president to come and collect the donation. Unfortunately, he was unable to come then, but the idea of a visit at a later stage remained alive.

Because the negative attitude of the Foreign Ministry had been made well known, it was impossible to invite Cabral through official channels. He himself had agreed to come if the visit could be arranged at a high level. So a special reception committee was called upon, with the widest possible political support.[117]

According to Pyhälä, Lohikoski and Mattsson, the formation of this committee was not difficult. It was decided to form a politically representative committee which was already in itself a sign of the large amount of support that the liberation movements had attracted among Finnish interest groups.

> For that reason, to form a committee to receive him was the important thing. Not the actual visit of Cabral, only. It was to make up the basis. And the small meetings started with some persons from some parties, and finally we got into the committee more or less the chairmen of every political party and the party secretary of every party. That was the important work, because this way they got involved in the question. And that gave us then the basis finally to make a demand to the Finnish Government.[118]

---

115. Oral questions by Erkki Tuomioja and Mirjam Vire-Tuominen 12.2.1971. Foreign Ministry's Archives.
116. Press reports 13.2.1971. Foreign Ministry's Archives.
117. Letter to Raimo Lintonen 13.9.1987. Personal archives of Mikko Pyhälä.
118. Interview with Börje Mattsson, 29.2.1996.

The political parties of the left came first. The stories of Mattsson and Pyhälä give a slightly divergent account of the role of the Social Democratic party. While according to Pyhälä they were the initiators of the whole affair, in Mattsson's memory the participation of the SDP was not so certain because the Communist Party was already involved. And PAIGC, like liberation movements in general, was seen as revolutionary—as communists, that is. Seemingly Mikko Pyhälä's account is more correct, because after the very first meeting the SDP took a leading role on the Reception Committee; the SDP Secretary General Kalevi Sorsa was elected chairman of the Committee.[119]

However, much more work had to be done on the right. The youth organisation 'Tuhatkunta' of the Conservative Party (Kokoomus) became involved instead of the mother party, because the latter had not yet formed a policy toward liberation movements. But the Kokoomus Party did pay its share of the budget, to the pleasant surprise of the Committee activists.[120] Furthermore, again surprisingly, such small and nationalistic parties as the Finnish Rural Party, which had recently gained in the elections by increasing its seats in Parliament from 1 to 18, were eager to join in.[121]

Eventually, most of the parties had joined the Committee one by one. The Centre Party was among the last. But in contrast to the Conservative Party, the Secretary General of the Centre party, Mr Mikko Immonen, was more sympathetic than its youth representative, Jorma Leskelä. The youth sections of the parties were known to take a more radical standpoint than the mother party. The Liberal Party of Finland, competing in the political centre, was perhaps an encouraging example for the Centre Party.[122] Mikko Immonen even took most responsibility for acting as host to the guest.[123] The fact that the Centre Party was also a member of the Reception Committee bore a particular importance in regard to the future. It was the party of the President, and the party with the strongest foreign political legitimacy and influence. To have an impact on its opinion was therefore of great importance.

The visit of Amílcar Cabral on 19–21 October was a success. In fact the whole process in connection with the arrangements was a success, because it had for the first time united the political parties around the question of ending colonial-

---

119. Minutes of the meeting, 7.9.1971, The Amilcar Cabral Reception Committee. Personal archives of Mikko Pyhälä.

120. Letter to Raimo Lintonen 13.9.1987. Personal Archives of Mikko Pyhälä.

121. "I think funnily enough, there was this Party for Small Farmers, which also came quite easily even if that was a right-wing party. But we used Amilcar Cabral's material where he talked about revolution of the farmers. So there was not a working-class revolution, it was really a revolution of the farmers presented in the material of Amilcar Cabral. Of course the small farmers thought that this was wonderful. They also wanted peasants to make a revolution in Finland, so they liked Amilcar Cabral a lot!" Interview with Börje Mattsson 29.2.1996.

122. Letter to Raimo Lintonen 13.9.1987. Personal archives of Mikko Pyhälä.

123. Minutes of the meeting 8.10.1971: The Amilcar Cabral Reception Committee. Personal Archives of Mikko Pyhälä.

ism in Africa. Amílcar Cabral was the first leader of the liberation movement who was treated as a statesman. His programme was very ambitious—and to everyone's surprise, it became more or less a reality.[124]

The biggest victory was the fact that Cabral was received by President Kekkonen. According to Pyhälä, Lohikoski had informed the President about the visit at one of the receptions Dr Kekkonen used to arrange for young activists, and he had shown positive interest towards the idea. When his office was contacted, an appointment had been booked. In contrast the Foreign Ministry's top civil servants had shown a clearly ignorant, even negative, attitude towards the visit. Only the Office of Development Aid had booked an appointment. But after Kekkonen's appointment was confirmed, a meeting was arranged with the Minister of Foreign Affairs.

In addition Cabral met several leaders of the political parties, as well as youth and solidarity organisations. A solidarity event was organised at the Old Student House on 20 October. In addition to Cabral's message, several political speeches were given and the Government's foreign policy, once again, severely criticised. This time, the foreign policy bureaucracy was identified as a main obstacle to change. MP Ilkka Taipale's[125] message clarified this:

> President Kekkonen has said that we cannot be neutral in regard to peace and war. Thus in this question we cannot be neutral. A civil servant of the Foreign Ministry, Keijo Korhonen, recently accused the youth of being immature. We know too well his and other civil servants' attitude towards the African liberation movement. But these people, they are already over-mature, their time is running out. We demand that part of the development assistance must be channelled to the African liberation movements: PAIGC, FRELIMO and MPLA.[126]

Cabral's visit was a victory in the world of images. If Janet Mondlane was white, American and a lady, Cabral was a true black African, considered by the establishment a 'civilised' one. With his intellectual thinking and good manners, he was able to shake the images that Finnish people were still holding onto as regards Africans and especially revolutionaries.

---

124. According to the programme, the Committee planned to station young people alongside the road from the airport to the hotel! It was not such a good idea because of the October weather in Finland, if not otherwise unrealistic. Minutes of the Meeting, 8.9.1971, The Amilcar Cabral Reception Committee. Personal Archives of Mikko Pyhälä.

125. Dr Ilkka Taipale, as a student of medicine, had studied in 1964 in Portugal, where he met several refugees from the colonies. He has founded several solidarity and peace campaigns and served during the period 1971–1975 as an MP of the Social Democratic Party. Presently, he is a doctor of medicine and an everlasting political activist on behalf of the poor and mentally handicapped.

126. A speech on behalf of the Central Union of Social Democratic Youth at the Solidarity evening for Guinea-Bissau by Ilkka Taipale, 20.10.1971. Foreign Ministry's Archives.

President Kekkonen's attitude is reflected in his answer to Carbral's invitation to visit Guinea-Bissau: "Thank you for the invitation. A visit would no doubt be interesting, but in the future I might meet a happier people."[127]

2.7. Political parties' international dimension

The radical youth movement entered the party-political structures through the parties' youth organisations. Finnish parties responded to the social and international pressure to show practical solidarity toward the poor and oppressed in the Third World. Communists and social democrats were traditionally more international in their approach. The Social Democratic Party, the strongest party on the left, achieved an election victory in 1966, which resulted in a left majority in Parliament. A social democratic Foreign Minister, Väinö Leskinen, had been nominated. This raised hopes among the young and radical.

But in practice the situation was problematic to the party, because in spite of the rhetoric, the foreign policy line could not be changed overnight. The policy changes were initially happening inside the party's own structures. The party set up a new body called the International Solidarity Foundation in 1970. In its first session it expressed open support for the liberation movements. A solidarity campaign was established to collect funds and material help for the people under colonial rule. But the official foreign policy line stayed intact; the Government did not commit itself to the support. Leskinen was accused of 'sitting between two stools'.

The party and its solidarity wing were in practice the hosts for representatives of the liberation movements. They were highly enough regarded, as the largest party in Finland, when the Foreign Ministry itself was not interested in inviting, or acting as host, to any of the liberation movement leaders, who were not regarded as 'statesmen'. The hosts also had the means to finance the visits.

One visit organised by the Social Democratic party and the Solidarity Foundation was for a delegation from FRELIMO. Joaquim Chissano and Anselmo Anaiva came to Finland in November 1970. Their programme also included an appointment with Foreign Minister Väinö Leskinen. During their visit to the Foreign Ministry's political department, they explained the situation on the war front. They also criticised the Cabora Bassa power plant project, as well as other attempts to support colonialism in Mozambique.[128]

The vice-president of SWAPO, Mishake Muyongo, visited Finland at SDP's invitation. His visit coincided with Finland's active period in the Security

---

127. Report of Cabral's visit. Archives of Mikko Pyhälä.
128. Pro memo *"Mosambikin vapautusliikkeen FRELIMOn edustajien käynnistä UM:ssä"* (The visit of FRELIMO's representatives to the FM), 10.11.1970, Jussi A. Muttonen. Foreign Ministry's Archives.

Council in 1970. He met representatives of the Foreign Ministry and expressed his appreciation of Finland's activities concerning Namibian question.[129]

The Social Democratic Party had already invited the president of MPLA, Agostinho Neto, for a visit to Finland in July 1970. He was also the first liberation movement representative to meet the Foreign Minister Leskinen. The visit was reported by the press, which was also interested in the image of the Finnish missionaries. According to Neto, the Catholic Church as a state church was not popular, but the attitude towards Lutheran missionaries varied among the people. He did not, however, consider the work of the church very promising or positive.[130]

The questions concerning the church's role that were presented during Neto's visit did not come out of the blue. At that time the work of the Finnish church in Africa was under serious consideration. The young and radical in and outside church circles had challenged the church's role in the missionary work in relationship to the liberation struggle. The next chapter will discuss the changing role of the church in more detail, while its relationship to the radical movement is returned to later on.

---

129. Saarela, 1980:194.
130. *Helsingin Sanomat* 7.7.1970, *Suomen Sosiaalidemokraatti* 7.7.1970.

Chapter 3
Proclaiming the Gospel or Politics?

In addition to the youth organisations, another institution of Finnish society started to experience the African liberation struggle in a very practical manner. Almost all the Finnish population (approximately 90 per cent) belongs to the state church or other Christian movements in Finland. When measured by regular attendance in weekly church services, only a small percentage are practising Christians, many of them elderly persons. But the large membership has meant that many people who otherwise would not have come into contact with the reality of the African continent, experienced it through the church. Its missionary work was carried out in the midst of the national uprising, in Ovamboland, in the territory of South West Africa.[131]

3.1 The Finnish Lutheran Mission in Ovamboland

> Of course I was delighted because the name of Finland was not strange to me as a Namibian, who was born and grew up in the northern part of Namibia, which is the part of Namibia where Finnish missionaries were very active since 1870. And in fact, the primary schools I went to, were schools organised and belonging to the Finnish missionaries in collaboration with the local people of the northern part of Namibia.[132]

The history of the Finnish mission is popularly known among the people of Namibia and Finland, but it also has an international reputation. In the history of Finland's relations with Africa, it has had a very special effect. In regard to liberation movements, and especially SWAPO of Namibia, the Finnish mission influence is without comparison. The role of the church—and especially the commitment of some of its servants—was instrumental in informing public opinion on the situation of the Namibian people. But the history of the mission's involvement is not without controversies and complications. For that reason, its activities will be given special emphasis in this study.

Finland had done missionary work in Ovamboland in northern Namibia since 1870. The Finnish Missionary Society's work was started there on an initiative given by the Rhenish Mission from Germany, which had already

---

131. When the missionary work began, the territory which later formed Namibia was legally no man's land. It was inhabited by various groups of African people. The area under discussion was not occupied by Germany until 1884, when it became known as South West Africa.
132. Interview with Nickey Iyambo, 20.8.1996.

started proclaiming the Gospel in the south western corner of Africa. The Finns started to work in the northern part of the territory, where only some explorers had visited before. The newly established Finnish Missionary Society—which was an independent association under the auspices of the Finnish Lutheran Church—was regarded by the Rhenish Mission as suitable for work in the primitive part of the area, where circumstances were extremely harsh.

The missionary work was done in a region which long remained outside the direct domination of the emerging colonial power, Germany. Finnish missionaries, especially Martti Rautanen in his capacity as an important adviser to several Ovambo kings, contributed significantly to that fact.[133] The colonial master of South West Africa after Germany was South Africa, which later consolidated its grip over Ovamboland.

The main aim of missionary activities was to introduce the word of God in its Lutheran interpretation. Later on, a social and health service function was added. Especially during the Rautanen era, which stretched from 1870 until the 1920s, missionaries had a role as go-betweens in their relations with the colonists and Ovambos. Sometimes it was also hard to avoid taking a stand on political questions or relations between the rulers and the ruled. But the main principle was to practise a policy of non-interference and to build their own Christian community amongst the Ovambo communities. The work was never easy, because there was a continuous struggle for power and influence between the local chiefs, the white administration, and the foreign missionaries. The missionaries were mostly able to manage, because they put a lot of effort into adapting to the local circumstances as well as learning and developing the local language.[134] They lived near the people as the only white people in the area, and gradually the locals learnt to trust them at least to some extent.[135]

The missionary work was greatly challenged by the birth of the liberation movement SWAPO. At the end of the 1950s, the missionaries were worried by the unrest, which had broken out among the Ovambo workers and the first nationalists, in relations with the South African administration. Most of the missionary reports condemned the actions of SWAPO. They were afraid for the continuation of their work. They reported uncivilised manners and false accusations made by the uneducated natives.[136] Nickey Iyambo, one of the early activists, explains the church's attitude:

> Because in the first place people did not know where the country was—something about *Ambomaa*, a little bit. But not really much in terms of the social and political difficulties the country was undergoing, because the duty of the missionaries was obviously to spread the good message of conviction and Christianity. It was not

---

133. Eirola, 1992.

134. The role of the missionaries has been studied and analysed by, e.g., Matti Peltola (1958) and Eirola (1992). Finnish missionaries collected and organised three local vernaculars—Oshindonga, Ukwanyama and Kuangali—in their written form.

135. Väisälä, 1980:231.

136. Juva, 1993:108–112.

very clear to them whether they also had to look into social difficulties of the country, particularly the political arrangement. They thought that was part of the local politics and they were from a far land and they should not really spend considerable energy on political issues, but rather consider spreading the Gospel of faith.[137]

Worried by the tense situation, the Missionary Society decided to make an inspection in the area in 1961. The inspectors chosen were the chairperson, Dr Mikko Juva,[138] (an academic historian and a theologian, who had been a member of the board since 1951), and the secretary of the society Aleksi Vallisaari. The delegation was hosted by the head of the mission in Namibia, Alpo Hukka. During the following seven weeks, the delegation familiarised itself with the situation in the territory, the conditions of the migrant workers, and the rural areas and people, as well as the mission stations and their work.

Mikko Juva, who had been actively involved in the colonial question and had also come into contact with the liberation struggle through participating in the work of the international Christian and student organisations, had from the start taken a positive attitude towards the liberation movement. He urged the missionaries to take the movement seriously. To his disappointment, he did not manage to meet anybody from the movement itself, which he understood to be a result of the reserved attitude the Africans had towards all Whites and their institutions. The inspection trip itself did in the end have a profound effect on the future work of the local church.

Mikko Juva was the first reformer in the Missionary Society circles. He had already met the head of the Evangelical Lutheran Ambo-Kavango Church (as the Finnish-formed local church was called) Leonard Auala, in 1959, when he was the first member of the Ambo-Kavango church who was allowed to travel to Finland.

> I had a discussion with him and I told him here in Finland, in safety and openly, that Finland has been for centuries under foreign rule, first Swedes and then the Russians, but when the time was ripe and we had had higher education, and the historical situation arrived, when we could declare our independence, we did it. And I'm quite sure that sometime in the future your country will achieve the same. ... So it was in such general ideologist terms I spoke to him, but Auala's reaction was a horrified one. And I understood it a few years later, when I learned what instructions Auala had received.[139]

Before the trip to Finland Bishop Auala had been given a lecture by the administrator of Ovamboland, emphasising that he must represent the views of the regime when he went to Finland. He had to promise on oath, in front of the

---

137. Interview with Nickey Iyambo, 20.8.1996.

138. Mikko Juva became a Professor, then Rector and Chancellor of the University of Helsinki; and after that the Archbishop of the Lutheran Church of Finland. He was also, for a brief period, the chairperson of the Liberal Party and an MP.

139. Interview with Mikko Juva, 24.11.1995.

policemen in the courtroom, that he would not say anything negative about the South African administration.[140] Dr Juva, for his part, was of the opinion that as a student of history he knew something about how nations develop, and thought that it was wise to tell Auala that he should not be afraid to think of future liberation.[141] He could not understand what a difficult situation he had caused for Bishop Auala at that time.

But then neither the Finnish church nor its Southern partner was ready to regard liberation as a realistic issue. During the inspection trip, though, Juva found out at the Teachers' Seminars at Elim and Ongwediva that the younger students were very keen to learn more about the ideological and political ideas of the day, as well as problems of colonialism and the intellectual and national independence of the continent. He had to reply to questions concerning Marxist ideology and the theory and practice of communism. Dr Juva, a Christian theologist, might have been the first foreigner talking about such forbidden subjects publicly and openly.[142] For the students, it was a surprise that somebody from the older generation was prepared to discuss with them subjects that many regarded as forbidden.

Mikko Juva thought that the only possibility for the black people was to follow the path of negotiations and passive resistance. The first reason for hope was the Ovambo nation itself. Although they were poorer than Blacks who lived in the police zone,[143] their communities had been able to develop relatively independently and they had not become a proletariat of the White people. According to him, the Ovambos of the day had dignity and a sense of freedom, which could not be met in the South.[144]

After the inspection, the group gave some recommendations to the Society. Many of them were concerned about the immediate needs and conditions of the missionaries for whom Dr Juva had developed a great respect during the trip. Even though he could not agree with the opinions of many of them, he admired the work they were doing. The Society's attitude toward SWAPO had improved a little. However, the majority of the missionaries were still against any such contacts. Many of them still had old patriarchal attitudes based on obedience to the authorities, including the South African regime.[145]

The attitude of the older missionaries naturally could not be changed overnight. The level and quality of action of the liberation movement did not convince many of the missionaries of its seriousness and power. Many of them

---

140. Ihamäki, 1985:117.

141. Interview with Mikko Juva, 24.11.1995.

142. Juva, 1993:110.

143. Southern and Central regions of South West Africa which were directly administered and controlled by the South African colonial government were called the police zone. The Northern parts—including Ovamboland—of the territory were under indirect rule.

144. Juva, 1993:112.

145. Väisälä, 1980:244.

were of the opinion that the current situation was merely turmoil caused by outside propaganda. The inspection group had worked out some guidelines to be followed by the FMS. The Society was not to take any active part in the politics of the country, but it was to follow very keenly what happened among the people of the country.[146] As soon as the movement got its leaders, the FMS should establish contacts with them. Soon thereafter, the FMS did establish contacts with Sam Nujoma. Yet, when Nujoma visited Finland for the first time in the mid-1960s, Juva and another supportive colleague—the Mission Leader Olavi Vuorela—paid for his tickets personally, being conscious of the negative attitude of the missionaries. Later on, Sam Nujoma became a regular guest of the Missionary Home in Helsinki.

The younger members were quite sympathetic toward the liberation cause, because it reflected many of the Christian values of freedom, equality and self-determination. Especially Aarne Hartikainen, the foreman of the printing press at the church centre in Oniipa, Ovamboland—where the only newspaper in a local language was edited and printed—was very sympathetic toward SWAPO. The attitude inside the missionary society developed gradually, not least because of the efforts of the enlightened chairperson.

In 1962, Juva published a pamphlet *Teollistunut Eurooppa ja teollistuva Afrikka* (Industrialised Europe and Industrialising Africa). Its purpose was to present the current situation in Africa, as well as to advise the Christian community what was expected of it in this situation. In this booklet, Dr Juva states three different mental factors which influenced the development of the modern African society, namely European political nationalism, European socialism and European Christian missionary work. Because there was no return to the past, the Christian community should take a stand in favour of the African liberation movement. Juva listed three standpoints which would help to form the church's attitude. Firstly, the liberation movement was not a rebellion against God—instead, the revolution provided a richer life for the oppressed people of Africa, as promised by God. Secondly, the church should make sure, that the movement only accepted peaceful ways of resistance. This would be achieved through the education of its leaders by the church. Thirdly, Christians should always look for reconciliation. With these standpoints in mind, Dr Juva came to the conclusion that White men were still needed in Africa. However, Africans did not need them as leaders but as professional assistants.[147] Juva's pamphlet was distributed in church circles and provided a standpoint for reformation of its opinion.

---

146. Interview with Mikko Juva, 25.11.1995.
147. Juva, 1962:13–14.

3.2. Taking a stand against racial segregation

Within the Missionary Society, the situation became a matter of dispute again in 1963, when Dr Juva proposed to the board that the Society should condemn all racial segregation and convey its stand confidentially to Bishop Leonard Auala and the missionaries. The idea of such condemnation had come from the international church bodies, whose discussions Dr Juva participated in regularly. The board was not ready for the statement and overruled it. The majority was of the opinion that racism was absolutely reprehensible but racial segregation was not. As a result, Dr Juva informed the board, that he would resign as chairperson. He did not want to continue to lead an organisation that was unsure of its policies as regards racial questions. After Olavi Vuorela and Bishop Martti Simojoki had formulated a compromise proposal, the board was able to accept it. The new proposal was similar in content to Dr Juva's proposal, and so he could continue as chairperson.[148]

SWAPO, however, was not yet convinced about the role of the Finnish mission. The debate continued in August 1965, when SWAPO representatives Emil Appolus and Andreas Shipanga visited Finland on their own to meet with the FMS representatives. Appolus, the information secretary of SWAPO, gave an interview, in which he accused the Missionary Society of having betrayed the African people. He compared Finnish missionaries to Anglicans, whose schools had been closed and missionaries expelled from the country. The Finns, however, were acting in cooperation with the oppressive regime. That was why the departure of the Finns would do no harm.[149]

Dr Juva replied in his interview by saying that the attitude of the Finnish missionaries had changed a lot during the previous 10 years. They did not have paternalistic attitudes anymore, but worked under Black leadership. But a letter from Aarne Hartikainen confirmed that SWAPO was partly right. Many of the missionaries could not yet understand the conditions of the black people. This was due to the South African propaganda, which had convinced the world that things were in order in South West Africa.[150]

Aarne Hartikainen was one of the first missionaries that were sympathetic toward SWAPO. He met Herman Toivo ya Toivo regularly, and respected him very much. Another missionary of the new generation was Mikko Ihamäki, who made personal sacrifices for the cause of Africans. It did not take long before the Ambo-Kavango church and the missionaries started to openly criticise the South African regime.

But above all, the missionary society's main work continued in the 1960s: educating Ovambo youth. The religious work was carried out more and more

---

148. Juva, 1993:114.
149. *Sosiaalidemokraatti* (Social Democratic daily) 22.8.1965.
150. Juva, 1993:115–116.

by the locals, under the leadership of Leonard Auala. Despite the difficulties that FMS had in understanding the demands of the new situation, it was convinced of its role in social and educational work. The Oshigambo High School educated many of the future leaders of SWAPO, who later on left for exile to be educated abroad. The flight of some of the students was assisted, this being the only way to rescue them from South African punitive measures. The missionary society also provided scholarships for young priests to study theology in Finland.

The SWAPO activists, many of whom had received their primary education at local missionary schools, do not have much that is negative to say about the church nowadays. A collection of statements from the Namibian interviews sound so similar:

> There is this historical church connection, which was the pressure point. The Finnish mission church, with strong sentiments and ties to Namibia, always wanted the government of Finland to do something, to do more.[151]

> ...Well, as there is some sentimentality about Finland, especially among the people from the North, because of the influence of the Finnish missionaries. So perhaps it was not difficult for young Namibians to accept to go for training in Finland because some of them were taught by Finns in many cases.[152]

> ...That most probably around that time the contact between Finland and Namibians really got increased, because even the missionaries that were in Namibia at that time were getting involved. Like the late Mikko Ihamäki, who was also asked to leave Namibia, when he went to Finland and was not allowed to come back. He was in fact the one who came to Zambia that time to fetch the first large group of Namibians [to study in Finland].[153]

3.3. Missionaries face problems in Namibia

By the time the UN was taking a firm standpoint on the Namibian question and the World Court's opinion on the termination of the mandate had been given in 1971, most of the missionaries had become more understanding toward the aspirations put forward by SWAPO, especially the plight of contract workers. Regarding their work as even more valuable in the growing repression, missionaries continued their activities in Ovamboland. After the closure of the Finnish consulate in 1971 on the recommendation of the UN, Finland's only presence in Namibia was through the missionary society. Side by side with the increasing political and military presence of the South African regime, the

---

151. Interview 26.8.1996 with Hidipo Hamutenya, Minister of Trade and Industry in Namibia and a long time member of SWAPO in exile. He worked at UNIN and was responsible for education.

152. Interview 22.8.1996 with Nahas Angula, Minister of Education in Namibia, member of SWAPO, responsible for educational projects during the years in exile.

153. Interview with Nickey Iyambo, 20.8.1996.

church gave its attention and sympathy to the local population. Its relationship with SWAPO became stronger, causing further problems.

In fact, the change in the church was not as very outward-oriented as the South African government always wanted to believe and argue. In 1960 at the church convention the first indigenous church leader, Leonard Auala, was elected. He was first and foremost a servant of his people in the spirit of God. His courage seems only to have grown when the South African regime intensified its segregation policy in the form of the homeland system. Bishop Auala started his political work gradually, on the basis that the church could no longer separate its message from the socio-political reality. But at the same time, he wanted to secure independence and space for the work of his church, which was getting harder all the time.[154]

In 1971, the conflict between the church and the regime was brought fully into the open, when the leaders of the two Lutheran churches, Bishop Auala and Rev. Gowaseb, sent an open letter to the South African Prime Minister Vorster to urge that the regime act according to the opinion of the International Court of Justice. One of the results of the letter was that the Finnish missionaries became dangerous in the regime's eyes. Foreigners were an easy target to blame for this disturbance. Bishop Auala's position was secured, thanks to his excellent ability to moderate between the people and the regime, though never forgetting on whose side he and his church stood.[155] The regime was of the opinion that there were 'White brains' behind the letter. Mikko Ihamäki, whose activities had been monitored for a while, and who was seen as a 'leftist with provocative opinions who interfered in the politics of the area' was suspected. He was also accused of mobilisation of the strikes which had occurred the previous year.[156]

Another person who was strongly criticised during the strike was missionary Rauha Voipio, who had just recently done the first socio-economic survey among contract workers. She wrote a booklet in Afrikaans, based on the survey, which clearly showed the misery of the contract system. Ms Voipio points out that it was written in a conciliatory spirit for the purpose of informing the White employees about the conditions, life and ideas of their

---

154. This story of Bishop Auala and the development of the Ambo-Kavango church is based mainly on the memories of Bishop Auala himself, collected and written by Kirsti Ihamäki (1985), the wife of missionary Mikko Ihamäki. They were eyewitnesses to the events until deported from Namibia in 1972.

155. Ihamäki, Kirsti, 1985:177–78. Teacher and SWAPO activist Erastus Shamena tells how Bishop Auala was speaking with a hidden message at the occasion to mark the publication of the Odendaal plan (the plan to divide the country into separate ethnic homelands) in Ovambo in 1968. "We have now seen with our eyes what we have long been waiting for", Bishop Auala said in the prayers. Mr Shamena himself got angry at first, when he thought that Bishop Auala was saying that people had been looking forward to it happening, before he understood that Bishop Auala in fact meant exactly the opposite.

156. Letter no 326/83 from the Legation in Pretoria to the Foreign Ministry, Kurt Uggeldahl, 2.10.1972. Foreign Ministry's Archives.

workers. In spite of that, the book was condemned by the White authorities and linked with the strike.[157]

As a result of the withdrawal of the residence permits of Mikko and Kirsti Ihamäki in 1972, preventing their return to Namibia, SWAPO reacted strongly and sent a letter to the Finnish Government. In his letter, Sam Nujoma noted that South Africa had stepped up its repressive and punitive acts towards the population, and that also endangered the lives of Finnish citizens. SWAPO urged the Government of Finland to review the matter urgently and to take all necessary steps to protect its citizens.[158] The missionaries and SWAPO had come a long way since the accusations of Emil Appolus in 1965, that the FMS was being indifferent.

The Missionary Society, as well, approached the Finnish Government. It wanted to secure its work in *Ambomaa*, because particularly its education and health services were necessary to the local population. Mikko Juva from the society was of the opinion that the South African government, though they would like to, could not throw the missionaries out completely for fear of the consequences. The church was the only institution that was maintaining peace and order in the community.

Nevertheless, the South African government was harassing the missionaries, which made the work unpleasant if not impossible. For instance, the printing press of the Ambo-Kavango church was blown up in 1973. According to Dr Juva, the Missionary Society did not practise any particular policy in Namibia, but served the people and the Ambo-Kavango church. The local church and its head, Bishop Auala, were leading the Christian community. Dr Juva requested that the Finnish Government express its support for the Society's and the church's work by, for instance, sending an official representative to visit their working area.[159]

As a result, Finland's chargé d'affaires in Pretoria, Kurt Uggeldahl, visited Ovamboland 5–12 July, 1974. It was emphasised that the visit was strictly private and the purpose was to get to know the Finnish Missionary Society's work in the area. During the visit Mr Uggeldahl was greatly impressed by Bishop Auala and was in general satisfied with the Society's work. According to him, the conditions in the area were depressing. At his meeting with Commissioner General Jan de Wet, it was agreed that the Missionary Society's presence in the area was important. Mr de Wet received Mr Uggeldahl's complaints on the growing military presence in the school area, which he denied any knowledge of. Flogging as a punitive measure, recently introduced by the South African created Ovamboland authorities, was explained as 'tribal tradition'. The

---

157. Voipio, 1980:117.
158. Letter from SWAPO to the Prime Minister of Finland from Sam Nujoma, 12.10.1972. Foreign Ministry's Archives.
159. "*P.M. Suomen virallisen edustajan mahdollinen käynti Namibiassa*" (Memorandum on the planned visit of an official Finnish representative to Namibia), Foreign Ministry, Antti Lassila, 30.11.1973. Foreign Ministry's Archives.

visit, which was meant as a sign of Finland's support for the missionary work, had opened up a chance for diplomatic channels to observe the area. The realistic picture gained of the conditions under South African rule had a great impact on the Foreign Ministry's Namibia policy.[160] Up till then, the situation had only been monitored from Pretoria, which was of course giving a distorted picture of reality.

In Finland, the clear expressions of solidarity by the Church and the Missionary Society were welcomed by the radical Africa movement. From time to time, the emerging discussion on the missionaries' role in Namibia started to turn around: criticism against the Foreign Ministry's rather passive policy was heaviest from the so-called conservative corners of the church and society. In fact, missionaries were regarded by some in the Foreign Ministry as already being too sympathetic toward SWAPO. But according to many missionaries, they were just consistent in their policy of serving the master of the day. The difference from the past was that the independent Ovambo-Kavango Evangelical Lutheran Church, which was now the employer of the missionaries, had taken a clear stand in favour of the popular opposition. It was estimated that most of the church members were also SWAPO supporters.[161] The missionary society's task, as well as the churches', was to unite the people regardless of their race, ethnic origin or political affiliation. That was God's message, after all.

In Finland, radicals of the day often found themselves on the same side as the church, defending the Namibian people's rights to self-determination. The Foreign Ministry, however, was not willing to assist SWAPO directly. Especially after Bishop Auala's letter and Mr Ihamäki's deportation, the SWAPO-sympathetic church people started to put more and more emphasis on information work in Finland. A suitable channel for that appeared to be the church's international wing, Finnchurchaid.

3.4. Finnchurchaid

Another church body was also involved with the liberation movements from the 1960s. It was actually this body which later came into more direct contact with SWAPO. The Missionary Society's main duty was proclaiming the Christian faith. Finnchurchaid was, on the other hand, a church body specialised in development and humanitarian work. While the controversies inside the FMS continued concerning its role in relation to the liberation struggle over the years, Finnchurchaid became very convenient for channelling direct aid to the struggle.

The Finnish Evangelical Lutheran Church started to call its foreign aid activities Finnchurchaid in 1965. In the beginning, the Finnchurchaid work was

---

160. "*Muistio, Vierailu Ambomaalla 5–12.7.1974*" (Memorandum on the visit to Ovamboland) Pretoria 17.7.1974, Kurt Uggeldahl. Foreign Ministry's Archives.

161. Väisälä, 1980:248.

included in that of the Lutheran World Federation's (LWF) National Committee in Finland. In 1974, when the church's foreign relations were reorganised, Finnchurchaid was formed as a separate unit. The activities of Finnchurchaid include foreign assistance, recruitment of workers for developing countries and technical aid, scholarship and visitors' programmes, and relations with foreign church assistance bodies, as well as information concerning foreign assistance.[162]

Finnchurchaid first came into contact with refugees from Southern African countries in 1966, when it collected money for the Mozambique Institute.[163] Its umbrella organisation, the Lutheran World Federation, has as its main assistance work been helping refugees, first in Europe, then gradually more and more in Africa. The financial support from Finland was collected from the member churches. During those years a lot of work was done in Tanzania, where many Mozambican refugees had settled. The Mozambique Institute was set up by Janet Mondlane, the wife of the leader of FRELIMO, Eduardo Mondlane, to look after the refugees. This connection between Finnchurchaid and the MI encouraged some of the more conservative students to join the *Taksvärkki-69* campaign.

In general, Finnchurchaid did not engage in any bilateral cooperation, because all the work was done through the international ecumenical bodies like the World Council of Churches (WCC), which is more involved in advocacy, information and policy-making, and the Lutheran World Federation (LWF), which gives practical humanitarian assistance. The aid to the MI was also channelled through LWF.

In fact, Finnchurchaid was considered quite a radical body compared with the mother church. That did not facilitate its fund-raising.

> The church itself was not at all one-sidedly favouring these projects. There was much resistance, and it was a small wonder that Finnchurchaid could continue. But at the same time it gathered all the church leaders to the committees. But Finnchurchaid had at the time such a reputation that those ordinary conservative Christian people did not accept it. So all the support went to missionary work, and we had a really difficult time to get funds for any purpose. Some strong characters like Mikko Juva went on and linked the activities with the Christian proclamation in such a way that also Finnchurchaid became acceptable.[164]

In that sense, Namibia was an exception to the rule. The FMS offered a natural link with Namibia for Finnchurchaid, which started to support Namibia. Finnchurchaid had already participated in education of Namibians in the 1960s. In 1969, together with the Missionary Society, it organised *Yhteisvastuu*

---

162. "*Kumppanuutta rakentamassa. Ulkoasiainministeriön ja Kirkon Ulkomaanavun yhteinen Namibian stipendiaattiohjelma vv.1975–1993*" (Building the partnership. The Namibian Scholarship Programme run jointly by the Foreign Ministry and Finnchurchaid). Kirkon Ulkomaanapu, Finnchurchaid, Helsinki, March 1994. Unpublished report, pp. 2–3.
163. Interview with Yrjö Höysniemi, 11.10.1995.
164. Ibid.

(Common Responsibility),[165] a fund-raising campaign for Namibia. The purpose of this was to support agriculture and vocational training in Ovamboland. The campaign was deliberately apolitical, targeted to the people of Namibia.

But at the beginning of the 1970s, Finnchurchaid increased its support to Namibian refugees. The situation had changed drastically and more Namibians were fleeing the South African repression. Finnchurchaid concentrated on helping those members of the Ambo-Kavango Church who had gone into exile. In November 1974, Finnchurchaid started a special fund-raising campaign on behalf of Namibian refugees. Rev. Mikko Ihamäki, after having been expelled from Ovamboland, started to go around churches and congregations to raise interest and support for the campaign. The money was then used to buy clothes and other necessities, which were channelled through LWF to Zambia.[166]

The reputation of Finnchurchaid caused some of the SWAPO-friendly missionaries to look for support from its structures. It was understandable that politically more sensitive work was done by Finnchurchaid, because the missionaries wanted to continue their educational and social duties in the area.

> The mission had various views and various faces, so that some of them did not pick up the problems at all. Then some of them were very conscious of the problem but they could not respond to it through our conservative missionary institution, through the normal channels, because the Missionary Society had to work there and they were very cautious in guaranteeing their own space for work.[167]

Later on, the Church and Mikko Ihamäki were crucial instruments in initiating and managing a specific scholarship programme for Namibian refugees, financed by the state.

---

165. *Yhteisvastuu-keräys* (The Common Responsibility Campaign) is an institution in Finnish society. This fund-raising campaign is organised every year by the Church. Money is collected in the churches, schools, streets etc. The Church bodies decide the recipients of the funds, and there are normally both Finnish and international targets.
166. *Kumppanuutta Rakentamassa* (Building the Partnership) (1994) p. 3.
167. Interview with Yrjö Höysniemi, 11.10.1995.

Chapter 4
Finland's Foreign Policy—Do Not Disturb!

> This kind of answer [not funding the student conference], which developed a lot of public discussion, actually hastened a reorientation in the policy. It was ambivalent there, and some people—Keijo Korhonen and a few other people, who were there, who were kind of hard-liners in this question—pushed it through, which finally backfired actually. It also reflects that in the political parties, there was a lot of support which the foreign office and the official decision-making could not resist in the long run if the civic society and political society were ready for that step. And we should also see that in the UN and elsewhere these questions became much more predominant. And because we co-ordinated our policy with the Nordic Countries, it was obvious that while the others had started [to support liberation movements], it was obvious that Finland could not keep its own line in these questions. There were many factors, but one factor definitely was that the liberation movements also made impressive gains, they became respected players in the international arena and they were granted status in different organisations.[168]

In this chapter, we try to describe and analyse Finland's foreign policy and its basic principles before 1973, and the change that occurred thereafter. The year 1973 is chosen because it was the year when the most important decisions in regard to the liberation movements were taken by the Foreign Ministry. It was decided then that the liberation movements could be supported by the Government. Before that, Finland was consistently and systematically refusing to directly support the liberation movements. It even went to great pains to discover new motives behind its status quo. In the background lay foreign policy doctrine, political realism, which was the leading principle amongst the foreign policy administration in particular. The political leadership initiated the change.

The analysis is done on three different but interlinked levels: 1. The official foreign policy of Finland i.e. its bilateral relations with other countries and its national stand on international issues; 2. Finland's policy in the United Nations, i.e. at the multilateral level; and 3. The informal NGO level. The analysis endeavours to show how all these interacted with and influenced each other.

According to Timo-Erkki Heino, the most important question in the foreign policy debate at the turn of the decade 1960s–70s—as well as in the sanctions question in the 1980s—was the question of decision-making, that is, who ultimately decided the foreign policy.[169] We take his assumption as a guideline. We analyse how the internal and external influences of the civil society found their way into the decision-making structures—that is, into the political parties,

---

168. Interview with Mikko Lohikoski, 22.12.1995.
169. Heino, 1992:111.

parliament and government as well as into the civil service. To have a real impact in a country like Finland, which was in such a special situation in the Cold War world, a new line had to have rather wide support including large sectors of society to push for policy change. In the question of supporting the liberation movements, that kind of a support did grow.

While this chapter follows a chronological order, the different levels are analysed simultaneously. Because the previous chapters introduced the main activities and approaches at the NGO level, including the foreign policy discussion that the activists initiated at the turn of the decade, this chapter concentrates more on the policy and its formulation at the official level. Finland's policies in the multilateral forums and in the Nordic context, as well as at domestic level, are examined in relation to each other in order to analyse the causes and consequences of the different actions.

Although the special emphasis is on the policy towards liberation movements, certain general policy questions must be introduced in order to understand the underlying foreign policy principles. The analysis concerning Finland's policy towards apartheid and South Africa is based mainly on the excellent study by Timo-Erkki Heino.[170] Many conclusions drawn from the development of Finland's standing on South Africa are applicable to its policy towards liberation movements, because the questions of apartheid and colonialism were closely connected. Finland's official foreign policy thinking concerning the whole of Southern Africa was naturally a strong reflection of its policy toward South Africa, and its viewpoints were influenced by diplomatic connections with Pretoria.

Heino argues that there have been two dominant approaches to foreign policy in Finland. The first one is a 'realist' approach, which was the primary approach adopted by the official foreign policy decision-makers. The 'realist' approach is based on the state-centred idea of the international order, where the dominant feature is the struggle for power, defence of the survival of the state, and pursuing of the national interest. The focus is on Finland's position in the Cold War and its requirements, especially national security in a narrow sense.

The second approach is a moral consideration of the role of Finland in the world of injustices. This is based on the idealist principles of moralism and cooperation in the international society. Having its roots in the first decades of this century when it influenced the establishment of the League of Nations, the moral approach was dismissed in the aftermath of the Second World War as an over-optimistic view of international relations. Realism took over and was efficiently strengthened by the era of the Cold War and bloc politics. The moral approach did, however, made a significant comeback in the 1960s, this time dominating the thinking of the new radicals, who were imbued with ideas of solidarity, common responsibility and a new economic order. They demanded

---

170. Heino, 1992.

that moral principles must be taken into account in foreign policy decision-making.

4.1. Finland formulating its position in the world after 1945

In general, the African question was not high on the foreign policy agenda before the 1960s. It was clearly a side issue. After Finland's independence, its foreign policy and diplomatic representation concentrated on Europe. Germany and Great Britain were important reference countries. With Africa still almost entirely under colonial rule at the time, Finnish diplomatic representation on the African continent was limited. By 1925, however, Finnish honorary consulates were established in five South African cities: Cape Town, Johannesburg, Durban, Port Elizabeth and East London. Trade was the connecting concern.[171]

The Second World War had a profound impact on Finland's foreign policy thinking. The partial *de facto* alliance with Germany during the war against the Soviet Union had resulted in substantial areas of Finland being annexed to the territory of the Soviet Union. The seriously damaged Finnish economy had to recover quickly in order to pay the war compensations and accommodate half a million internal refugees from Karelia. Industrial development—which speeded up all over Europe—was the key to development as well as some structural adjustment from an agrarian economy to a modern one.

New markets were sought all over the world. Since 1949, Finland had had a permanent diplomatic mission in Pretoria. Her exports to South Africa were mainly forest industry products, and she imported fruit from there. Prior to the 1950s, South Africa's racial policies did not in any way affect Finland's relations with the country. Finland's main interest was still in promoting trade. Her internal economic development was not to be harmed by any humanitarian violations. That was not even an issue. Only in 1955, when Finland became a member of the United Nations, could the Foreign Ministry no longer ignore the question of apartheid.

UN membership forced Finland to deal with global issues and perspectives instead of the former inward oriented policy, which concentrated almost fully on the Soviet Union, Scandinavia and Europe. Joining the UN in 1955 was not a clear cut decision for Finland, either. It was feared that it would harm her precarious position. For that reason, Finland accepted in its UN policy in the 1950s a principle called 'Enckell's corset'.[172] This meant not getting overly involved, but trying to further solutions which might gain support from all the superpowers and when this was not possible abstaining from taking a stand. Finland emphasised its strong policy of neutrality and endeavoured to remain

---

171. Heino, 1992:19–20.
172. After Ralph Enckell, the Finnish Ambassador to the UN.

outside East-West conflicts. Another important principle was to strive for a common Nordic policy.[173]

When Finland, for the first time, spoke out on its view concerning apartheid, there was no ambiguity in regard to the question of racism and apartheid in the Finnish policy. In Finland's first official statement in the UN on apartheid in November 1959, Ambassador Max Jacobson stated that the equality of all, without regard to race, was deeply rooted in Finnish tradition, law and social practice. Racial discrimination violated the sense of justice of the Finnish people.[174] Immediately after it joined the UN, Finland had been elected as one of the nine members of the South West Africa Committee, which had the task of collecting information on the territory and conducting negotiations with South Africa over Namibia's future.[175] In 1958, Finnish delegates had for the first time participated in discussions on Namibia in the General Assembly, explaining that the relations between Finland and South Africa were most friendly and satisfactory. Finland agreed about the need to continue negotiations with South Africa, reflecting the pragmatic Finnish policy in the UN.[176] The relations continued as usual, bearing in mind that the missionaries were operating in Namibian territory.

Regardless of its anti-racial sentiments, Finland still did not want to get involved. Her problem was thus not the substance, but her interpretation of the rules and regulations of international law at that time. When the UN was discussing whether dealing with apartheid was within its competence, the Finnish delegation took the stand that apartheid was an internal question and should therefore not be dealt with. Finland held on to that principle for a long time, although the other Nordic countries had chosen the other side emphasising the human rights principle. Finland stressed that it did not favour the line of protest that the other Nordic countries had adopted.[177]

Finland's standpoint was a logical consequence of its relationship towards the Soviet Union. It wanted to stay behind the legal agreements accepted by the international community in order not to make any mistakes.

> When Finland formulated its policy on different issues—for example, whether to support this or that, here or there—it was not only the issue of that country. It was considered also whether that example could be used to pressurise Finland to take a stand in another situation, which could be seen as an analogical situation, to take a stand which it did not want to take. So it was always in mind that once the world was divided in this Cold War situation, that if we take this step, we are more vulnerable, for example, to pressure to take a stand on another issue, one which we

---

173. Heino, 1992:23-24.
174. ULA, 1959:116.
175. Saarela, 1980:184.
176. Ibid., p. 185.
177. Ibid., p. 187.

would like to avoid. Therefore it's better to abstain from the first step, if it leads to another one which is undesirable.[178]

4.2. A medical doctor, not a judge

This policy of neutrality was clearly spelled out by President Kekkonen, when at the General Assembly in 1961 he presented Finland rather as a medical doctor than a judge. "It is not for us to pass judgements, not to condemn. It is rather to diagnose and try to cure".[179] For the first time since Enckell's corset Finland had formulated its UN policy. This speech served as a basic principle of Finland's stand in international affairs for years to come.[180] During the first decade of Finland's membership of the UN, 1956–65, Finland's policy was cautious and reserved. Finland refrained from making initiatives to be discussed at the UN and did not even put forward its own candidates for important positions there. Its low profile was also reflected in the low number of speeches in the forums of UN.[181] Attempts to act as bridge-builder became a reality towards the end of the decade, when the effects of the 1961 Berlin crisis and that of Cuba in 1962–63 had receded and a period of 'detente' began to emerge. According to a professor of political science, Jan Magnus Jansson, Finland lived through a period of confirmation of its neutrality.[182]

In regard to South Africa, after the Sharpeville massacre in 1961, Finland's attitude was only slightly reformulated. Finland voted in favour of the Resolution condemning apartheid. According to Heino, Finland's basic position on the South African question was not deeply affected by that resolution, but rather there was only a temporary policy shift.[183] As proof of this, it abstained from voting for the part of the Resolution where apartheid was seen as a threat to international peace and security. According to its general guidelines, Finland supported peaceful means of ending apartheid, emphasising negotiations with the South African government and being sceptical towards sanctions. According to Finland's stand, the General Assembly did not have the mandate

---

178. Interview with Mikko Lohikoski, 22.12.1995.

179. The 3rd Special Session of the United Nations General Assembly and the sixteenth session and its resumed session. Publications by the Foreign Ministry. Helsinki 1962, p. 163.

180. "In Finnish foreign policy the old saying was that Finland is not a judge but rather a doctor. I think that type of an approach also within the UN stressed the importance of rather making a change in substance than just flying the Finnish flag. That's why it might seem that Finland didn't appear very much, although things did happen." Interview with Tauno Kääriä 29.8.1995. He was serving as a coordinator for the Nationhood Programme 1980–83. According to him, the 'doctor' approach was still dominant in Finland's policy. He is presently Finland's Ambassador to Bangkok, Thailand.

181. Möttölä, 1984:292.

182. Saarela, 1980:187.

183. Heino, 1992:29.

to decide concerning security matters and sanctions, but rather that right was only held by the Security Council. Furthermore, Finland held on to the principle of universalism, according to which no country should be forced to resign from UN membership.[184]

UN membership also demanded that Finland take a stand on questions of colonialism. At the beginning of the 1960s, when many African states gained their independence and joined the UN structures, the remnants of colonialism were brought onto the agenda. There was a continuous debate in the UN concerning Rhodesia and Namibia as well as the Portuguese colonies. Finland's behaviour followed the general rule: always abstain when possible. It was reluctant to become involved. It preferred to maintain its trade relationships with Portugal and England. Finland's passive attitude towards Namibia at the beginning of the decade was not criticised even by the Missionary Society, which was the only other relevant reference point to Southern Africa. The society was still holding on to the status quo and securing its work in the area. Neither was the diplomatic representation pointing to any need for a change— on the contrary: the marketing effort had just begun to yield results.[185]

But Finnish civil society was awakening to the Southern African question. The young radicals and leftist politicians were calling attention to the colonial and apartheid problems. They wanted Finland to include human rights and moral questions on the foreign policy agenda. When the colonial and apartheid question began to gain more attention in the international community, the NGOs used its resolutions in their national campaigns.

Taking the radical groups in the UN as a framework to urge for economic sanctions, some of the interest groups in Finland responded to the boycott calls. In October 1963, *Kuljetusalan Ammattiliittojen Federatio* (Federation of Transport Workers' Unions) and its major member union *Merimies-Unioni* (Finnish Seamen's Union) headed by its leader Niilo Wälläri, started a blockade of South African ships and goods in Finnish ports. The boycott was inspired by initiatives of the international trade union movement and SYL, the National Union of Finnish Students. This time the blockade was called off practically before it started.

In the following year, the Boycott Committee of Finnish trade unions, under Wälläri's leadership, sent a letter to the Government calling attention to the violations of human rights in South Africa and pressing for a decrease in the trade between Finland and South Africa.[186] With the establishment of the South Africa Committee in 1965, the public action against South Africa was intensified. Together with the trade union boycott committee, it started a consumer boycott of imports from South Africa. This 'brandy boycott', named after one of

---

184. Viemerö, 1975:77–87.
185. Heino, 1992:27.
186. Letter to the Government of Finland, Niilo Wälläri 30.12.1964. Foreign Ministry's Archives.

the most popular South African import products 'Kap Brandy', was especially directed towards the state-owned alcohol monopoly. During the boycott, the students organised public events, including a particularly successful teach-in in May 1966 at the University of Commerce in Helsinki, to heighten awareness of the South African situation.[187]

This time, the boycott came into effect. The activities of the trade unions and the growing public protest were a clear warning to the importers and for the foreign policy decision-makers. The legation in Pretoria was not at all happy about the negative publicity that Finland received due to the boycott. Finland was worried about the trade possibilities.

> The Finnish Seamen's Union's import ban on alcohol is the first political act from Finland's side which has caused loss in Finnish exports. "All depends on the Finnish Trade Unions", said Mr Sole (director of the Foreign Trade Department in South Africa). "If they continue their boycott actions, the trade cooperation with Finland must be reassessed. Trade cannot be unilateral. There are enough partners to trade with. On the contrary, Finland's radical UN policy would not affect the trade relations".[188]

Until now, Finland had succeeded in not harming its good reputation in the eyes of South Africa, despite its protests—albeit rather mild—in the UN. Though South Africa was tolerant toward protests in the multilateral forums, there was a limit. Bilateral relations should continue unharmed, was their message. Generally speaking, talk and resolutions in the international forums were regarded as relatively harmless, ineffective as such. But influence grew out of concrete action, be it a small thing like an effective boycott in a small country of a single brand of imported alcohol. Fortunately for Finland's trade promoters, the boycott died down and it was business as usual. But the civil society had managed to show some of its strength, which was effectively exploited later.

Meanwhile, the Finnish legation followed the events in South Africa through normal diplomatic channels. Their picture of the events was rather distorted, because of the views of the representatives. Contacts with the government were regular. The most worrying development was the security situation, which was getting more attention when the liberation movements' armed wings started their first, although quite modest, sabotage actions. The South African Government's new security arrangements were closely monitored and reported to the Foreign Ministry. In contrast, the understanding of the racial problem was very superficial, to say the least. The Government's segregation measures were praised as appropriate, and the black population's position was considered to be improved by moderate political reforms. The radical policy of the black organisations was not understood, but criticised.

---

187. Personal communication with Raimo Lintonen, a student activist of the time, now a senior researcher at the Institute of Foreign Policy in Helsinki.
188. Report from the Finnish Legation in Cape Town, Tauno Nevalainen 23.1.1967, on a meeting with the South African government representative. Foreign Ministry's Archives.

> The racial question in South Africa will be solved by natural evolution in the course of time. This artificial urgency might mean a disaster for millions. Instead, constructive negotiations in the international forums, even threatening resolutions, might help to speed up the development. Effective sanctions or military intervention would mean that this still peaceful part of the world would be thrown into chaos and great disaster.[189]

4.3. The policy change in the UN after 1966

For Finland, among others, the year 1966 was a point of no return. The policy change came about through several factors. Some changes were made by the Foreign Ministry to its Southern African policy. It was no longer correct that South Africa should be highlighted as a trading partner; thus, as a consequence, the marketing efforts went underground.[190]

What was more important in 1966, was that the left-wing parties gained a clear election victory in the Finnish parliamentary elections. This naturally encouraged the radicals who were critical of the government. The victory led to the first ever left-wing majority in Parliament. It was followed by the formation of the Left and Centre party government called the 'popular front'. The critical Social Democrats were finally in power. This change of power was to become an important factor in Finnish policy towards Southern Africa in the coming years.

Another important issue to have an impact on Finnish foreign policy the same year was the Namibian question. The International Court of Justice had abstained from deciding about the status of Namibia after Ethiopia and Liberia had appealed for an end to the South African mandate. Instead, the UN General Assembly decided by an overwhelming majority to end the mandate and to set up a legal administrative authority for the territory. The Nordic countries, including Finland, voted in favour of the Resolution and Finland's Ambassador Max Jacobson was elected as chairman of an ad hoc committee which was to deal with the South West African question.

The Committee's work ran into problems when a common understanding on the Namibian question was not reached. Finland was pointing out the fact that the Committee's proposals had to be in line with the possibilities for their practical implementation.[191] However, the majority in the General Assembly voted in favour of establishing a Namibia Council. But the superpowers blocked the Committee's proposal that the UN should take Namibia under its control.

---

189. Report from the Finnish Legation in Pretoria, Tauno Nevalainen 1.10.1964. Foreign Ministry's Archives.

190. Letter to the Finnish Foreign Trade Association from the Foreign Ministry, Osmo Orkomies 31.10.1966. Foreign Ministry's Archives. According to the recommendations, the South African trade should no longer, in effect, be promoted in public.

191. Saarela, 1980:189.

Finland abstained from voting. Furthermore, the incompetence of the International Court of Justice led to another, equally important development—namely, that SWAPO started the liberation war against the colonial regime. Finland's line was consistent: she abstained from voting on most of the resolutions. Only when 37 SWAPO activists, including Toivo ya Toivo, were detained by the South African government, did Finland vote in favour of the Resolution which condemned the act.

As a consequence of its membership of the Committee, Finland's policy in the UN was significantly activated for the first time. Her standpoint was secure, though, because the Namibian question was dealt with by a majority vote. When there was a risk of running into conflict between the superpowers, Finland abstained. Finland carefully conformed to the resolutions of the UN, which it followed by the book. For example, in the Rhodesian question, when the Security Council for the first time adopted mandatory sanctions against UDI (the Unilateral Declaration of Independence) in Rhodesia, Finland adapted its national legislation accordingly. It was easy, because there was no trade between Finland and Rhodesia.

Despite all this, the motives for Finnish policy change could, however, be brought into question. Or what else could be indicated by the following letter from Risto Hyvärinen to the chargé d'affaires in Pretoria?

> It is also important to realise the role of the South African question in present-day international politics. In my opinion it is not a moral question but expressly a question of expediency. Nevertheless, it might be expedient to occasionally behave as if we were morally concerned. It has to be remembered that the interests of our overall foreign policy surpass our relations with South Africa. In spite of that—and partly just because of that—I find it expedient to maintain relations, especially economic relations, with South Africa and even improve them.[192]

Trade was the preference. It was not to be disrupted in any way. Pretense was used to cover it up, when necessary. But it had become politically unwise for Finland to be associated with the decreasing number of countries who refused to condemn apartheid by supporting UN resolutions. The South African question was a matter of image, not a true moral question for Finland. But the questions of realism and moral had already emerged within Finland's own decision-making structures. The young radicals had, with growing intensity, started a discussion on the values underlying the foreign policy. The election victory of the left encouraged more discussion in the national press and official forums. The Missionary Society was assessing its position in regard to the South African regime.

Despite that, not even in the Namibian question did Finland's role really become further activated before 1970. Until then, she had followed the policy of

---

192. Personal letter from Risto Hyvärinen, the head of the Political Department of the Foreign Ministry, to the chargé d'affaires Tauno Nevalainen, 11.4.1968. Foreign Ministry's Archives.

the other Nordic and leading Western countries. Since the establishment of the Namibia Commission, Finland's position had been cautious. According to the Finnish UN representative, Max Jacobson, Namibia existed only as 'a state on paper', because South Africa was *de facto* controlling the territory. This determined Finland's policy on the question, because it epitomised the conflict between words and reality, a conflict which continuously weakened the credibility of the UN as a medium for international cooperation. Finland's priority to support the functionality of the UN had prevented her from playing a more active role in the process.[193] The question rose in priority only when Finland was serving as a member of the Security Council in 1970–71.[194]

4.4. The foreign policy debate in Finland

The change in Finland's national foreign policy had to be awaited for some time longer. Her policy in the UN did not affect the bilateral relations with the countries in question. In fact, one can argue that the UN had become another excuse not to act unilaterally. According to Kimmo Pulkkinen:[195]

> The Government and Foreign Ministry saw the United Nations as a vehicle, as an instrument through which and by which Finland could materialise her policy and deliver political statements. In retrospect, without criticism, I may say as my personal opinion that perhaps we tried to ride with this kind of policy a little bit too long. We kept many issues only on the UN level avoiding direct contacts and not taking a national position on them. Questions relating to the Southern Africa and the liberation movements were these kinds of issues.[196]

The South African regime itself was, however, strengthening its position in the world. It was unashamedly refusing to comply with the demands of the international community and relying on its influence on bilateral levels. The Western powers were, after all, with their strong economic partners, effectively blocking in the UN Security Council strong measures against South Africa. But unilateral boycott actions spread around the world. A sign of intensified bilateral relations between Finland and South Africa—one of the countries still unsure of its position—was the establishment of a South African legation in Helsinki in 1967. Worried about the growing public protest against apartheid, the South African Government began to defend itself. The legation was

---

193. Jacobson, 1983:71.
194. Halinen, 1988:111.
195. A young official whose first tasks in the Foreign Ministry included dealing with the liberation movements' assistance in 1971. Before joining the Foreign Ministry, he was active in the UN Student Association. In 1973–74 he served at the Finnish Embassy in Dar es Salaam under Ambassador Ahtisaari, also being responsible for liberation movement contacts. Presently, he is the Finnish Ambassador to Mexico.
196. Interview with Kimmo Pulkkinen, 11.8.1995.

effectively disseminating information, as well as sponsoring studies and trips to South Africa among its supporters in Finland.[197]

In general, as described above, the end of the 1960s became a period of active foreign policy in Finland. The concept of an active foreign policy was based on the view that neutrality and the endeavour to remain outside East-West conflicts were insufficient. The active phase brought with it 'the external tension' between national interests on the one hand and individual moral standards on the other.[198] Although there was quite a wide consensus on the foreign policy line being shaped by President Kekkonen, there were some disagreements around the relationship between neutrality and the obligations of the YYA-pact with the Soviet Union. The core question was, whether the active pursuing of neutrality could violate the YYA's security aspects. Another issue which was debated was the tension between 'idealism' and 'realism'. In one respect, it was a question of determinism versus voluntarism, i.e. whether Finland should actively promote changes in the international system or merely lean on its status quo role which had recently been confirmed in the East-West controversy. In practice, the question was about Finland's position in the Third World problematique and in global peace and development issues.[199]

The younger generation were the most active promoters of the 'idealistic' line of foreign policy. Especially students with language skills and training in international affairs were interested in global issues and wanted to move in the wide world beyond Finland. Thus, many of them had acquired experience of international affairs through NGO activities. They criticised the 'realist' line in foreign policy, which was based on the principle of national interest and practised by a hierarchical administration. Foreign policy was not exposed to democratic discussion outside expert groups inside parties and small papers and some books. Parliament's role in foreign policy decision-making was rather insignificant. And, more importantly, the foreign policy doctrine was based on a narrow concept of national interest.

The younger generation forced foreign policy into public debate, which—according to Heino—was the most intense debate ever witnessed in Finland.[200] This debate between the 'gang of doctors'[201] (the Foreign Ministry's top officials, many of whom held centrist or conservative views) and their opponents in the 'lads' league'[202] (who were leftist or social-democratically

---

197. One product of a successful South African promotion is Heikki Brotherus' book: What is happening in South Africa? 1964.

198. Heino, 1992:43.

199. Möttölä, 1993:65.

200. Heino, 1992:43.

201. Heino lists the central members of the 'gang of doctors' who were President Kekkonen's close foreign policy confidants and aides: Risto Hyvärinen, Aimo Pajunen, Keijo Korhonen and Max Jacobson. Heino, 1992:44.

202. Heino uses the translation 'little league' for the Finnish word 'nappulaliiga'. We found it more appropriate to translate it as 'lads' league'. Central figures in the 'lads' league' were: Jaakko Blomberg, Pertti Joenniemi, Jaakko Kalela, Paavo Lipponen and

oriented young academics or politicians) was centred around the emphasis in foreign policy. The 'lads' league' had actually grown up around UNTA and Committee of 100. They demanded 'a new foreign policy' which would be open to discussion, well-planned, effective, and infused with fresh ideas and personnel, as well as leftist in its analysis and approaches.[203]

> It was a question of bringing new moral values into the sphere of foreign relations. The debate circled around the question, whether foreign policies should be concerned solely with the national interests as narrowly defined or whether there were other values of broader dimension, which Finland should promote in her foreign relations. This was the fundamental issue, in my opinion; not only the national liberation as such, but the question whether we should take responsibility for wider international issues than just the issues of our close neighbourhood.[204]

The 'lads' league' not only discussed, but also worked in other ways. The growing NGO sphere and its international connections provided an opportunity for the young radicals to create their own foreign relations, independently of the attitude of the official circles. The Southern African liberation struggle and policy toward the liberation movements was only one—but an important—question where these two lines, the 'realist' and the 'idealist', came into conflict.[205]

Former Minister of Foreign Affairs and Finnish Ambassador to UN, Dr. Keijo Korhonen has recently defined some arguments in the debate.[206]

Osmo Apunen. However, there were many others who are mentioned elsewhere in this study.

203. Lipponen, 1966a and b.

204. Interview with Ilkka Ristimäki 19.8.1995. Living next door to Nickey Iyambo at Domus Academica student dormitory in 1965, he translated into Finnish Nickey's story of his escape from Namibia across the African continent. Ristimäki was secretary and chairman of Helsinki UN Student Association in 1965–67 and later joined the Bureau for Development Assistance in 1970. He served as an adviser to the Tanzanian Ministry of Finance and Planning, before joining Martti Ahtisaari's staff at the Office of the UN Commissioner for Namibia in New York in 1977. He is presently Finland's permanent representative at OECD in Paris.

205. Other questions were mainly in the field of security policy and relations with the Soviet Union. The debate hovered around the role of military force vs. international co-operative structures, and their relative weight. From today's perspective, it seems that the co-operative attitude got the upper hand and clearly dominates the Finnish approach. This is, of course, due to the profound changes in international society. On the other hand, it is not surprising, because its early proponents now hold power over the foreign policy of Finland. One example of the debate is Blomberg & Joenniemi, 1972.

206. Korhonen, 1989. Korhonen works presently as a university professor in Arizona, USA.

4.5. Support from the official ranks

4.5.1. Finland's development aid becomes established

Although the official foreign policy decision-making apparatus was mainly in the hands of the 'realist' civil servants, there was a small sector inside the administration, that was more sympathetic toward the 'lads' league'. A Bureau for Development Assistance[207] was established in 1965. The department proved to be an important communication channel between the NGOs and the official administration.

Finland had already started multilateral development assistance at the end of the previous decade. The activity expanded to a common Nordic assistance in the form of a joint project in Tanzania. According to the recommendations of the Government's committee for international development aid, Finland ought to give development aid like other countries having high technology and a good economy.[208]

Development aid was more or less an image question, but also an important political vehicle. But at that time, however, this political dimension was not debated publicly. No selfish motives were publicly connected with the development aid. Having experienced several changes in its more than 30 years of existence, the Finnish development policy is once again under public scrutiny. During this process, interesting issues have been brought out, which also throw light on the motives behind that policy during the early years of its existence. Especially the relationship that development aid has to the general foreign policy line is interesting from the point of view of this study.

This led, according to Korhonen, to overestimating foreign policy, and populism:

> Finland's relations with South Africa have, in fact, ceased to be foreign policy in the strict sense of the term. They instead have added a new dimension to domestic and party politics while becoming an important instrument of self-congratulation in the realm of foreign policy. ... Central principles of the policy of neutrality and UN-policy weighted less than populist satisfaction.[209]

For Korhonen, the essence of foreign policy is enlightened self-interest and the primary means for guarding it is security policy. He did not want Finland to become too deeply involved in world affairs, especially not in economic terms.

According to Korhonen the generations that became politically active in the 1960s had no experience of the fear, deprivation and insecurity of the Second World War. They took peace and security for granted. In Korhonen's "rude"

---

207. The Bureau was later called the Office for Development Cooperation.
208. Kansainvälisen Kehitysavun komitea. (Committee for International Development Assistance). Helsinki 1963.
209. Korhonen, 1989:93.

characterisation they were the "spoiled heirs of a tolerant society". This generation looked for international arenas where they would participate in the "awakening and salvation of the proletarian masses of the South".[210]

According to Jaakko Iloniemi[211]—the first director of the Bureau and the author of the one-man committee report on Finnish development aid in 1995—the political position was a relevant element in the thinking of those responsible for development aid and foreign policy.[212] Development aid, being clearly in the area of foreign relations—even when directed toward territories with which previous contacts had been few—was to follow the line of the general foreign policy. And in fact, it was to be ensured that it was justified by several motives, in order to avoid its being connected with either East or West. The growing international activity, which development aid entailed, was to open more channels for Finland to the world community away from the shadow of the Soviet Union.

The Bureau for Development Assistance employed notable figures in its ranks. Iloniemi, who was himself a former secretary general of the National Union of Finnish Students, was joined by Martti Ahtisaari, director of YKA (Students' International Assistance), who had gained experience of development aid in Pakistan while employed by the Swedes, and Kari Karanko.[213] The Bureau was first operated from the premises of Finland's UN Association, one of the participants in the development policy discussion.

Martti Ahtisaari's familiarity with Swedish development aid and its administration, SIDA, was regarded as an important asset. According to him, Finnish development aid was a response to the global challenge of how to solve the problem of poverty. It was supported from very different starting points: on the one hand, the leftist ideas of solidarity and support for liberation movements; and on the other, the liberal cosmopolitan thinking represented by the Swedish minority in Finland. Equally important was the basic Christian world view of common responsibility. Politically, Finland wanted to belong to the progressive Nordic framework.[214] Finland's social structures, cultural framing and political opportunities connect it in a permanent way with Sweden, Norway and Denmark. The multiple justifications were regarded as important in order to secure the widest possible acceptance for the activity.

From a modest start, the development aid grew steadily. In 1972, the Bureau for Development Assistance became a department of the Foreign Ministry to

---

210. Korhonen, 1989:86, translation by P. Peltola.

211. He served for years in Finland's diplomatic corps in Washington and elsewhere. Although working in the private sector nowadays, Jaakko Iloniemi is still regarded as an important background figure in Finland's foreign policy design.

212. Iloniemi, 1995.

213. An officer of development aid for 25 years, presently the head of evaluation and planning. He was working in Dar es Salaam from 1971, and thereafter in Lusaka as a development aid officer, being in constant contact with the liberation movements.

214. Ahtisaari, 1994:59–60.

practise development aid in the form of projects, technical aid and staff recruitment. The development aid budget had increased rapidly: the funds multiplied fivefold between 1968 and 1972.[215] NGOs' influence in increasing development endeavours was significant. The 'development idealism' of the popular movements had mobilised support to increase development assistance. Finland was activated into global cooperation, pursuing a reformist development strategy, i.e. one that aimed to promote negotiated solutions to the conflicting interests between the industrialised and the developing countries. Solidarity toward the UN system became more evident. In development cooperation, Finland preferred social programmes. Justifications were drawn from the ethical and social democratic standpoints.[216]

Nevertheless, the hidden agenda also influenced the development aid. According to one researcher, Lauri Siitonen, the strongest justification in Finnish development policy has been the political dimension: neutrality and support for multilateral institutions with the aim of securing world peace.[217] Development policy has been a vehicle for practising the basic foreign policy doctrine. For that reason, the political authority has remained in the political department.

> We have had very strict borderlines between the aid and career diplomats. This has been a very significant characteristic of Finnish foreign aid throughout these years. There has been a division between the career diplomats and the aid officials. These things have been somehow mixed during the years, but there is still this basic sort of main line there, that the aid officers are not supposed to touch upon the politically sensitive areas although they seem to know much more about the content of that.[218]

According to Karanko, the divisions between the political and aid departments have caused situations where decisions were made separately, not in unison. What is clear, though, is that the development aid was used as a foreign policy tool. Development aid was an area where Finland, while restricted by its geopolitical position, was able to manoeuvre to a certain extent.[219]

When choosing partners, the East–West dimension was a crucial background factor. In the beginning, Finland was determined to avoid those partners who were strongly labelled as belonging either to the Eastern or the Western camp. This changed at the end of the 1960s, when strong political pressure groups and the example of Sweden led to a reassessment of the policy in the direction of showing solidarity toward those who had chosen the socialist path of development. This was due to the NGO pressure groups, which attracted sympathy, and their advice was listened to in the development aid depart-

---

215. Siitonen, 1981:65–66.
216. Siitonen, 1981:82.
217. Ibid.
218. Interview with Kari Karanko, 25.8.1995.
219. Iloniemi, 1995:13.

ment. Accordingly, the African liberation struggle was followed and understood in the department, although it was not in a position to offer any financial or political assistance.

The political department, on the other hand, was not always pleased with the new tendencies in its own ranks. A former chargé d'affaires to Pretoria, Tauno Nevalainen, and others, expressed worry about Finland's economic relations with the developing countries. He criticised the way in which the administration of development aid was organised or, rather, not organised. The development aid department was getting far too many resources to deal with rather unimportant matters, while the resources for economic relations with very important neighbouring countries were not allocated in a sufficient amount. Besides the younger political elite did not understand the African situation deeply enough, and was too hasty in looking for solutions. According to Mr Nevalainen's understanding, the leaders of Africa only needed economic and technical help.[220]

Nevalainen, surely, was not alone in his views, although similar viewpoints were not openly expressed. Rather, they materialised in an indifferent attitude.[221] As a result, the development assistance did not actually live up to its promises. Although it increased rapidly money-wise, its share of the GDP did not reach the goal of 0.7 per cent until the late 1980s. And content-wise, Finland's development aid policy was two-faced: radical global reforms were supported in the multilateral forums, but bilateral assistance remained modest compared with other Nordic countries.[222]

4.5.2. Children's parties allow communication with the top

This did not bother the NGO activists for long, however. Meanwhile another, even more influential path to the inner circles of foreign policy decision-making opened for the radicals right from the top. As early as 1968—when the radical students occupied their own Old Student House in Helsinki to protest against the elitist policy of the Student Union—President Kekkonen, whose visit to the Old Student House was prevented by the occupation, showed sympathy toward the radicals. His policy was to integrate rather than alienate. He, too, needed support for his new openings in foreign policy.

This strategy, which proved to be right, enabled the young radicals to present their policies directly to the President at special 'children's parties', a derogatory but popular term for the regular receptions at the presidential residence in 1968–71. From now on, discussion especially on Third World questions reached the whole population through all the media. Researchers studying

---

220. Memorandum, Tauno Nevalainen 17.9.1971. Foreign Ministry's Archives.
221. E.g. Mikko Lohikoski told how the Foreign Ministry was not at all interested in his travel reports on the liberated areas. Interview with Mikko Lohikoski, 22.12.1995.
222. Siitonen, 1981:135.

radicalism in Finland have been convinced that this integration strategy prevented further frustration and radicalisation of the youth movement,[223] unlike in other European countries e.g. in West Germany and Norway, at that time. It was important to create structures through which the youth leaders could express their aspirations.

The impact was not only one-sided, however. It is not always understood or known that President Kekkonen was not only clever, but sincerely interested and sympathetic. According to Juhani Suomi, a prominent historian with a virtual monopoly over President Kekkonen's personal diaries, the late president was often more radical in his foreign policy than was his own government or foreign policy administration. He showed interest in development in Southern Africa and the points of view of the liberation movements and events on the fronts.[224] The travels of Mikko Lohikoski and his colleagues were presented to and discussed with the President Kekkonen, and he was regularly informed about the news from the field. A sign of his sympathy was the ease with which the appointment with Amílcar Cabral was arranged. "So he [President Kekkonen] had a great readiness for certain decisions of his own. He could follow his advisers, but he could also do exactly what he wanted," says Börje Mattsson, one of the organisers.[225]

Ilkka Ristimäki, an activist of that time remembers:

> In regard to the President and his position vis-à-vis youth organisations, the visit of the Shah of Persia to Finland [in 1969] created an interesting situation. This visit led to major demonstrations by the youth, perhaps the most violent demonstrations I can remember from the sixties in Helsinki. They were aimed against the Shah, but indirectly, of course, they turned against the President, who had invited the Shah and who was now hosting him. For the youth organisation behind the demonstrators, this was a curious situation. As far as I can remember, in the minds of the demonstrators, it was somewhat difficult to understand, why Kekkonen, who was such a hero for these youth as the leader of the policy of neutrality and good neighbourliness towards the Soviet Union, was here rolling out the red carpet for the Shah of Iran. This revealed another dimension of Kekkonen, which was confusing for the youth activists. One can now ask, whether there was some kind of Freudian aspect in relations to Kekkonen, who was such a strong father figure and was always trusted as a kind of good guy. Now how could this father deceive his

---

223. See, for example, von Bonsdorff, 1986. A journalist, Tapani Suominen, has recently written a doctoral dissertation (University of Oslo, 1996) on the far left political movements in Finland during the 1970s. By studying press articles concerning the radical movements, he concluded that the movements' access to the public discussion prevented their radicalisation and marginalisation. The political leaders of the time also effectively exploited the idea of the radical movement and integrated its activists. (*Ilta-Sanomat*, evening press, December 1996). A book based on the dissertation has been published (in Finnish) by Tammi: *Ehkä teloitamme jonkun*. Helsinki 1997.
224. Interview with Juhani Suomi, 17.10.1996.
225. Interview with Börje Mattsson, 29.2.1996.

children by inviting into his house somebody who was so strange to the ideals of the children?[226]

As Ristimäki mentions, the improving relations with the Soviet Union were greeted with satisfaction among the young radicals. In addition, many of them had by now joined the far-left organisations, where friendly relations with the country they regarded as a model were placed on a pedestal. President Kekkonen, as a leader of the foreign policy was given the praise. And support did not only come from the far left, but also from among other political groupings, even from the conservative Kokoomus, liberal Swedish People's Party and the Centre party—which, as the party of Kekkonen, was very outspoken in its Soviet support.

4.6. The 'rebel' civil servants

President Kekkonen's apparent sympathy did not, however, materialise in any concrete political changes concerning the Southern African policy, let alone the Namibian question. Other foreign policy events closer home kept him fully occupied. After all, the core of Finnish foreign policy remained in European affairs. Finland decided to conclude a free trade pact with the European Community. 'Detente' in the superpower relations resulted in intensive activity in global affairs. The German question and European Security arrangements allowed Finland to play a role in between the blocs. Bilaterally, the Soviet Union and Finland went through an active phase. In the UN context, Finland became a member of the Security Council in 1970, and Finland's candidate was a serious contender for the post of UN Secretary General.

Under the mainstream development, what was more important than immediate practical changes was the general atmosphere of President Kekkonen's sympathy, which allowed the NGO activists to present openly hardening criticism toward the foreign policy line. And the criticism did not remain outside the official structures, but became a debated matter in Parliament. In 1970, the proportion of parliamentary questions concerning developing countries out of all the foreign political questions increased threefold from the previous year (from 8 to 25 per cent). The two following years were even more active in that respect: in 1971 and 1972, development questions constituted 44 per cent and 47 per cent of all the questions. South Africa and the liberation movements were on the agenda several times.[227] The Government's and Foreign Ministry officials' incapability to respond to the changing international circumstances was under criticism.

The Foreign Ministry had started a training course for future diplomats known as KAVAKU. In 1970, for the first time, NGO activists had an opportu-

---

226. Interview with Ilkka Ristimäki, 19.8.1995.
227. Tuomi, 1976:241.

nity via this channel to apply for recruitment inside the Foreign Ministry. Formerly known as a fortress of Centre and Conservative party officials, the Ministry now allowed NGO, student and leftists activists to participate in the training course. This 'rebel KAVAKU' shook the old habits and traditions of the Foreign Ministry. And what was more, many of the candidates were accepted for a diplomatic career.[228] A new generation had entered the decision-making structures of Finland's foreign policy.

> What we remember about President Kekkonen's policy and his way of action in general those years was that he gave the younger people a certain freedom and certain areas to take care of. This understanding might have been so informal that probably the practice was never even introduced to the President. Therefore most likely it is not recorded anywhere. Africa must have been one of those issues that the President left to young activists. At least he did not prevent us from speaking about those issues. The President may have considered Africa as a 'secondary issue' and thought that it does no harm if the boys play a little with it. This openedup for us the freedom and opportunity to seek support for African issues.[229]

The young officials were now bound by foreign policy doctrine and bureaucratic procedures.

> Definitely, everyone in the Foreign Ministry down to the youngest attaché knew what issues are such that they must be submitted to superiors in the line of command. Surely, if President Kekkonen would have considered African issues somehow dangerous or would have been afraid that Finland might burn her fingers in playing with the Africans, he could have prevented it simply by saying: stop it. But he didn't. On the other hand, I remember how Kekkonen often bypassed normal bureaucracy and gave certain issues to student groups or political activists as if thinking: let them talk about it, let them prepare the ground for it. The question of the liberation movement might have been one of these issues.[230]

According to some critics, the recruitment of the radicals was simply a 'sell-out', a strategy to silence some of the criticism.[231] But the decision-making apparatus, for its part, probably started to change as well, because now the new thinking made more inroads into the system. The Ministry also represented the composition of Finnish society more widely.

> The fact that a new generation of people was entering the Foreign Ministry meant that the debate which had been going on in the Finnish society—among the public and in the media—since the mid-60s, was now brought to within the walls of the

---

228. There were 30 participants in the course, of whom 16 were admitted to the diplomatic service. Among them were, for example, Kirsti Lintonen, (Finland's first Ambassador to independent Namibia in 1990–95, later first female under-secretary of state in the Foreign Ministry (Department for Development Cooperation), Kimmo Pulkkinen and Rauno Viemerö. Mikko Pyhälä entered the Foreign Ministry through the next KAVAKU.
229. Interview with Kimmo Pulkkinen 11.8.1995.
230. Ibid.
231. Lipponen, 1985, quoted in Heino, 1992:44.

Ministry. Not that we would have lobbied or demonstrated or anything, as was suggested from some directions. Every official in the Foreign Ministry has and had also in the past always his or her political views as a private citizen. This was not normally affecting the way he acted in his capacity as a civil servant. It was the same in our case. The new blood flowing into the Ministry was not different in that respect. They had their views the same way as the old guys had their views. The difference was that now the composition of the staff at the Foreign Ministry was perhaps better reflecting the overall spread of opinions in the society than before.[232]

4.7. Finland as a member of the UN Security Council

In 1969, Finland was elected as a member of the Security Council for the first time, for the period 1970–71. Finland had activated its UN policy and was looking forward to another possibility of making known its policy of active neutrality, introduced by President Kekkonen at the turn of the decade. Finland adopted the role of an active mediator, trying to discover and propose compromise solutions between the conflicting parties. It was fully according to the role that Kekkonen had formulated for Finland. This was a big disappointment to radical NGO circles in Finland, who would have rather seen Finland more as an initiator.

Fortunately, though, in the Namibian question Finland saw some room for manoeuvring. It clearly activated its Namibian policy, adopting a policy of 'serving' neutrality.[233] Finland allied with African and Asian states in order to establish a special committee to deal with the Namibian question. In consultations with the African states Finland proposed that the Namibian question should once again be referred to the International Court of Justice. This time, the answer of the ICJ was rapid and positive: the South African occupation of Namibia was ruled illegal in 1971. In the same context, Finland made a proposal that a special Namibia Trust Fund should be established, which would seek pledges from member countries to be used in Namibian development. The emergency programme for financial and technical assistance—started in 1968—as well as training, would then be financed by the Fund. An additional element would be a scholarship programme for Namibians. The Fund was established and became operational in 1972.

Some of Finland's activity in the Namibian question was a result of the influence of the Missionary Society. As described in the previous chapter, the Foreign Ministry started to get a better understanding of the Namibian situation through its contacts with the missionaries, who themselves had—at least for the most part—changed their minds about the South African policies in the region. That did not, however, indicate that Finland recognised SWAPO or other libera-

---

232. Interview with Ilkka Ristimäki, 19.8.1995.
233. Halinen, 1988:117.

tion movements. Its opinion was as before: no support should be given for violent movements. Instead, the international community should do its utmost to assist the constantly increasing number of refugees who had fled outside Namibian territory.

The Namibian question did get attention, especially because the Court's opinion opened a new phase in the conflict. Finland could more freely vote in favour of firm resolutions condemning South Africa. Yet, it did not support any type of sanctions unless accepted by the UN Security Council.[234] On the domestic front, the liberation movements were not accorded any understanding at the Foreign Office, as the denial of funds for the SYL students' conference indicated.

The active phase in the UN culminated in the contest for the post of the Secretary General, in which Finland was seriously putting forward its own candidate, Ambassador Max Jacobson. In this respect, all diplomatic relations were used to support the candidacy. Mr Jacobson's activities in African affairs were reinforced. That naturally increased Finland's readiness for new openings in the African question. This corresponded well with attempts by the African countries to seek more support for issues that they considered important—that is, the colonial question.

4.8. Outside influence intensifies

4.8.1. The OAU visit to Finland in 1971

Pressure to change the policy orientation also increased from outside. Finland had always regarded the Nordic frame of reference as important in its global policy. The other Nordic countries had for some time had closer cooperation with the liberation movements. Their governments' policy in the UN was more radical. Sweden, especially, had a longer (social democratic) tradition of solidarity work, developed through building up the welfare state and not hampered by the devastation of war. Sweden was also not subject to restrictions due to foreign alignments or affiliations, and thus was able to express rather unreserved support for the liberation struggle—in contrast to Nato members Denmark and Norway, as well as Finland with its particular neutrality. All the other Nordic countries had more often voted together in favour of the radical resolutions, where Finland had preferred to abstain. Though Finland continuously stated that it wanted to act in accordance with the other Nordic countries, in actual fact it followed a few steps behind.

At their respective national levels, the other Nordic countries had already established bilateral relations with many liberation movements. Sweden started to support the liberation movements in the Portuguese colonies in 1969. The Mozambique Institute was already given governmental assistance in 1964.

---

234. Ibid. pp. 87–88.

Norway decided to support the Institute as well as MPLA in 1969. Denmark was reassessing its bilateral relations with South Africa, and was about to start assisting the liberation movements. Its first assistance programme was launched in the fiscal year 1972–73. This naturally concerned Finland, which wanted to maintain its policy in cohesion with the other Nordic countries, but was not yet ready for any real changes in its national foreign policy.

The independent African countries and their cooperation body, the Organisation of African Unity, OAU, had started to take the struggle against colonialism and apartheid more seriously—especially after the UN, at its 25th Session in 1970 had passed a strong resolution to end colonialism. The OAU was looking for more political and financial support from overseas. It had established a special Liberation Committee and a Fund to assist the movements. In this connection, Finland received a delegation from the OAU in October 1971.

The preparation for this visit had started in the previous year, when the initiative came from OAU Secretary General Diallo Telli. He made it known that he wished to pay a visit to the Nordic countries in order to express his appreciation of their activity in the African question. In Finland's case, the OAU Secretary General was referring to Finland's policy in the Security Council and to Max Jacobson.

In this respect, Finland became concerned because it was preparing to put forward its own candidate for the vacancy of UN Secretary General.[235] A positive attitude was taken towards the visit, and a special contribution for the liberation movements was planned. The Luthuli Foundation, which had been set up in Addis Abeba the previous year, was identified as a suitable beneficiary. Sweden had been the founding member of the Foundation and had donated a sum equivalent to 160,000 FIM for its scholarship programmes.[236] Finland decided to contribute 50,000 FIM and to publicise the donation in connection with the OAU visit.

In the end, Mr Telli's visit in the spring had to be cancelled due to other commitments. Instead, a large and high-ranking delegation led by the then OAU President, the President of Mauritania, Ould-Daddah, was planning to make a tour in the Nordic countries. The visit was to be made at a high level. It would take place right after the UN Special Session on Namibia, which was expected to react according to the decision of the International Court of Justice concerning Namibia's legal status.

The delegation was welcome in Finland, and the preparation of the programme was given special attention. The OAU made it known that they wanted especially to discuss the Nordic trade with South Africa. For Finland, which was actively pursuing its trade with South Africa, that was not an easy subject. The national daily *Helsingin Sanomat* had already commented on the coming

---

235. Letter from the Ambassador in Addis Abeba, Joel Pekuri, to the Foreign Ministry 21.1.1971. Foreign Ministry's Archives.
236. "*P.M. Suomen tuki Luthuli—säätiölle*", (Memorandum on Finnish Support to the Luthuli Foundation), Jussi A. Muttonen, 19.1.1971. Foreign Ministry's Archives.

visit in September, saying that the Foreign Ministry was handling the visit 'with a long stick', i.e. carefully, because the discussion on the South African situation would not be pleasant.[237] But the visit was instrumental for Finland in connection with the Secretary General contest.[238] It was important to indicate that Finland's candidate would be supportive to the African cause.[239] This being so, Finland was able to swallow somewhat sharper criticism than usual.

However, stronger forces were mobilised against Finland's dream of a Secretary General. As far as we know, Mr Jacobson's candidacy was stopped by the Soviet Union at an early stage. In a Cold War world, there was no room for Finland to increase its role beyond certain limits.

Anyway, the OAU visit materialised and produced other important results. During the visit, the delegation held talks with President Kekkonen and the Foreign Minister, Väinö Leskinen. The African situation, the Namibian question, and sports and trade boycott against South Africa were brought up. The delegation expressed its satisfaction with Finland's activity in the Namibian question, and asked for more support for the decolonisation process in Africa. President Kekkonen reminded them of Finland's well-known policy of neutrality and support for decolonialism. He reaffirmed his country's non-acceptance of violence as a means of solving international conflicts, and welcomed the proposal for a dialogue inside South Africa.

At the meeting with the Foreign Minister Leskinen, Finland's policy of not directly supporting movements which used violent means was reaffirmed. Instead, he claimed, Finland channelled its support though UN funds. However, Leskinen informed the OAU delegation that Finland would consider channelling assistance to the OAU Liberation Fund for humanitarian purposes. Furthermore the delegation thanked the private organisations which had supported the liberation struggle.[240]

As a result, in the following year, 1972, Finland decided to include the OAU fund among its humanitarian aid channels and a first contribution of 24,000 USD was made.[241] Finland was the first Western country to contribute to that fund. The decision was remarkable also in the sense that Sweden had decided not to channel funds via the liberation fund—the reason being simply that it preferred to support the movements directly, even though it was supporting the work of the liberation committee itself. So far, Sweden's example in choosing the appropriate channels had always been crucial to Finland, so in that respect Finland's unilateral contribution to the fund was quite unique. On the

---

237. *Helsingin Sanomat*, national daily, 12.9.1971.
238. Saarela, 1980:194.
239. Jacobson, 1983:329.
240. "P.M. *Afrikan yhtenäisyysjärjestön OAU:n valtuuskunnan vierailu Suomessa 6–8.10.1971*" (Memorandum on the OAU visit to Finland), Matti Kahiluoto, 25.11.1971. Foreign Ministry's Archives.
241. Memorandum, Embassy of Finland, Dar es Salaam, 11.1.1973. Foreign Ministry's Archives.

other hand, though, Finland clearly preferred an international fund to individual movements as the recipient of its contribution, thus keeping at a distance from the liberation movements.

4.8.2. Liberation movements approach the Finnish Government

Meanwhile, the liberation movements had increased their influence in the Nordic countries. Until then, only SWAPO had had a permanent representative in Finland. Alongside his studies, Nickey Iyambo was mobilising Finns on behalf of Namibia. He tells here about his gradual strategy to mobilise Finnish society:

> Slowly but surely we expanded the horizon from the student organisation to the mass organisations of Finnish society, particularly the trade unions and indeed the political organisations. And in those days, it was the political organisations of the left of the political spectrum that were more forthcoming than those of the right political spectrum. Now after that, it was the time to expand this to the academics. And soon we found Africa and African affairs discussed in seminars, seminar papers prepared, and that people even introduced some texts where African history, Africa politics, African sociological perspectives and information were discussed. And because of that, I realised quickly that indeed, soon or later, we would get to involve governments of those countries as well. By the time we talked to governments, we then had assistance from the citizens of those countries, students in particular, members of political parties of the left political spectrum, and soon thereafter academics. They were not many people that came up in the beginning. But soon thereafter, a few African research papers were produced. That is how the interest was developed.[242]

As we have seen, the presence of Nickey Iyambo was an inspiration to many activists and a source of information. Nickey Iyambo's work was occasionally supported by a visiting delegation from SWAPO. For instance, Sam Nujoma visited at the invitation of the Africa Committee in 1969. When Mr Iyambo started to study medicine, in 1971, SWAPO assigned a representative to Stockholm.

Janet Mondlane was the main organiser for Mozambique. No other FRELIMO representatives were needed in Finland, because in connection with the Operation Day's Work campaign, *Taksvärkki*, a lot of information on Portuguese colonies and the struggle was disseminated.

> And my job was to mobilise and dynamise these Nordic governments to understand what this struggle meant for the independence of Mozambique. That was really my job. FRELIMO didn't get into it until later on. I began in Sweden in 1965, and worked very hard almost up to independence, really up to independence.[243]

---

242. Interview with Nickey Iyambo, 20.8.1996.
243. Interview with Janet Mondlane, 18.7.1996.

In 1970, MPLA from Angola opened an office in Stockholm. The representative, Antonio Neto, visited Helsinki from time to time. The Angolan situation got a lot of publicity after Börje Mattsson's and Mikko Lohikoski's visit to the liberated areas. Discussion centred around the question of which liberation movement was the 'true' popular movement. The far left organisations were strongly promoting MPLA, mainly because it was the closest ally to the Soviet Union. On the diplomatic front, on the other hand, FNLA was being monitored. Other liberation movements like ZAPU, ZANU and ANC visited Finland during special events at the invitation of different organisations.

The representatives of the liberation movements had learned their lessons on foreign policy well. They approached the Government of Finland with great care, aware of Finland's delicate international position.

> Finland was very traumatised and neurotic by the fact that it had this border with the Soviet Union. And it seemed to determine a lot of Finnish policy. At least this is what I was told at the time. At the same time, they were walking the tight-rope with their Western allies. But really I sympathise with Finland, and I think it made the political life a bit difficult. I felt there was a lot of resentment about the Soviet Union—about what had to be done and what positions could be taken. But one must say that if they had to work with or please or be careful with the Soviet Union, the liberation movement wouldn't have disturbed that at all, because the Soviet Union was involved with liberation movements. Like at that time the whole Eastern bloc. But it was very difficult for the so-called Western bloc to be allied or seem to be talking with these revolutionary movements. ... I remember Erkki Liikanen explaining to me the complications of the foreign policy. It was something that I could understand and take into account, because I came from a society with a much wider way of looking at the world—I wasn't confined to the Mozambican viewpoint. So it was easier to cultivate the Nordic countries.[244]

The Mozambique Institute never applied for or received any funds directly from the Finnish Government. The MI was satisfied with the cooperation with students. When Janet Mondlane met the government representatives, she lobbied support for the struggle in general, that is for FRELIMO.

For the representatives of the liberation movement, it became clear that the good relationship with the Soviet Union was an insufficient, if rather necessary, asset for seeking support from Finland. Finland was not another satellite of the Soviet Union, although influenced by it. In the world of *Realpolitik*, even though it was easier for Finland to support movements which were on good terms with its big neighbour, Finland also had to be careful to earn the acceptance of the Western world. Thus it always wanted to emphasise the humanitarian aspect in its policy, and as a result preferred international humanitarian channels for expressing its support. Even though some NGOs used as a model the Soviet Union's policy of supporting the liberation struggle through all means, this approach could be turned upside-down when Finland's foreign policy officials

---

244. Ibid.

were approached. One had to bear in mind the other side of Finnish foreign policy: it was also important to minimise the influence of the Soviet Union.

This paradox was well known by SWAPO representative Nickey Iyambo, who was introduced to Finnish society and Finnish political thinking right from the bottom. He came, after all, to study political science.

> What we were told those days was that Finland also had a very delicate political situation of its own. Being a country sandwiched between East and West means that although Finland has been for a long time a Western country, it had the then Soviet Union as a neighbour under a different political system than Finland's. It was cleverly balancing its own position between the East and West, Finland of course being a Western country. So I think because of its policy of neutrality there was sometimes, should I say, a disinterest as far as remote issues were concerned, in this case Namibia. It was a question whether Finland had something to gain if it takes an active participation and side in African politics. Because those countries that did colonise Africa, of course, had all the monopoly of information that was spread all over the world. You had a trade between Finland and South Africa. And Finland, unfortunately, had to balance between what it was getting in trade with South Africa and to compare it with the simple word and statement of Nickey Iyambo, who was a student of Finland.[245]

In the Namibian and South African cases, as Mr Iyambo rightly points out, the South African trade aspect played a significant role. SWAPO, which was heavily supported by the Soviet Union and other socialist countries, was carefully evaluating the benefits it could obtain from Finland, among other Western countries.[246] In that regard, it had to respect Finland's more delicate international position as compared to Sweden's, for example.

> Finland recognised that she was a neutral country, but with a superpower border. Because of that neutrality Finland was unlike Sweden, which had what you want to call an active neutral policy in terms of speaking out. Sweden was neutral but always ready to speak out openly. Finland chose the road of quiet diplomacy, so to speak. This is maybe the difference between Finland and Sweden. Open vocal, neutral policy approach for Sweden and quiet diplomacy kind of an approach for

---

245. Interview with Nickey Iyambo, 20.8.1996

246. Very little research has in fact been done so far on the relations between the different liberation movements and the Soviet Union. Although it is common knowledge that the movements were heavily supported militarily and economically by the Soviet Union, which considered them as ideological allies, the scope and various forms of the aid as well as the interaction in policy-making between the movements and the Soviet Union has not yet been documented and analysed. Vladimir Shubin, a former official of the Soviet Afro-Asian Solidarity Committee, is presently engaged in research on ANC–Soviet relations at the University of Western Cape, South Africa. In his paper (Shubin, 1994) he argues that the Soviet Union was never actually directing the movements politically, but relied on the movements' own analysis of the Southern African situation and provided support at their request (p. 9). The Soviet Union kept up a direct link with ANC from 1963, in addition to the South African Communist Party, SACP, which was ANC's ally. He points out that since 1963, the Soviet Union had been willing and in a position to render assistance in several fields when not many countries were ready to do so (p. 2). South Africa, however, always wanted to prove that both ANC and SACP were taking orders from the Soviet Union.

Finland. And when Finland realises that most probably she would be involved in the humanitarian causes, I think that was an even more comfortable position for Finland. And of course we also were quite realistic, because it was obvious.[247]

SWAPO used a strategy that was adapted to the country in question and pragmatic in its approach, in order to secure the widest possible international support.

> We knew it would have been pointless, it was not even a measure to discuss, to request or ask arms from any Western countries. It was clear. So we made therefore the distinction that when it comes to education, we can ask help from anybody including the socialist countries. But in addition to education, from the socialist countries we can ask arms. When it came to the West, we knew the question of requesting arms was out, but we could ask for scholarships and financial assistance. So we then said if that continues, we get scholarships and arms from the socialist countries, scholarships and financial assistance and other political support from both of them, wherever possible depending now what is the issue at stake. We were really comfortable with that. ... Of course we condemned, we did condemn any relationships that there were between the West and our colonisers, we did condemn when those relationships were economic relationships, or military relationships or perhaps financial relationships in terms of trade. Those were condemned by us, but they did not go so far that, for instance, as cutting off the contact with them. There were always ways and means of continuing talking to these people.[248]

Nickey Iyambo met often with his colleagues in the Soviet Union, where many were studying and undergoing military training. But as to mobilisation in Finland, his expertise was superior. "I was a Master of Finnish politics and Finnish international relations. There wasn't anything that they could tell me."[249] Iyambo felt he recognised the Finns' need to mirror themselves through the Soviet Union. And exactly for that reason, he preferred to apply an independent strategy in terms of Finland, not treat it as a satellite.

4.9. Winds of change from the field

4.9.1. Chargé d'affaires to Pretoria dismissed

While the Foreign Ministry was still holding firmly onto the status quo in its foreign policy toward the Southern African question, it started to receive different messages even among its own ranks. First of all, a new chargé d'affaires, Jaakko Lyytinen, was assigned to Pretoria in 1969. His style differed fundamentally from that of his predecessor, whose one-sided view he criticised more or

---

247. Interview with Nickey Iyambo, 20.8.1996.
248. Ibid.
249. Ibid.

less openly.[250] Lyytinen's reports on the events in his station country bypassed the official rhetoric and tried to present the reality behind the facade. In 1971, for instance, he reported the difficulties which occurred among the missionaries when the World Council of Churches made an about turn in its opinion on South African apartheid and condemned the South African policy. Many priests were expelled from the territory by means of false accusations.[251] Lyytinen also paid a lot of attention to the liberation movements, as well as political trials and prisoners—such cases were steadily increasing.

Lyytinen's opinions on the South African situation did not please many. In the decision-making apparatus, heavily influenced by the trade community, his messages raised concern. According to them, humanitarian questions were internal matters, not to be bothered with at all. This was indicated in the same context as when the new department of development aid was criticised. When he proposed that the status of the diplomatic representation should be lowered to a consulate, he simply went too far. Lyytinen was called back from Pretoria. In the end, he was dismissed from the Ministry in 1973.

This incident soon became an object of public debate. In Finland it is normal practice that nobody is dismissed from public service without serious misconduct. The Swedish press reported his case and claimed that Finland was seriously considering breaking off diplomatic relations with South Africa.[252] The Government was asked about the reason for his dismissal. This even prompted debate in Parliament on Finland's South African policy line. Any connection between his dismissal and his proposal on the diplomatic representation was, however, denied. He himself considered it certain that his views were not liked by the trading companies, and that he was being harassed.[253] No official explanation for his dismissal was given. Diplomatic relations and trade connections continued as usual. The documents concerning Lyytinen's case are not open to public investigation. Lyytinen himself is no longer here to tell his story. His case, again, refuelled the public discussion on Finland's Southern African policy, hastening its demise some time later.

Finland's missionary work had been another reason for the diplomatic mission to behave well in the eyes of South Africa. Despite the flourishing trade relations and passive diplomacy, the missionary work in Namibia had in fact run into serious trouble. That was because the church itself no longer wanted to be a passive bystander as regards the events in the area. The church's critical attitude toward the illegal administration in Namibia had grown side by side

---

250. "A few years ago the legation seemed to report that there are no dissatisfied blacks in this country. The view of the undersigned is exactly the opposite." Report to the Foreign Ministry, Legation in Pretoria, Jaakko Lyytinen, 19.10.1970. Foreign Ministry's Archives.

251. Report to the Foreign Ministry, Legation in Pretoria, Jaakko Lyytinen, 24.3.1971. Foreign Ministry's Archives.

252. *Dagens Nyheter*, Swedish daily newspaper, 18.11.1973.

253. *Kansan Uutiset*, Finnish daily newspaper, 19.11.1973.

with the debate in the international forums. In 1971, the church leaders had openly handed a letter to the South African Prime Minister to demand South African withdrawal from Namibia. The printing press of the church was bombed. Finally, in October 1972, the best-known advocate of SWAPO in the Finnish Missionary Society, Mikko Ihamäki, was denied entry to Namibia when he intended to return to his duty in that country. When in Finland, among church members there, Rev. Ihamäki started to use his expertise in mobilising understanding and support for the Namibian people, becoming rather successful. In the conservative church circles, the Finnish government's position of not expressing clearer support for the people of Namibia was becoming a target of criticism.

All this also worried the diplomatic mission, although Ovamboland was not under its surveillance. The consulate in Walvis Bay had been closed down when the UN had terminated the mandate and assumed responsibility for governing the area. However, Finland's host country in Pretoria, South Africa, was the *de facto* government of the area and did not want to let go. Finland's image was in danger, once again, because of the critical missionaries. Finland went to great pains in order to accommodate the double pressure, because ending the diplomatic relations was totally out of the question.

4.9.2. Active Finnish community in Dar es Salaam

In Dar es Salaam, the Finnish community came into close contact with the liberation movements. Dar es Salaam was host to most of them and the OAU liberation committee was situated there, so it was natural to communicate with the movements' activists. Tanzania promoted their cause, and this support was personified in President Nyerere's vocal support. Also in connection with the *Taksvärkki* Campaign, the links of the Embassy and the Finnish expatriate community with the Mozambique Institute and FRELIMO increased. As a matter of fact, the members of the expatriate community assisted the movements in their spare time.

> The community of the Finnish expatriates and their spouses in Dar es Salaam was very active. A few months after I had arrived with my wife, we spontaneously organised a study group of those members of the community, who were interested in development and liberation issues. That must have been sometime in February or March 1974. It was called the Action Group Jumatatu after the Swahili name of the day of the first meeting. We were especially involved with FRELIMO, as the organisation had its headquarters in Dar es Salaam. We had many contacts with the FRELIMO camp, they came to address our study circle and we donated blood and did volunteer work for the organisation. There was an accountant among us who helped them to keep their accounts. This was very pragmatic and practical support to FRELIMO civilian headquarters.[254]

---

254. Interview with Ilkka Ristimäki, 19.8.1995.

Finland had found it expedient to recruit people with practical experience of developing countries to its new missions in developing countries. In 1973, Martti Ahtisaari from the Department of Development Cooperation was nominated as Ambassador to Tanzania. He was assisted by the young attaché Kimmo Pulkkinen, who had entered the Foreign Ministry through KAVAKU and dealt with the African question as one of his first tasks. They continued strengthening the links which Kari Karanko—the development aid officer of the Embassy since 1971—and missionaries Marja-Liisa and Lloyd Swantz[255] had already built with SWAPO and other liberation movements in the 1960s.

SWAPO's activists had found their way to Tanzania (then Tanganyika) at the beginning of the 1960s. The Old Location demonstrations in Windhoek and the growing protest among the contract workers in Cape Town and inside Namibia became too much for the regime to tolerate. Small numbers of activists left for exile. The first Namibian ones came from Cape Town, ending up in Tanganyika, considered a friendly country. American missionary Lloyd Swantz, who was assigned to Dar es Salaam to organise religious and humanitarian work among the refugees, actually accommodated Sam Nujoma when he first came as a refugee from South West Africa in 1960. Dr Swantz and his wife, Marja-Liisa, helped for quite some time with clothes, bread and later even with a house and an office for the approximately 100 so-called 'students' in the early days of SWAPO in Dar es Salaam.[256] Mikko Juva, familiar with the Namibian situation and SWAPO, visited Dar es Salaam a few times in the context of his duties in the international Christian organisations. Their personal understanding of and sympathy toward the still rather modest SWAPO organisation had a strong influence on the diplomatic representatives later posted in Dar es Salaam.

According to Martti Ahtisaari, the atmosphere in Dar es Salaam was characterised by development optimism and trust in the future.[257] While the Ministry in Helsinki was still thinking of opening links with the liberation movements, its staff members in Dar es Salaam were already doing it in practice. They had several times passed requests from different liberation movements over to the Foreign Ministry and inquired if the Ministry would take a stand on the matter. According to them, assisting the liberation movements would not do any harm. But their hands were tied, and their actions limited to only personal and volun-

---

255. Lloyd Swantz represented the Evangelical Lutheran Church in America (ECLA) in Dar es Salaam as a pastor of the Azania Front Church 1960–1975. He has continued his work under the auspices of the church after finishing his PhD in anthropology. Dr Marja-Liisa Swantz did her PhD in anthropology and worked at the University of Dar es Salaam. In 1982, she became Director of the Institute of Development Studies, with which she had been involved from its beginning. Presently she works as a visiting professor of WIDER, the United Nations Research Institute in Helsinki. Their closest colleagues in Dar es Salaam included Barbro Johansson, a Swede, Otto Immonen, a Finn, and the American Edward A. Hawley.

256. Interview with Lloyd Swantz, 25.3.1997.

257. Ahtisaari, 1994:60–61

tary assistance. In any case, their open communication with the liberation movement representatives helped the Foreign Ministry to start considering the movements as partners.

4.10. NGO letter to the Foreign Ministry

The train kept moving rather fast in the NGO sector. After the *Taksvärkki* Campaign, the Students' Conference and Cabral's visit, it had become evident that political parties were ready to increase support to the liberation movements. The Social Democrats, still a leading party and the holder of the Foreign Minister's portfolio, had for a long time indicated a change in their attitude. The movements themselves had gained considerable victories in the international arena and earned more recognition. The Namibian question faced a new phase with the court ruling in 1971. Only the Foreign Ministry administration was firm in its policy.

The NGOs' own financial and material support to the liberation movements increased steadily in scope and extent. After its conference, the National Union of Students, SYL, continued its collection of funds for PAIGC and included also MPLA, FRELIMO and SWAPO. The International Solidarity Foundation donated funds to MPLA, FRELIMO, PAIGC, SWAPO and ZANU. The Africa Committee, together with the Emmaus Association, started to collect clothes for MPLA. The students of medicine planned to co-operate in collecting medicines for Angola. Financially, these were small fish, compared with the need for resources demanded by the liberation struggle.

It was evident that state funds were needed to secure continuous and large-scale financial support for the movements. Discussions centred around the method whereby this support would materialise. Liberation movement representatives (Janet Mondlane from the MI and a delegation from ZAPU, among others) visited Finland and met officers in the Ministry, presenting repeated demands for aid with no results.

But in fact, in the Foreign Ministry some preparations were already under way. The Ministry gave general guidelines to its diplomatic missions on its policy toward revolutionary and independence movements. The Finnish diplomatic representatives should treat the liberation movements recognised by the UN Resolutions in a flexible and sympathetic way.[258] The four-page guidelines were very detailed, and had understandably required a lot of work from the political department to determine what was the difference between a rebel group and a 'seriously regarded' liberation movement! However, for the first time ever, it was preparing to take the movements seriously.

The NGO activists were quite well aware of the events in the Ministry. Kalevi Sorsa, who had been the chairperson of the Cabral Reception Committee,

---

258. Administrative Circular Letter No. 15, Helsinki 4.5.1971. Foreign Ministry's Archives.

became Foreign Minister in 1972. He had been a strong advocate of the liberation movements, criticising his colleague, the former Foreign Minister Leskinen, for employing double standards.[259] But he lacked the courage to push for change in the policy on liberation movements on his own initiative. But if there was a clear proposal and pressure from outside, it would be regarded in a positive light, he advised.

Based on that, the Africa Committee made a proposal, that all political parties and the relevant NGOs should prepare and sign a memo on the liberation movements to petition the Finnish government to recognise those movements and channel aid to them. The Cabral Reception Committee was set up again, and a comprehensive memo was written by Mattsson, Pyhälä, Marianne Tarkka and Kristina Vanajas. Pyhälä soon joined the civil service, and abstained from his NGO activities. In the Ministry, however, he was given the tasks of assessing and reporting on the events on the liberation front.[260]

The petition letter was handed to the Foreign Ministry on 23 August 1972.[261] Referring to the UN 25th Session on Colonialism, it demanded that Finland should clarify its stand on liberation movements in the Portuguese colonies and start giving bilateral humanitarian development assistance to FRELIMO, PAIGC and MPLA. Finland should also make preparations for the next General Assembly in the spirit of the UN Resolution. Portuguese colonies were chosen as the focal point, because there the struggle was most advanced. The petition was signed by the political parties from right to left, as well as the church and a few of the most important NGOs—in practice, all important representatives of the civil and political society.

After a few days, Minister Sorsa gave a mandate to his ministry to review the situation. In the Foreign Ministry, several reports had already been made concerning, for instance, the position of the liberation movements in the eyes of international law[262] and the international organisations, as well as their foreign assistance.

A Working Group was set up in January 1973, simply to write up a positive recommendation on aid, according to the chairperson of the group Matti Kahiluoto.[263] The composition of the group was extraordinary, because its members represented political parties from right to left, not only the state administration. This was done to secure the largest possible political support

---

259. See Chapter 2, note 116.

260. *P.M. Ulkomainen tuki Afrikan vapautusliikkeille* (Memorandum on Foreign Support for the African Liberation Movements), Mikko Pyhälä, 15.1.1973, Foreign Ministry's Archive.

261. A letter to the Foreign Ministry from the Africa Committee and undersigned NGOs. 23.8.1972. Foreign Ministry's Archives.

262. Memorandum on the position of the liberation movements in international law, Henrik Räihä, 21.6.1971. Legal department of the Foreign Ministry. Foreign Ministry's Archives.

263. Interview with Matti Kahiluoto, 24.8.1995.

and smooth implementation of the recommendations. Around the same time, on 9 January 1973, the Foreign Affairs Committee of Parliament had recommended that the development cooperation should also include humanitarian and social support for the liberation movements recognised by the UN.[264] Ilkka Ristimäki, who joined the office for development assistance in 1970 and was the secretary of the working group, says:

> During that period the Foreign Ministry set up a working group to determine guidelines regarding possible Finnish assistance through bilateral or multilateral channels to the various liberation movements of Southern Africa. The working group was led by Matti Kahiluoto of the Political Department and I was appointed as its secretary. The working group did not actually do much work. Its essential role was to provide a wide political backing and consensus among the parties for a new policy, which I quickly formulated into a text. From now on Finland was going to provide humanitarian assistance to the economic, social and educational activities of the liberation movements. Essential elements of the consensus were that on the one hand Finland was not promoting or supporting the use of violence and on the other hand the Finnish humanitarian assistance was not to be interpreted by anybody as support to or approval of the use of violence. That was the crux. The text was short, but the change was crucial. Through this advice by the working group the "battle of aid or not" had been concluded. It was now politically legitimate for the Finnish Government to support the liberation struggle in Africa.[265]

4.11. Foreign political justifications behind the policy change

As Ilkka Ristimäki describes, one of the first starting-points for Finland in dealing with the liberation movements was still to avoid supporting violence. It was one of the leading principles in Finnish foreign policy and it had to be worked into any policy reformulation as well. How could a government support a rebel movement which was waging a war against a legitimate member of the international community? In this respect, it surely helped that the international community had clearly decided about the self-determination of the people in the colonies and created ways of channelling humanitarian assistance to the movements of these people. Still, it was an extraordinary decision, because it implied channelling money directly to these movements, not to an international body able to control the flow of funds. The decision becomes more extraordinary when taking into consideration the fact that although the Southern African struggle was relatively unimportant in relation to Finland's international priorities, it needed to be dealt with in the context of the Finnish foreign policy doctrine, which had not been designed to be applied to a situation of that kind.

---

264. Foreign Affairs Committee of Parliament, Letter to the Government 9.1.1973, personal archives of Mikko Pyhälä.
265. Interview with Ilkka Ristimäki, 19.8.1995.

> It was not something different from the general policy line, maybe on the contrary. We tried to see and tried to tackle, treat this particular issue of liberation movements in Southern Africa with the same principles and along the same lines as the foreign policy in general at that time. We have to remember that these were the years also when we struggled and kept neutrality as a main and really leading guideline in any and all foreign policy issues. And in that sense, because neutrality was developed of course first and foremost for the, what we now call, near-area politics for Finnish relations with our neighbours and superpower conflicts. When trying to apply those principles to a far away issue and problem like liberation movements in Southern Africa, it again now, saying it in retrospect, was not so easy to fit into the picture. And through this process, it became obvious that we have to diversify that general neutrality approach and identify a more direct approach to particular issues like the liberation movement. And in that I think the humanitarian assistance came in very handy.[266]

Humanitarian assistance became a tool to deal with the liberation movements. In other words, to include the Southern African struggle in Finnish foreign policy, new ways of international action had to be developed. Finland decided to render internationally accepted humanitarian assistance to the people under colonial rule. The very act of channelling the assistance directly to the movements implied recognition of them or at least an acceptance of their demands for self-determination as justified. And the process of selecting the movements which were supported was a decision determined by political calculations, as we will see in the next chapter. Moreover, the political sensitivity of the liberation movement aid was also highlighted by the fact that all decisions above the level of technical administration of aid were made at the political department of the Foreign Ministry.

Coming back to the questions put forward at the beginning of this chapter—that is, how Finland's policy change came about—we shall try to come to a conclusion. We have shown the process by which the public opinion developed to become more favourable to the liberation movements. It had not been enough that the young radicals in the universities and their respective NGOs had pushed for the policy change and a new foreign policy. Neither had it been sufficient that the liberation struggle was getting more and more understanding and support in the multilateral forums. Finland's national policy had held firm, and the UN had served conveniently as a forum for rhetoric but also for important contacts and as an outlet of multilateral efforts. Changes in the field, in Finland's diplomatic missions, had played a part as well, but critics had to be careful. Trade relations had actively worked against bringing any other values into the foreign policy by promoting economic cooperation above all.

The liberation movements themselves, who adapted their strategy in awareness of Finland's delicate international position, were suffering to some extent from their alliance with the Soviet Union. Finland did not want at any cost to be seen as one of the satellites. The Finnish mission in Ovamboland and its mother

---

266. Interview with Kimmo Pulkkinen, 11.8.1995.

church gradually became important advocates of the black Namibian people and their organisations, especially SWAPO. But they alone could not have brought about the change. The Nordic countries served as one reference group, but all of them—with different international affiliations—had in the end created their own line, Finland notwithstanding.

Finland continuously stated that racism, colonialism and apartheid were foreign to its people. The equality of all and the right of all peoples to self-determination were leading principles in building the modern Finnish welfare state. But it seemed to be difficult to enter these moral questions in the foreign policy agenda. Realist thinking was so justified in the Cold War situation that no deed was allowed to contradict its demands.

In conclusion, as regards the Finnish foreign policy principles—neutrality and good neighbour relations with the Soviet Union, as well as compliance with international declarations, such as those of the UN and an attempt to be one of the Western countries in the Cold War years—it became clear that any policy change should be justified by the largest possible section of the international community and, more importantly, by both superpowers. That acceptance was reached in the UN, where a growing majority of the democratic countries were voting against colonialism and in favour of the people's self-determination. Agreement on the moral principles behind the liberation struggle was reached in the international forums. That gave Finland a basis for a policy reformulation. However, problems remained of how to implement these policies in concrete situations. For the realists, it could have been enough that Finland directed its support via multinational channels, not to the movements directly. The movements were, after all, seen as being on the side of the East, because of the heavy military support flowing from the Soviet Union and its allies and because of the movements' ideological basis.

Thus, additionally, changing the national foreign policy to be favourable to the direct support of the movements, was linked to the international power game, which had its impact in the divided political system in Finland. In the Cold War years, even internal political questions were subject to international power relations. This was especially true of the Africa Committee, which played a significant role in mobilising support for the liberation movements. Overall, most of the Africa solidarity movement was inspired by the socialist ideologies.

Exactly for that reason, the reformulation of Finland's policy to be supportive of the liberation movements demanded pressure from all sectors of Finnish society, an alliance from right to left. This would ensure that left-leaning liberation movements were regarded first and foremost as morally legitimate protest channels of the oppressed. This succeeded. It was both the right and the left, the church and the leftist parties, the political and apolitical, the young and the old, that lobbied for support. Not to forget the Centre, which was the leading party in defining Finnish foreign policy in relation to the Soviet Union. It was not overly interested in supporting the movements, but with the leadership of

President Kekkonen and a number of other leaders, it did not totally reject the idea. Thus, in order to avoid a situation where a policy of supporting the movements would be associated with any of the camps, it was to be carefully justified by all.

This alliance which was formed was to perform an even more important role in the South African sanction question, as we will see in Chapter 6. It also ensured increasing financial assistance to SWAPO and later ANC.

As to the decision-making question that Timo-Erkki Heino put forward, we can conclude the following. We have seen that in order to have an impact on Finnish foreign policy-making—which rests so heavily in the hands of the President, and the Government, and its foreign policy administration, and where Parliament's role is small—there had to be powerful public pressure which would not be neutralised by any excuses. The changing political power relations in Finland played their role in the first place, allowing the radical views to be formed as elements of the political parties' programmes of action. The change was especially significant in the Social Democratic party, which became the largest party in Finland and, as a consequence, was able to formulate the government policy. It did help, too, that the President himself was interested in this particular question. He allowed the change to happen, because there was broad support. Furthermore, the humanitarian support for the African liberation struggle became quite a new asset of foreign policy. It gave Finland a chance to play a significant role in African affairs, which further strengthened her policy of active neutrality at the beginning of the 1970s, when the period of 'détente' provided Finland with more space to manoeuvre in international affairs, at least regarding the Third World. This resulted in Finland's particularly important role in Namibian affairs, as we will see in the next chapter.

Chapter 5
Finland Supporting Liberation Struggles

This chapter deals with one of the purposes of this study, the financial assistance given to liberation movements. At the beginning, we present the quantitatively small, but on the other hand significant contributions to the liberation movements in the Portuguese colonies. They opened the way for Finland, among other Nordic countries, to become a important supporter of independent Mozambique, for instance. We believe that through these seemingly small decisions a new though quite undefined line in Finnish liberation movement policy was built up step by step. The fruits of this more positive standing towards the liberation struggle were gathered in Finland's substantial assistance and role in the Namibian question as well as her firm commitment to isolate apartheid-practising South Africa. The Namibian question is dealt with in this chapter, while the South African problem will be presented in the next.

Despite FINNIDA's growing resources and expertise in development and humanitarian aid, the political department of the Foreign Ministry kept firm in deciding about matters considered politically sensitive. The Namibian question and also the South African problems were divided between 'politics' and 'aid', however artificial this dichotomy may seem from today's perspective. The Foreign Trade Department, too, had an interest in sharing the growing resource flows to Africa, which is most evident in the case of South Africa and Zimbabwe. The NGOs, for their part, united behind the support and although doing battle ideologically from time to time, continued to push the government for new initiatives and greater assistance.

5.1. The decision of principle in 1973

As a result of the NGO petition and the working group in 1973, the Finnish Government decided to "give humanitarian aid also through the national liberation movements. Humanitarian aid which is not aimed to support armed or violent activities could be given through the liberation movements."[267] By then, the support on behalf of aid had become so wide that the first press release on the positive outcome of the working group discussions was distributed before the Government made the formal decision.

This decision of principle formed a basis for cooperation between the Finnish Government and national liberation movements. The aid could first be

---

267. Decision N:o 5/1973. The Foreign Affairs Committee of the Finnish Government 27.3.1973. Foreign Ministry's Archives.

directed to the liberation movements in Portuguese colonies, namely PAIGC in Guinea-Bissau, FRELIMO in Mozambique, and MPLA, FNLA and UNITA in Angola. It could then be extended to the movements in South West Africa/ Namibia (SWAPO) and Southern Rhodesia (ZANU and ZAPU) as well as ANC in South Africa.[268] The Government's decision was aimed

> to support African people living under colonial rule, to the refugees of these areas and the victims of apartheid. This aid should be channelled through the UN specialised agencies, OAU and national liberation movements. The decisive factor in channelling the aid to the various liberation movements is that the aid must reach the largest possible number of people. Thus Finnish aid ought to be given especially through such movements which are widely accepted and whose educational, public health and other administrative network can effectively distribute the aid to the people.[269]

In order to select the particular movements, the Government decided to rely on the decision of the UN and the OAU (Organisation of African Unity). The decision applied to those movements that were referred to in the Resolutions of the General Assembly of the UN and that were recognised by the OAU.

After the formal decision of principle, Finland's policy toward liberation movements changed considerably. Humanitarian support became an important instrument of development aid and was handled by the Department for Development Cooperation, FINNIDA. Many NGOs took advantage of the increasing resources and lobbied for more aid for their own as well as official projects.

5.2. The independence of the Portuguese colonies

The Government's decision on direct aid was taken in March 1973. It was very carefully limited to strictly humanitarian assistance which should be donated in kind. No cash donations were authorised. It was believed that material and equipment could be more easily monitored. The first beneficiaries were PAIGC and FRELIMO. The rapid unfolding of events in the Portuguese colonies nearly nullified the Finnish aid. Independence for these colonies was just around the corner and the liberation movements were becoming future governments.

The Foreign Ministry's first financial contribution to PAIGC 50,000 FIM, was allocated right after the decision. Another donation was made the following year, 300,000 FIM. According to the statistics, the money was channelled through the OAU for UNESCO's literacy programme. It was used to print textbooks. The statistics available do not really reveal whether PAIGC was given any assistance directly in cash or kind to that value. Finland did not continue to

---

268. These were the movements that were considered as possible recipients of Finnish aid. Concrete decisions on assistance were to be handled case by case, as a result of which not all of the above mentioned movements were funded. See below.

269. Press release on the Government's decision 3.4.1973. Foreign Ministry's Archives.

support Guinea-Bissau after its independence in 1974, because that was considered administratively inexpedient and difficult.[270]

In February 1974 the Foreign Minister, Ahti Karjalainen, visited Ethiopia, Kenya, Tanzania and Zambia. It was the first time ever, that a Finnish Foreign Minister made a series of official visits to Africa. Carefully prepared and given wide public documentation, the visits were considered to be of central importance in Finland's unfolding African relations. Up till then, Finnish public opinion concerning Africa had still been rather weak, apart from in the university towns where the NGO activists had done their information work. The awareness had been growing among the activists of the Missionary Society, too. The consequences of the visits were important. During them, Finland's official Africa policy was formulated for years to come.[271] In the programme, meetings with the liberation movements were also arranged. For FRELIMO, it was the first official meeting with the Finnish Government. Dr Karjalainen was able to inform this movement that Finland had decided to assist it directly.[272]

The fate of the assistance to FRELIMO was actually quite interesting. The active Embassy in Dar es Salaam had several times asked the Foreign Ministry's opinion on FRELIMO's request for assistance. The Embassy had, after all, established contacts with FRELIMO as a form of voluntary assistance. Having now been informed about the decision of principle, the Embassy approached FRELIMO asking it to come up with a concrete request. Due to bureaucracy, the matter was still open when it became evident in 1974 that Mozambique would gain its independence under FRELIMO's leadership. Now Finland was in a hurry to make a donation in order to be entered into the records of contributors.

> Late summer and early autumn 1974 we were still in Dar es Salaam considering how to channel the aid and what kind of aid to give to FRELIMO when a political decision was made in Helsinki. That time Ambassador Ahtisaari was on home-leave in Finland and I was in charge of the mission. We were discussing the question with the Foreign Ministry, because normally embassies cannot decide these kinds of things by themselves but instructions and guidelines must come from the Ministry. With Mr Ahtisaari we took the position that we'd better give the Finnish contribution quickly and we'd better give it in cash. We did realise that this was contrary to general principles of humanitarian assistance. But there was the time factor and the deadline was approaching that if we don't act soon we will miss the train and FRELIMO and Mozambique will be independent and Finland would never appear in the statistics of giving assistance to the liberation movement FRELIMO. The struggle with the Foreign Ministry was to get the acceptance for a cash contribution. Finally we got it and FRELIMO got its cheque.[273]

---

270. Memorandum, 30.4.1975. Foreign Ministry, Department for Development Cooperation, Pekka Malinen. Foreign Ministry's Archives.
271. Personal communication with Kari Karanko.
272. *A Voz da Revolução*, No 21, Janeiro-Abril 1974, Arquivo Histórico de Moçambique, Maputo.
273. Interview with Kimmo Pulkkinen, 11.8.1995.

Samora Machel and Marcelino dos Santos received a cheque for 100,000 FIM in October 1974.[274] Mozambique got its independence on 25th June 1975.

MPLA had also approached the Finnish Embassy in Dar es Salaam in 1973. In a carefully designed written application, MPLA requested financial support for food, for building a food storage depot, a cash donation for administrative and transport costs, and funds for an education programme. The request was forwarded to the Foreign Ministry. MPLA renewed its request in February 1974, when no response had yet been received.[275]

It had meanwhile become public that MPLA was in the middle of an internal conflict. A faction was attempting to challenge the leadership of Agostinho Neto. The Finnish Government came to the conclusion that the position of MPLA compared with other movements had seriously weakened and Agostinho Neto's days seemed to be numbered.[276] Seemingly for this reason, Finland was still hesitating with the assistance. According to two documents, Finland finally gave a donation of 90,000 FIM to MPLA.[277] But no concrete evidence is found to confirm the statistics. Instead, another memorandum argues that Finland made a donation to FNLA to the value of 50,000 FIM. Unfortunately there are no documents to confirm this statement, either.[278] The donation probably did not become a reality, after all.

All in all, it seems that FNLA was intended to get 90,000 FIM out of the sum of 300,000 FIM which Finland had granted for UNESCO's textbook project for PAIGC, among others. In any case, this uncertainty reflects the situation in

---

274. Telegram from the Embassy in Dar es Salaam to the Foreign Ministry, Martti Ahtisaari, 10.10.1974. Letter from the Embassy in Dar es Salaam to the Foreign Ministry, Kimmo Pulkkinen 11.10.1974: " I hereby send for your information, a photo and a press release on the occasion of handing over the cheque to FRELIMO. The money was 100,000 FIM, which the Ministry gave, after our long 'battle' as a cheque." Foreign Ministry's Archives. Interestingly, in the same letter Mr Pulkkinen states that he did not know how the 1974 assistance to PAIGC (300,000 FIM) and SWAPO (300,000) was handled. Foreign Ministry's Archives.

275. Letter (SAM 226/109) from the Embassy in Dar es Salaam to the Foreign Ministry, Kimmo Pulkkinen 9.7.1973 and letter (SAM-78/38), Martti Ahtisaari 5.3.1974. Foreign Ministry's Archives.

276. Telegram from the Embassy in Dar es Salaam to the Foreign Ministry, Martti Ahtisaari 3.6.1974. Foreign Ministry's Archives

277. *"Muistio, Kehitysyhteistyö Portugalin entisten Afrikkalaisten siirtomaiden kanssa"* (Memorandum: Development cooperation with the former Portuguese colonies in Africa), Foreign Ministry, Department of Development Cooperation, 30.4.1975, Pekka Malinen; and Memorandum, 6.11.1975, Political Department, Foreign Ministry. The documentation indicates that UNICEF was given 300,000 FIM for a literacy campaign, of which 90,000 FIM went to MPLA. Foreign Ministry's Archives.

278. *"Muistio No 268, Kansallisten vapautusliikkeiden kautta annettava tuki"* (Support through the national liberation movements) 4.5.1983. Foreign Ministry, Political Department. This document is the only one that lists the support for PAIGC, FRELIMO and FNLA. There is no further documentation on how and why the above-mentioned groups were chosen and how the aid was channelled. Interviews could not unfortunately reveal more on the matter. No request from FNLA can be found, either. Foreign Ministry's Archives.

Angola and Finland's standpoints on the matter. Finland never made any serious commitment to the Angolan cause despite strong NGO pressure—mainly from the Africa Group, who lobbied for MPLA, for ideological reasons as well as for the reason that the activists had visited the liberated areas of MPLA.

Consequently, after the Portuguese revolution, Finland waited to see how the internal situation in Angola settled down. Representatives of MPLA did intensive lobbying and paid a visit to Jaakko Iloniemi in November 1975. In the following year, an MPLA delegation visited Finland and had an appointment with Prime Minister Martti Miettunen and Foreign Minister Kalevi Sorsa. Nevertheless, Finland recognised the independence of Angola only after the international community had reached a common standpoint in February 1977. Because of the unclear situation in Angola, no development cooperation agreement with it has been signed to this day. Angola received attention in the Finnish foreign policy mainly in the respect that liberation movements, especially SWAPO, were hosted in its territory. Angola was soon in the midst of a full civil war, from which it is still suffering.

The situation in Mozambique was completely different. There was no internal struggle and the transition to independence was carried out peacefully, in spite of the fact that most of the white people decided to return to Portugal. In April 1975, a seven-member delegation from FRELIMO visited Finland to discuss future cooperation. They met, for instance, Prime Minister Kalevi Sorsa and Minister for Foreign Trade Jermu Laine. During the visit, Finland announced a donation of 300,000 FIM from its humanitarian budget to FRELIMO. Finland promised to assess possible development cooperation in a positive spirit.

Interestingly, despite the top-level meetings and a promise of assistance, the visit produced a scandal in protocol. The delegation complained to their host, Paavo Lipponen, that they were not treated in the way future statesmen should have been. Lipponen filed a complaint to the Foreign Ministry accusing it of not showing enough courtesy to *de facto* heads of state. The discussion continued later on in Dar es Salaam too between Martti Ahtisaari and Marcelino dos Santos. This minor and, practically speaking, quite insignificant episode reveals that Finland's civil servants had not yet realised that today's guerrillas may be tomorrow's statesmen.

In the end, the Foreign Ministry decided to recommend development cooperation with Mozambique. It was adopted as a target country and a development credit was granted in the following year. The deteriorating conditions and the economic crisis in Mozambique, however, led to a situation where the credit was converted into a grant, which was soon followed by a number of other contributions. Over the years, Mozambique has become one of the main recipients of Finnish development aid.

> After the independence the bilateral project assistance started in a common Nordic framework. The first project was a big agricultural project, MONAP, which was

started in 1977. The next was the support for the transport sector, which was an overall support to all SADCC countries. The construction of the port in Nacala started in 1984 as a bilateral project.[279]

The Nordic countries' joint and bilateral support to Mozambique continued and Mozambique became an important recipient of aid in Southern Africa. According to many, the substantial support to Mozambique was seen in connection with the regional political situation. Assistance to a country next to the apartheid regime carried important political implications, though Mozambique was also a host of liberation movements until 1990.[280]

5.3. NGO aid increases

The NGOs were naturally happy about the 1973 decision of principle, on which they had such crucial influence. The NGOs, always on the move, were already directing their attention elsewhere. The struggle against apartheid and against the South African illegal occupation of Namibia was intensified.

But at the same time, assistance programmes for Portuguese colonies continued. The LKS (Students for Medicine), in their medicine collection for MPLA had by late 1973 managed to collect equipment and medicine worth 200,000 FIM. The Africa Committee opened a bank account to collect funds for transport of the goods.[281] To beat the heavy transport costs, the Committee approached the Department for Development Assistance for help.[282] The goods were sent via GDR, where the Solidarity Committee (Solidaritätskomittee der DDR) took the responsibility for sending them forward to Angola and having them distributed by the Angolan Red Cross. The Foreign Ministry decided to pay the transport costs from its humanitarian budget.[283] Thus, for the first time the Foreign Ministry was channelling its humanitarian funds through an NGO to be used in liberation movements' assistance. Unlike in the question of the Students' Conference only three years before in 1971, the NGOs and the Foreign Ministry had struck a common note.

---

279. Interview with Keijo Ruokoranta, 30.8.1995.

280. Interview with David Johansson, 6.10.1995. It is well known that despite the South African and Mozambican governments' so-called Nkomati Agreement to stop supporting the ANC and Renamo respectively in 1984, members of ANC were still residing on Mozambican territory. Furthermore, the Mozambican economy was suffering severely from the South African destabilisation policy in the region.

281. Archives of the SRP collection in the People's Archives

282. Letter from LKS/Angola Group to the Foreign Ministry, Reijo Salmela, 24.10.1973. Foreign Ministry's Archives.

283. *"Muistio 6/4721 KD-73, Humanitaarinen apu kehitysmaille; Helsingin Lääketieteen kandidaattiseuran pyyntö kuljetusavustukseksi Angolan vapautusliikkeille"* (Memorandum on support towards transport costs of the LKS's Angolan project), Department of Development Cooperation, Pirkko Juntti, 14.2.1974. Foreign Ministry's Archives.

The Africa Committee launched an information campaign on Southern Africa and published a special issue on African decolonisation in 1973. The Youth Festival Movement[284] decided to organise fund-raising for the African liberation movements. The campaign collected 101,000 FIM. Also the Central Union of Finnish Trade Unions (SAK) donated 14,000 FIM to the Angolan trade union movement.[285]

The NGOs had for years lobbied for a system of co-funding of development projects. The Ministry set up a working group to consider the possibility and to design an appropriate system. In 1974, a decision was made that the NGOs' development cooperation and information work could be supported in such a way that the NGOs collected a certain share of the budget of their own projects (40 per cent) and the government funded the rest of the project. The government justified the assistance via NGOs by the fact that these complemented the official aid by assisting areas and groups which could not be reached by the government aid.[286] For information projects, 100 per cent funding from the government was available on application.

NGOs which were busy organising campaigns to popularise the liberation movements, immediately took the opportunity to apply for the government funds. The International Solidarity Foundation and the Social Democratic youth organisation (called Young Eagles) were granted information funds to organise a Southern African Campaign in 1975.[287] In addition to that the Africa Committee's material donations were among the first which were co-funded in the 1970s.

The National Union of Finnish Students' fund-raising for PAIGC and SWAPO was assisted with a sum of 54,000 FIM. SYL applied for and was granted funds the following year too, when 60,000 FIM was given for its scholarship programme.[288] It had established a separate fund for development cooperation in 1976. Contributions to the fund were collected from the students, who could make voluntary donations when paying the university registration fee. Establishment of the fund and the voluntary already 'taxed' students in this way. Students' contributions to the fund grew steadily and soon some individual student unions followed the example, when student interest toward the Third World became more widespread. Students ran projects on behalf of the liberation movements and financed scholarship programmes. SYL's grant from

---

284. The Festival Movement was a cooperation forum of youth organisations of the left and centre. It had a close relationship to the youth movements of the Soviet Union and in other socialist countries, and summer festivals and other cultural and solidarity events were organised together with them.

285. Tuomi, 1976:159.

286. "Kansalaisjärjestöjen kansainvälisen toiminnan komiteanmietintö" (Committee report on the international activity of NGOs). Komiteanmietintö 1974:24. Helsinki.

287. Letter 27/39 Keh 74, Unto Korhonen. Foreign Ministry's Archives.

288. Memorandum, 16.2.1976, Department for Development Cooperation, MES; and Memorandum, 22.3.1979, Department for Development Cooperation, Leo Olasvirta.

the government became automatic over the years, and the liberation movements were always the core beneficiaries of its solidarity work.

At the same time, the NGOs intensified their pressure in relation to the South African question. In 1973, the consumer boycott against South African imports came to the fore again. This time, the 'orange boycott' was targeted on fruits. In April 1973, the UN-OAU conference on Southern Africa was held in Oslo. NGO representatives from Finland (Börje Mattsson and Jaakko Kalela) participated with financial help from the Foreign Ministry. Public opinion against the South African regime grew steadily until the Soweto massacre, in June 1976, caused a public outcry about Finland's stable policy towards South Africa. The South African question will be dealt with in more depth in Chapter 6.

As to the Namibian question, NGOs lobbied the Finnish Government to continue its active policy of looking for solutions towards independence. The relationship with SWAPO was established on a new level when Finland started its direct support to SWAPO. Demands for education programmes were intensified. Finnchurchaid's role in promoting the Namibian cause had become more active when Mikko Ihamäki, unable to return to Namibia, concentrated on information work in Finland.

The churches' role in supporting SWAPO was emphasised when Finnchurchaid launched a special campaign to support Namibian refugees in 1974. The campaign was co-funded by the Foreign Ministry. The budget for NGOs grew substantially in 1977, reaching as much as 2 million FIM. Out of that sum, 1.5 million was channelled via missionary organisations. Their health and education work became ever more valuable in Ovamboland, where local conditions were deteriorating rapidly. The church had organised its work among Namibians in such a way that the Missionary Society continued its social work in Ovamboland and Kavango, while the independent local Ovambo-Kavango Lutheran Church (ELOK) was able to carry out the religious work on its own. On the other hand, Finnchurchaid also directed its work outside Namibia to places where there was a lot of need for assistance among the refugees.

5.4. Finland's Namibia policy in the UN becomes more active

As described in Chapter 4, Finland had begun to pursue a substantially more active Namibian policy in the UN. On Finland's initiative, Namibia was legally transferred to being under the authority of the United Nations after the Court's opinion was given in 1971. A special Namibia Commission, which had already been established in 1966 by decision of the General Assembly, accepted more responsibility for the territory's affairs, under the leadership of a Commissioner. SWAPO, which was gaining ever-increasing international recognition, had its position secured in 1973 when the UN recognised it as an authentic representative of the Namibian people.

During the early 1970s, Finland officially adopted the 'policy of protest' in the Namibian question. This was easy, because it was in line with world opinion. In accordance with the UN recommendations, Finland closed its consulate in Walvis Bay in Spring 1971. In that context, Ambassador Lyytinen had a chance to visit the South West African territory. He noted that the South African regime practised a similar repressive policy in the area to that inside its own territory. The majority of the population held a bitter, alienated, even hostile attitude toward the administration, and readiness for 'Black power' was imminent.[289]

Thus, following on Finland's more active role in the Security Council and its success in getting the ICJ's opinion on the Namibia matter, its policy changed rapidly. It strove for membership of the Namibia Council, to which it was elected in 1974. A strong role in this policy shift was played by the pressure of the political parties and the NGOs, as well as the Church's influence, as we have seen in the previous chapters. Finally, in 1973, Finland mentioned SWAPO by name for the first time in a speech in the UN. Later on, an active Ambassador in Dar es Salaam, Martti Ahtisaari, pushed for more openings in the question. He co-operated closely with SWAPO in Tanzania and Zambia, to which he was also accredited as Ambassador.

Sam Nujoma visited Finland in 1974. The Finnish Government made its first donation to SWAPO when 100,000 FIM was granted to be used for its agricultural school and health programme in Zambia. Discussions on closer cooperation with the movement were held. SWAPO was in great need of educational opportunities for its growing number of refugees.

Finland's Namibia policy was now practised actively on two levels. On one hand, it made initiatives and sponsored proposals in the UN. For example, the UN had decided to establish a special institute of higher education for Namibians in Zambia. Finland had sponsored the initiative and made a substantial financial contribution to the fund. There was still, however, a need for more. In the following year, Finland donated 400,000 FIM directly to SWAPO, to be used in education. This was a sign of Finland's growing bilateral interest toward Namibia. SWAPO, recognised as the authentic representative of the Namibian people, was becoming the main—later the only—beneficiary of Finland's Namibia support.

The quickly initiated good relations between SWAPO and the Finnish Government worried the other Namibian organisations. A delegation of SWANU visited Finland in March 1975. SWANU, which was losing its battle on the diplomatic front to SWAPO, was in great need of funds and political support. Its delegation was received by the political department, but no meetings at a high level were arranged. In the discussion, SWANU pointed out that all Finland's liberation movement aid in regard to Namibia was then going to

---

289. Report of the Finnish Legation in Pretoria to the FM, Jaakko Lyytinen, 13.5.1971. Foreign Ministry's Archives.

SWAPO, although SWAPO was not the only Namibian organisation. They criticised SWAPO for monopolising the representation in the international forums and not co-operating with the other movements. The ideological differences were pointed out. SWANU complained that they did not have any say in the affairs of the UN Institute for Namibia (UNIN) nor did it offer them anything. The discussion did not produce any concrete results.[290] SWANU never received any financial assistance from Finland apart from the South Africa Committee's donation in 1967.

Soon, dark clouds gathered over the Namibian question. The battle for Namibia was far from over. SWAPO's diplomatic struggle continued, while South Africa was busy preparing its internal arrangements in Namibia. At that time, South Africa's repressive measures resulted in a growing number of exiles to SWAPO's external wing. This could not happen without political and organisational problems in SWAPO's structures. SWAPO became sensitive to any acts which could mean supporting a solution promoted by the South African regime.

At the same time, the preparations for the UN Institute for Namibia were well on the way. Finland's ambassador to Tanzania, Mr Martti Ahtisaari, represented Finland in the Senate. It was a practical channel for Finland to monitor the developments in the Namibian question at large. SWAPO's internal problems became known by the international community. It was believed there were three different factions in SWAPO. No common negotiations could be held. Mr Nujoma was even hospitalised because of overwork and stress.[291]

According to Ahtisaari, the Namibia Commissioner Sean MacBride gave the following advice to SWAPO's different factions: "do not in any case dissolve the organisation at this point". If they wanted changes in leadership, Mr Nujoma should at least remain as a figurehead. Dissolution would, first and foremost, disturb the Namibian people's cause.[292] The Nordic countries stuck to that attitude when a serious conflict inside SWAPO escalated and finally led to imprisonment of the so-called rebels. We will come back to these events later in this chapter (5.10).

Meanwhile, Finland's bilateral aid to Namibia took the form of a special programme for Namibia. Namibia and SWAPO were the entities that owned the greatest share of popularity and support in the context of the liberation struggle. The public opinion was thus in favour of a growing contribution. In

---

290. Memorandum. No 7/3878, Political Department, Foreign Ministry, Reijo Uusiniemi 10.3.1975. Foreign Ministry's Archives

291. "P.M. YK:n Namibia Instituutin johtokunnan ensimmäisestä kokouksesta Lusakassa 24–25.7.1975" (Memorandum on the first board meeting of the UN Namibia Institute). Finnish Embassy in Dar es Salaam, Martti Ahtisaari 28.7.1975. Foreign Ministry's Archives.

292. Report to the Foreign Ministry, No R-1691/504, Finnish Embassy in Dar es Salaam, Martti Ahtisaari, 28.7.1975. Foreign Ministry's Archives.

this context, the government had the courage to start a venture never tried before in Finland's Third World policy.

5.5. The Namibia scholarship programme

The background of the scholarship programme can be traced from the following incidents. Bishop Leonard Auala was a regular visitor to Finland. The church had started a scholarship programme with the Ambo-Kavango church some years back. In 1969 the first student had arrived in Finland to study theology. In 1974, when Bishop Auala was again in Finland, there were serious talks on extending the scholarship programme and having it funded by the Government. The Missionary Society made a proposal to the Finnish Government in November 1974.[293]

On his way to Finland, Bishop Auala had for the first time visited SWAPO's refugee settlement in Zambia, where his host was Sam Nujoma, whom he had only met for the first time in 1970. Sam Nujoma, too, had visited Finland in 1974 to discuss cooperation with the Finnish Government, and a provision for education had been made. Although the camps lacked a lot of materials, the greatest need was for educational opportunities. The SWAPO representatives had a good relationship with the Finnish Embassy in Lusaka, where Kari Karanko was working as a development officer. And naturally, Nickey Iyambo was an encouraging example and an active promoter of scholarship programmes. In this way, the church's and SWAPO's interests were in harmony and the Finnish Government could be approached with a solid idea. After all these meetings and discussions, an idea had matured: to start a bilateral education programme which would bring Namibians to study in Finland.

> In a European or Scandinavian context Finland was special in the sense that it accepted people to go and study there under its sponsorship [in a government's specially designed programme]. And it also went out of its way to assist students actually to acquire basic qualifications. Many of our students, when they left the country, they had not even finished their grade twelve of matric. But some of them went there, did their language, some of them even went to the high schools to just get a solid background. Finland was also one of the countries which was ready to bend its rules to allow people to do their things there. Those who studied there, could study courses which are very difficult within the European context to get: medicine, dentistry, geology, and this kind of things. It is not easy to get to study those subjects. People even went there to study nursing. In Finland nursing is taught in Finnish, not too many countries can accept you to go there and study a thing like that which is so local. But they really went out to accommodate us in that respect.[294]

---

293. Letter from the FMS, 3.11.1974. Foreign Ministry's Archives.
294. Interview 22.8.1996 with Nahas Angula, at that time responsible for SWAPO's education programmes, and presently the Minister of Higher Education for the Government of Namibia.

For SWAPO, the scholarship programme was most welcome. In the Foreign Ministry administration, there were many who were sceptical about the idea. Finland's important reference country as regards development cooperation, Sweden, had invited some, later prominent, students to study there, but not in the form of a coherent programme. What Finland was trying to do was to set up a specially designed comprehensive education programme, which was something new in Western Europe. The logistical, cultural, educational, linguistic and other problems seemed overwhelming. But there were also many who thought that this could be absolutely the best way to use the bilateral assistance, which until then had been used for buying materials (sewing machines, petrol and the like). Many other countries were already making material and financial donations. But no other country had the special asset Finland had: the hundred-year-old relationship and knowledge of Namibia because of the missionary work.

> And the idea was first to have them here in a sort of basic adjustment training—Finnish language and all these types of things. We were not at all doubtful on teaching them the Finnish language, because we thought that, well, Namibians already know so many languages, so that an additional language wouldn't be a problem. And it could open them a door into our high learning institutions and technical institutions. So that was not a problem. And they were also willing to learn that language, because they had a sort of interesting tie to Finland, especially those who were from Ovambo.[295]

Even if the Government could finally accept and finance the initiative, it was not willing and able to administer it in practice. In this respect, Finnchurchaid came in very handy: they already had some experience in working with scholarship programmes. Another benefit was that Mikko Ihamäki, who had spent ten years in Ambomaa, was currently working for Finnchurchaid in Finland.

> Most probably during that time the contact between Finland and Namibians really got increased because even the missionaries that were then in Namibia were getting involved. ... There was a positive evolution taking place: the increased contacts between us, members of the liberation movement, and realisation from the Finnish government that it had to increase its participation in humanitarian endeavours. Therefore it made the proposals of the UN Institute for Namibia, and [then a decision to be] willing to be directly involved in increasing humanitarian assistance for Namibia in terms of scholarships. Again the Finnish missionaries—when it comes to Namibia culturally or socially—knew it better than anybody else in Finland those days. I think that provided a platform.[296]

Mr Karanko adds:

> We got to know them [the Namibians] very well and we organised together with Mikko Ihamäki the selection of the students. Mikko came from Finland specially

---

295. Interview with Kari Karanko, 25.8.1995.
296. Interview with Nickey Iyambo, 20.8.1996.

assigned by the Foreign Ministry to interview these students with their own languages and he knew very well about the educational standards in Namibia, so he couldn't be fooled by anybody. And the students came and they told that I have passed the secondary education or I have passed the middle school or something like that. He knew exactly about what this was all about and we were able to recruit quite a nice group of students to Finland.[297]

A partnership agreement between the Foreign Ministry and Finnchurchaid was signed in November 1975. According to the agreement, Finland would pay the costs of 20 students in Finland, including the administrational costs. Finnchurchaid would be responsible for the administration itself. The task was considered quite delicate—the students were all members of the liberation movement, and Finland was a sovereign state, that had diplomatic relations with South Africa, which SWAPO was fighting against. The Finnish Foreign Ministry would be responsible for selecting the students—together however with the Finnchurchaid when needed. Contacts with SWAPO functioned through the Foreign Ministry.[298]

The programme was to start at the beginning of the following year. The idea was to educate professionals for the needs of the future government of Namibia, but also for the needs of the refugee camps. The programme objectives would be reviewed annually. In principle, the agreement was to educate Namibians no matter what their political affiliation was, but in actual fact they were all SWAPO students, because they came from its refugee camps in Zambia.

The students were selected in good cooperation with SWAPO and Finnchurchaid's Mikko Ihamäki, who was commissioned by the Foreign Ministry. The practical arrangements for the programme were enormous, definitely enough to scare the sceptics. Mr Karanko's house in Lusaka was turned into a recruitment centre, where students were brought by lorry for interview. Their qualifications, medical condition and so on had to be checked. In the final phase, SWAPO changed some of the students, showing that it wanted to control the programme after all.[299] Finnchurchaid had recruited a secretary to administer the programme in Finland. Visas, residence permits and accommodation, not to mention warm clothes, had to be arranged. Educational institutes were contacted to accommodate the students for the first year to study the Finnish language and culture.

In January 1976, a group of 18 Namibian youngsters arrived from Zambia in the middle of the Finnish winter. As was proved later on, this group was the most promising of all the groups to come; Elia and Maria Kaakunga, Leake

---

297. Interview with Kari Karanko, 25.8.1995.
298. Agreement between the Foreign Ministry and Finnchurchaid, Helsinki, November 6, 1975. Foreign Ministry's Archives.
299. Interview with Kari Karanko, 25.8.1995.

Hangala and Raimo Kankondi,[300] among others, were to proceed to university studies and to have an important influence in shaping the Namibian future. The optimistic Namibians and their Finnish hosts did not know that they would have to wait for independence for another 15 years. In the coming years altogether 64 students were to join the programme.[301]

The programme had its ups and downs. Apart from the normal practical problems which occur in every exchange programme, where people from different cultures interact, there were also more delicate crises to overcome. One of the problems occurred right at the beginning of the programme, when some of the students were accommodated in the same premises as some Namibian businesswomen, who came to an international conference. The incident, which precipitated a written protest letter from SWAPO and an apology from the Missionary Society, was an indication of the atmosphere of paranoia and anger to which the Namibians had been exposed under the apartheid regime.[302] Ideological differences played a role as well.

> The students were rather ignorant as far as the political struggle is concerned. And they were very much concerned about the socialist way of development in their own countries. Mainly because of this very close connection [with some organisations from the far left], the antagonistic feelings had grown up towards the Missionary Society and also the Foreign Affairs. [We thought that] we cannot let the SWAPO people blame the Missionary Society, which has been so much supportive for their cause, and which is very much liked by SWAPO people inside Namibia. So we cannot tolerate that they come here and they give statements which are utterly rubbish. We considered the Missionary Society our allies in supporting African liberation at large.[303]

By then, ideological differences had started to split the solidarity movement. A number of the students and activists from the second wave of the radical movements of the 1960s had joined the far-left organisations. The most signifi-

---

300. Elia and Maria got married in Finland and had three children. Elia served as SWAPO representative to Finland until he was killed in a car accident in Namibia just prior to the election in 1989. His doctoral dissertation was published at Åbo Akademi in 1990, after his death. Maria, who finished a Master's degree in education, returned to Namibia and now serves the new Government as a civil servant. Leake Hangala, who completed his PhD in geology in Finland, was the permanent secretary of the Ministry for Mines and Energy before becoming the Director of Nampower, the electricity company of Namibia, in 1996. Raimo Kankondi became a biologist and a doctor of veterinary science, and served as the permanent secretary for the Ministry of Fisheries until his death in 1994.

301. *Kumppanuutta rakentamassa* (1994) (Building the Partnership) p. 1. The student groups arrived as follows: 1976:SWAPO I, 22 students; 1979: SWAPO II, 3 students; 1983: SWAPO III, 10 students; nurses, 21 students; FM/Finnchurchaid group 3 students.

302. Letter SFR/00/034/77 from SWAPO to the Minister for Foreign Affairs of Finland, Peter Mueshihange, Lusaka 3.6.1977; *Muistio* (Discussion memo) Finnish Embassy in Lusaka, 11.7.1977, and Letter from the Finnish Missionary Society to the Political Department in the Foreign Ministry, Alpo Hukka, 22.7.1977. Foreign Ministry's Archives.

303. Interview with Kari Karanko, 25.8.1995.

cant move had been the affiliation of the Africa Committee to the Finnish Peace Committee, which was falling more and more into the hands of the minority Stalinist faction in the deepening division of the Finnish Communist Party. Its consequences were also felt in the Africa Committee, which showed a growing tendency of trying to 'own' the liberation struggle in Finland. Fair enough—they had, in any case, been among the first to start popular campaigning for the movements. But now, with the growing ideological differences, the liberation struggle was used as a weapon in Finland's internal political power game.

Thus it was mainly the internal situation in Finland, the battle between different leftist parties—or rather their factions—which had an impact on different solidarity organisations and in that way on SWAPO students too. The Soviet Union was very sympathetic in the eyes of SWAPO students, reflecting the considerable military aid flowing from socialist countries. Socialism, in its Soviet interpretation, was the model for SWAPO's political thinking in the 1970s and for several years into the 1980s. In Finland, only the minority communists represented this ideological strain. Conflicts arose when SWAPO insisted on running its programmes through organisations like the Finnish Peace Committee and its Africa Committee, which were dominated by minority communists.

As a result of the ideological power struggle, the youth organisation *Teiniliitto* had also suffered from overpoliticisation, overbureaucratisation and loss of credibility. The officials were accused of misuse of funds, and that also affected its fund-raising activity, *Taksvärkki*, which had to be stopped. As a consequence, *Teiniliitto* was dissolved in the mid-1970s, resulting in the loss of one of the original promoters of the liberation struggles.

In the end, the wide consensus supporting Namibia prevented the conflicts from growing too serious. The alliance—which had proved so effective in mobilising for the liberation struggle and lobbying for change in the official policy—survived despite some difficult moments. Namibian independence, under the leadership of SWAPO, was a unifying aim for all the groupings from right to left.

The scholarship programme was a success. Fifty-eight students obtained a professional diploma or a university degree. Only six students had to cancel their studies because of illness or poor performance. The number of dropouts was small when taking into consideration the difficult background of the students and the great cultural difference. No systematic study has been done on how the students' careers have proceeded. Many of them have managed well in their professions and some have obtained high government posts.[304]

In retrospect, many who did not support the programme at all when it started, are among those who praise it most today.

> Within FINNIDA there was a doubt about having these students here at all. There was a doubt about having them here, there was some kind of doubt about them

---

304. *Kumppanuutta rakentamassa*, 1994:8 (Building the Partnership).

causing problems. Because there was no knowledge about the future, when Namibia is going to be free. What are we training these for? What are they becoming? In individual cases it was OK, everybody accepted in the early 60s, that Nickey Iyambo was very good. And then we had, all of a sudden, 20 Iyambos here, another 20, and they were all over and they caused some problems. You have 40 people here or 50 people and somebody is just not fitting well, somebody is getting crazy and so on.[305]

From the Finnchurchaid point of view problems were also recognised.

> Well, the programme had some problems and difficulties, because we were implementing it, but the pre-Christian rule says that, the one who is paying for it—in this case FINNIDA—will also rule quite a lot. And there were some tensions in that sense. And that is why I was very grateful if and when the personnel were changing; that was one exception, where I really liked FINNIDA people to change as quickly as possible. But there were some people who didn't change and performed their duties well.[306]

Mr Höysniemi refers, like Mr Karanko, to those reluctant officials, who did not believe in the programme and its participants. According to Mr Höysniemi, the practical arrangements for the programme were easier to handle, because the church had some experience with Chilean refugees, who had been received by Finland a few years before. The popular support for Namibia was greater and its students were received more warmly compared with the Chileans, with whom Finns had no previous connection. Mr Höysniemi also reminds us of SWAPO's role:

> At the same time we had very good support and even guidance from SWAPO itself and these group leaders with SWAPO representatives. Nickey Iyambo was representative here in Finland for quite a while. And then there were some others in Sweden and they were authoritative persons, who came here and they took care of the worst cases, if there were some; in fact, there were some not so good cases. But SWAPO had a good disciplinary grip, so that helped quite a lot.[307]

5.6. Other cooperation with SWAPO

The scholarship programme was the most visible part of Finland's support to SWAPO. In 1975-1978 it swallowed the whole aid budget. But as the Namibian situation faced a deadlock and the battle got complicated after the promising settlement in 1978 went wrong, SWAPO was allocated more funds for its refugee work. A Committee which was reviewing Finnish development aid

---

305. Interview with Kari Karanko, 25.8.1995.
306. Interview with Yrjö Höysniemi, 11.10.1995.
307. Interview with Yrjö Höysniemi, 11.10.1995.

explicitly recommended an increase in Finland's humanitarian support for the liberation movements.[308]

The government gave direct financial support to SWAPO according to a jointly agreed plan. SWAPO purchased goods for the camps and was obliged to report to Finland on the use of the funds. The government was unwilling to enter into a project agreement with SWAPO. At the same time, the development cooperation budget exceeded the administrative and technical capacity of FINNIDA. Consultant firms were allowed to implement projects which they won through a process of tendering. But in SWAPO's case this was not expedient, because of the particular character of the receiver.

NGOs, however, were very committed and experienced for doing the work. SWAPO had already entered into agreements with many NGOs to start project activities instead of the pure delivery of goods. For instance, construction projects were started by *Taksvärkki* and the International Solidarity Foundation.

> The consultant system, which came up in Finnish aid policy in the early 1980s, was because we couldn't increase the number of personnel in FINNIDA to the extent the aid increased. So we relied on contracting out literally all programmes, whereas in liberation movements' assistance only the education materials programme was contracted out to the publishing company, Otava. Sometimes also the foreign affairs officers are somehow devoted and involved also mentally in these matters, but not very often. But NGOs were. And that was an asset in this programme, because they did it very well, they cared about the people they were working together with. Had we had another model, had we employed consultants or agencies to do this job for us, it could have been more outside work. It could not perhaps have been such a good sort of learning together process as it was when it was done by the NGOs and various organisations.[309]

For instance, the government assisted the *Taksvärkki* Campaign in the shipping of the equipment to the camps in 1979.

Finally, in 1983 the Namibia assistance, which had been distributed through various channels and was still increasing, was designed in the form of a special Namibia Education, Health, Nutrition and Research Programme.[310] This included first the scholarship programme, in which connection a new nurses' training programme was started; production of the primary education material for the camps' schools: funding the extension education programme in the context of the UN Institute for Namibia and funding the research programme, which was for the most part run by the University of Joensuu. Only the educational material production was contracted outside.

By the end of the 1970s many new organisations had entered into contact with SWAPO. This was mainly thanks to Nickey Iyambo, whose energy in

---

308. "Kehitysyhteistyökomitean mietintö" (Report on the Development Cooperation Committee), Komiteanmietintö 1978:11. Helsinki.
309. Interview with Kari Karanko, 25.8.1995.
310. "*Humanitaarisen avun toimialaselvitys*"(Evaluation of Finnish Humanitarian Aid), 1985:56.

promoting the Namibian cause was endless. For instance, an alliance of the Finnish adult education associations adopted a project in the SWAPO camp Kwanza Sul, after Nickey Iyambo—then a student of medicine—participated in one working group session. He pointed out the lack of proper equipment and medicine in the camps. This 'Suitcase for a Doctor' campaign started in 1976 and led to a decade-long commitment of peace education activists to the Namibian cause. A warm personal relationship developed between Nickey Iyambo and the 'grand old lady' of peace education Helena Kekkonen. The Peace Education Institute, which grew from the alliance, started the 'Without Homeland' project with SWAPO in 1982 to raise funds for scholarship students inside and outside Finland.[311] This project was instrumental in popularising the Namibian struggle, because a lot of information work and fund-raising was done in schools all over Finland and in other institutions, which were not that familiar with the solidarity questions. Later on, some trade union groups and retired people built and shipped three buses for SWAPO.

5.7. Trade unions join in

Finnish trade unions were latecomers to Third World affairs. In particular cases, the unions had been quite active, as proved by the example of Niilo Wälläri and the early activities of his Seaman's Union in the1960s. The solidarity movement for Africa recognised the potential of the trade unions, and they joined in especially in the boycott actions. After Wälläri's death, no other union—individually or jointly—started on its own initiative any relevant actions before the 1980s, despite calls from the international community. However, when the need for actual solidarity work world wide was realised at the central organisation level in the unions, its scale and influence began to grow fast.

The first project was in Africa, for Namibia. In 1979, the Central Organisation of Finnish Trade Unions (SAK) started to support the building up of Namibian trade unions affiliated to the National Union of Namibian Workers (NUNW), which is the trade union arm of SWAPO. The work was mainly education and it was done in SWAPO refugee settlements in Angola, and by holding seminars elsewhere in Southern Africa (i.e. at UNIN) and in Finland. It included support for the building and maintenance of Nduuvu Nangolo Trade Union School in Kwanza Sul, and the establishment of the trade union mouthpiece *The Namibian Worker*, which was printed at the ANC printer's in Luanda from 1983 onwards. During the years 1983–89, five courses of ten months each were conducted at NNTUC. A total of 109 persons graduated from those courses. All the teachers were Namibians. In addition, several 6-week seminars,

---

311. Personal archives of and communication between the author and Helena Kekkonen. A Licenciate of Technology Ms Kekkonen has been working for adult education, concentrating especially on peace and development questions. She was the founder of the Peace Education Institute in 1981.

led by Finns, were held for the same people and others. There was a scholarship programme, too, whereby six scholarships were granted for several years each for studies at Finnish and foreign universities. The programmes cost about 8 million FIM.[312]

The work spread into other areas, including a highly successful brick factory and carpentry workshop in Kwanza Sul settlement, built and run by the Workers' Cultural Union of Finland (TSL). During its four years of existence, the factory produced enough bricks to enable several hundred small houses to be built to replace the dilapidated tents that were the earlier homes of refugees. In 1986, the Finnish Ministry of Labour organised two courses on Labour Administration in Angola and Finland for future labour officials. Many of these projects applied for and were granted funds from the NGO co-funding system of FINNIDA. SWAPO projects were, actually, particularly encouraged, because the humanitarian budget was steadily increasing.

Many of the NGO projects were implemented in close cooperation with the other NGOs, each taking responsibility for certain sectors of the work according to their areas of interest. SYL continued its assistance campaign. A new phase was started when SWAPO came up with the idea of preschool education. A kindergarten teachers' training project was started and a kindergarten building was constructed on the premises of a health and education centre in Kwanza. The Africa Committee started its health programme and sent doctors to Kwanza Sul in 1981. A notable characteristic of the NGO assistance was, that there was a lot of co-ordination and cooperation. Despite the ideological and power struggles in the home country, these did not affect the actual project work and there was friendly coexistence in the field.

> It was funny at that time that there was quite a lot of [institutional] co-ordination missing. There was this normal 'jungle drum' where you got the information and rumours that somebody is now going, there is some project starting and so forth, very small pieces from this and that. But it worked, I mean, always people made contact with each other, when somebody was going to Kwanza Sul or SOMAFCO [the ANC camp in Tanzania]. Then we sent something there. It was quite fluent, there were not major problems.[313]

Over the years, the government and SWAPO held annual negotiations on the aid package. The NGOs always participated in the talks. At the beginning of the 1980s, the tendency to link development assistance with Finland's export interests led occasionally to comical situations where SWAPO rejected Finland's

---

312. The effort of SAK is described in the doctoral dissertation of Pekka Peltola (1995). Projects were run by Ilkka Tahvanainen, Jukka Pääkkönen and Pekka Peltola among others. Pääkkönen and Peltola, former journalists, combined the project work with producing articles and documentary films for the Finnish media.

313. Interview with Ms Tuija Halmari, 8.2.1996. She worked in SYL as development officer after 1985. Presently she works at FIDIDA, the development NGO for disabled people, and is active in the framework of KEPA.

offers, for instance SISU trucks.[314] After all, SWAPO was receiving plenty of international aid and could already afford to choose what it wanted. In this particular case it preferred Volvos from Sweden!

5.8. Nordic cooperation

Nordic cooperation in questions relating to the liberation struggle was further strengthened when Finland, the last in line, reformulated its policy toward the movements. In the international arena, the Nordic countries continued to support the view that peaceful solutions to the conflict should be sought. Although they recognised SWAPO as a representative of the Namibian people, and sought cooperation with it, they had as well declined to endorse SWAPO's armed struggle as a legitimate part of the UN policy as proposed by the Third World countries since 1976.[315]

During its Security Council membership, Finland had played a leading role in initiating solutions to the Namibian question as well as proposing programmes of assistance. Thereafter, it had accepted the co-ordinating role for the Nordic Countries in the Namibian question. That was also due to Finland's special relationship to Namibia through the mission work. The communication between the Nordic capitals was always intense when the Namibia sessions in the UN approached. Attempts to formulate common policies were emphasised in order to increase their political importance and power.

> There was also division of labour between the Nordic countries. Because Finland was a member in the Council for Namibia, we had a sort of special role vis-à-vis Namibia. All countries had a special role in UN, and the different countries had different seats.[316]

But common policy was not a must, and sometimes also difficult to achieve, because of each country's different priorities in foreign policy and positions vis-à-vis international organisations. Sweden was by far the largest donor. Denmark and Norway had to view their positions in respect to NATO—and in the case of Denmark—the EC. Finland's willingness to act was dependent on a mixture of domestic public opinion, foreign trade considerations, and its hope of showing the standpoint of a good non-aligned member of the United Nations. All in all, the Nordic countries managed to create a special 'Nordic group' in the Namibian question. Its initiatives were always welcomed in the UN.

In regard to the assistance for Namibia, the Nordic countries increased their contributions to the UN Fund and programmes for Namibia. All the Nordic

---

314. Memorandum no 699, Foreign Ministry, Political Department, Office for International Organisations, 9.7.1985, PL/Sh. Foreign Ministry's Archives.
315. Namibia, 1981:11.
316. Interview with Tauno Kääriä, 29.8.1995.

coutries, with the exception of Denmark, had bilateral programmes with SWAPO. The determination of all the Nordic countries to contribute to the cause of a free Namibia was confirmed when a joint Nordic administrative plan of assistance for an independent Namibia was drawn up at the time, when Resolution 435 promised a quick solution to the territory's problem.[317] Finland was given administrative charge of the programme, and the plans were rather substantial. But the plan itself was buried while Namibian independence was being continuously postponed. Meanwhile, Nordic support to SADCC (Southern African Development Coordination Conference) was given preference. When Namibian independence was finally achieved, the joint Nordic policy had been forgotten.[318] Only occasional meetings and informative discussions remained. All the countries started their individual assistance programmes for independent Namibia.

5.9. Finnish nationals at the service of Namibia in the multinational forums

Finland's Ambassador to Dar es Salaam, Martti Ahtisaari, had over the years developed a good working relationship with SWAPO. This was further strengthened when he became a member of the UN Institute's Senate. The Namibian question was approaching a solution—so everyone thought—when Ahtisaari's role became more closely linked with the Namibian question. In Summer 1976 the Namibian Commissioner, Sean MacBride, announced that he intended to resign from his post in the near future. The official reasons were ill heath and working difficulties with the Namibia Council—especially with its chairperson. There was speculation centring around his resignation and especially his successor. Apart from the Secretary General, the Namibia Commissioner was the only UN civil servant who was appointed directly by the General Assembly. Thus, wide international support was needed behind the candidate.

Martti Ahtisaari was Sean MacBride's own proposal for the post. In July he had proposed the idea to Ahtisaari, who informed his employer about the matter. The Foreign Ministry was not pleased about the idea at that point, and instructed Mr Ahtisaari not to comment about the matter. In addition to the international power game, the attitude of SWAPO was known to be an important factor in the appointment. According to Sean MacBride, SWAPO had always had a positive view as regards Ahtisaari and Finland. Finland's defeat in the election for Secretary General in 1971 was well remembered, and this made the Foreign Ministry cautious. Finland's policy was not to take a vocal role in matters as complicated as the Namibian question. There was no certainty that the situation would be resolved quickly and smoothly. South Africa was pursu-

---

317. Namibia, 1981:15.
318. Personal communication with Kari Karanko. Nordic assistance plan for Independent Namibia, papers and documents. Foreign Ministry's Archives.

ing its own internal settlement, and SWAPO stayed firm on its policy. Finland decided to follow the well-known 'wait and see' policy and not to start any campaign for Martti Ahtisaari.

In September Ahtisaari was called back to Finland for an official visit. SWAPO had indicated that they wanted him for the post, not only because he was a Finn, but because of his personal capabilities. Their choice concerned the person, and the nationality was not an obstacle. Actually, Finland had already filled its quota in the UN high civil service, but this was seen as a problem to be overcome. In mid-September, a SWAPO delegation visited Finland and requested the Finnish Government to make Ahtisaari available for the post. The delegation, headed by vice-president Mishake Muyongo, emphasised to Foreign Minister Sorsa that Ahtisaari was a person whom they knew and trusted. Sean MacBride paid a visit to Finland soon after SWAPO did and informed the Finnish Government on the Namibia process. He also stated that Ahtisaari would surely get support from many African governments, because SWAPO was backing him. Finland started to warm to the idea, at least a little.

The whole matter was kept confidential until October, and negotiations were held via diplomatic channels. By then, it had become quite certain that Martti Ahtisaari's nomination would succeed. In October, SWAPO had officially informed the OAU that it wanted to propose him. A few days later the BBC reported MacBride's resignation and approached Ahtisaari to confirm the speculations about his candidacy. In Finland the Social Democratic newspaper was the first to publicise the news.[319] The Foreign Ministry confirmed the matter. However, before the nomination was brought to the General Assembly, there were attempts to look for other Nordic candidates. Norway proposed their own candidate. This caused some unrest in Finland, but actually Martti Ahtisaari's nomination was already clear. At the 31st General Assembly, he was chosen as Namibia Commissioner.

Interestingly, in the same connection Finland stated more clearly than ever its commitment to a solution for Namibia and spelled out sharper criticism against South Africa. President Kekkonen himself participated in formulating Finland's speech for the General Assembly, which the not-so-committed Foreign Minister Keijo Korhonen was to present.[320] Korhonen's personal disinterest in African questions and commitment to a realist foreign policy line was well known.[321] Finland's Namibia activism had really reached its peak: the bilateral scholarship programme was in its planning stage. To show more goodwill, Finland also decided to take a new initiative on behalf of Namibia. It proposed the establishment of a Namibia Nationhood Programme, for education, research and manpower training. The programme was designed and

---

319. *Sosialidemokraatti*, 23.10.1976.

320. Interview with Juhani Suomi, 17.10.1996.

321. He was one of the 'gang of doctors' who were vigorously against any reformulation of the foreign policy toward a more moralist line. Coming from the Centre party he was, though, trusted by President Kekkonen. See also Korhonen, 1989.

launched by the General Assembly and placed under the charge of the Namibia Commission.

Martti Ahtisaari's appointment was the newest achievement of international merit for Finland. The country had accepted an active role in the Namibia question since its membership of the Security Council. Through Ahtisaari, Finland's role in the process was reconfirmed. Although he was an international civil servant, it was natural that he should invite more Finnish nationals to work with him.

> Of course the fact that Ahtisaari was the Commissioner gave it additional focus, although as an international civil servant he was working as a UN staff member. But still he was a Finn, and that added to the Finnish profile. So I think that we did have a very special profile in the UN.[322]

Ilkka Ristimäki was assigned to design the Nationhood Programme in 1977 as a consultant. Later on, he entered the UN service to administer the programme. He was followed by Tauno Kääriä in 1980 and Veikko Tupasela in 1983. As part of Finland's financial assistance to Namibia, the Government took responsibility for the expenses of the experts. Veikko Tupasela relates:

> I should think that it did help [that I am a Finn]. The Namibian and Finnish connection was already so well established by the missionaries. Also because of Finland's initiatives in the Council and Fund for Namibia it probably was easy to deal with the Namibians on one hand and on the other the UN community as such. The fact that Finland was a member of the Council and also the Fund, for Namibia Committee and also some of the other standing committees, Finland was in many places kind of a spokesman for the Nordic countries in many meetings. And there was, of course, co-ordination with other Nordic countries here in UN headquarters. When talking about the financial assistance, all the Nordic countries were very active and they were the biggest donors of all the accounts of the Fund for Namibia. Finland was the major donor for the Nationhood Programme for Namibia, because it had been active in its establishment.[323]

At the height of Finland's ever-strengthening role in the Namibia question, SWAPO's internal crisis had also reached its peak. In retrospect, it is interesting to analyse the crisis from Finland's point of view and to see how certain issues coincided.

5.10. SWAPO's internal crisis in 1976

SWAPO was under an unbearable burden after the exodus from Namibia really started in 1974. At the same time, international negotiations were well on the way. The young activists and intellectuals from Namibia were shocked by the state of affairs in exile. Logistical and administrative structures were weak,

---

322. Interview with Tauno Kääriä, 29.8.1995.
323. Interview with Veikko Tupasela, 4.9.1995.

morale low, and internal democracy almost absent. SWAPO had never been ideologically very homogeneous. Ethnic differences, and unclear organisation of power for SWAPO-inside and SWAPO-exile, as well as different ways that the struggle was experienced by different generations, had divided the movement into several different factions. Burdened with fears of internal settlement without a role for SWAPO, the leadership was not in a position to assess its own organisational state.

The critics—the youngish activists from inside just arrived in exile, the confused PLAN soldiers and some others, independently of each other—demanded a party congress, which was due to be held during the five years from the SWAPO meeting in 1971. They thought that at an internal congress the situation could be discussed and solutions considered. But their demand came at the wrong time and in the wrong place. The congress was out of the question. Sam Nujoma left Zambia and the daily affairs were run by people intolerant of criticism and inexperienced in personnel administration. Zambia, which had just suffered from a crisis caused by ZAPU-ZANU rivalries, did not want to tolerate any more unrest in its territory. After unsuccessful attempts by the critics to meet and discuss with the SWAPO leadership, the situation reached a deadlock. Finally, at SWAPO's request, the sharpest critics were detained by the Zambians and put into prison 'for protection'. When the worst tension was over, the more prominent ones (Andreas Shipanga and Solomon Mifima) were transferred to Tanzania and given a chance to ask for exile in other countries. Some of the detainees actually spent two years in prison. Some died and some are still missing. SWAPO-inside held a conference where the incumbent leadership-in-exile was re-elected and power was effectively transferred to its hands.[324]

The Nordic countries followed the events inside SWAPO very keenly. All the countries had programme officers in Lusaka, who had developed close and confidential relations with SWAPO activists. During the crisis, some SWAPO members were hiding in the residences of Nordic officials, such as Mr Karanko's:

> This was a very difficult time. We knew them very well, because we had very close connections to these SWAPO people, although we were not taking any part in their inside activities. But we knew about them and they were discussing about this struggle and they were discussing with us about the situation in Namibia as such and they were discussing about their own situation.[325]

The church personnel working among the Namibian refugees tried to take a mediating role. But the Namibian Rev Ilonga, for example, who criticised SWAPO's policy too openly for SWAPO to tolerate, was deported from Lusaka together with his Finnish wife.[326] Tension had got so high that they needed

---

324. For a more detailed account of the events, see e.g. Leys and Saul, 1994 and 1995.
325. Interview with Kari Karanko, 25.8.1995.
326. Memorandum, 24.6.1976, Salatiel Ilonga. Foreign Ministry's Archives.

physical protection before their departure. All incidents were reported to the Foreign Ministry in Finland regularly.[327] Its leading guideline was that Finland among other Nordic countries, should wait and see and not interfere. The assistance programmes, and especially the preparations for the scholarship programme, continued as normal. Martti Ahtisaari, who was informed on the situation by Sean MacBride, among others, relates:

> We were aware of what was going on, but I don't think it had any major impact on our policy. It was simply an indication that there were difficulties in perhaps catering for different views in the organisation. The liberation struggle, as I have very often said, it is not the most democratic phase in the life of an organisation, because you are bound to have very authoritarian ways of running the organisation. ... I mean, that is a hard fact of life that democracy is not very high on the list. ... I think that the difficulty comes when you are too close to the recognised power. It's very, very difficult to actually show and take a sort of distance, and then very easily you say that this is an internal matter.[328]

Martti Ahtisaari the then Ambassador to Tanzania, thus covers how the relations to SWAPO were and takes a sort of distance to them, and also to the recently appointed Ambassador Unto Korhonen in Lusaka. It is interesting to speculate, in what respect Finland's quiet policy of non-interference was influenced by the fact that Mr Ahtisaari had been asked to become Namibia Commissioner soon after the problems in SWAPO reached their peak. It is fair enough to say that it at least strengthened Finland's already adopted position of not interfering in SWAPO's internal problems. Ahtisaari had taken the advice of his predecessor MacBride, who was strongly of the opinion that SWAPO should not be allowed to fall to pieces at that particular moment.[329] Thus, in actual fact, the international community—which had a few years before granted SWAPO the status of the authentic representative of the Namibian people at the UN—ended up accepting clear violations of human rights under its own wing.

For Finland, the situation was not so problematic, but for Sweden, it was. Finland had consistently avoided statements on human rights, which was yet another reflection of Finland's policy of neutrality and realism in the shadow of a big neighbour who had problems in its human rights record. Actually bound by its own increasing role in the Namibian process, Finland could not make a different analysis of the situation inside SWAPO and come to another kind of conclusion. There was a risk of weakening the liberation alliance and thus playing into the hands of the opposite force, in this case the powerful and violent South Africa. Thus the harsh measures of SWAPO could have warranted less understanding, had the situation been a different one. Glen Lindholm says:

---

327. Report from the Finnish Embassy in Lusaka, 24.5.1976, Kari Karanko. Foreign Ministry's Archives.
328. Interview with Martti Ahtisaari, 29.1.1996.
329. Report to the Foreign Ministry, No R-1691/504, Finnish Embassy in Dar es Salaam, Martti Ahtisaari, 28.7.1975. Foreign Ministry's Archives.

> Well, I think every movement has got one or several crises. And it's always a question of what kind of a leadership you have. Once you have a liberation movement, then in reality it's very difficult to have a democratic system in such a movement. It doesn't mean that the liberation movement should give away the model of democracy, but during the fight I think it is difficult to have several leaders.[330]

The arrested SWAPO members were given a chance to ask for asylum in the Nordic countries. No official requests were made to the Finnish Government concerning this. But in fact, one of the persons involved, Jimmy Amupala, found his way to Finland—though he kept a low profile, unlike those who were accommodated in Sweden.

5.11. SWAPO and Finland towards independence

The 1976 incident strengthened the authoritarian character of SWAPO. The fruits were to be reaped soon thereafter. When the independence process became complicated after the optimistic transition arrangements fell apart in 1978 because of the South African double agenda, SWAPO's fears increased. Although its international position had grown stronger when the UN recognised it as the "sole authentic representative of the Namibian people" in 1976, SWAPO became more paranoid about being left aside, when Namibia's future was being shaped. And, in fact, the whole agenda changed when the East-West rivalry was connected with the Namibian case. The USA wanted to take the lead in the Southern African question, especially after the Soviet Union together with Cuba had gained an influential position in shaping Angola's, and to a lesser extent, Mozambique's social development towards a socialist regime.

For Finland, it was a nightmare come true. The policy of staying away from superpower rivalry was still high on Finland's agenda. Suddenly the Namibian question, in which Finland had been so much involved had become just that. Martti Ahtisaari was appointed as UN Special Representative for Namibia, on top of his position as the Namibia Commissioner, and he had difficulty in managing both roles. As Special Representative, his task was to act as a conciliator and compromise-builder, which meant wider contacts especially with the Western powers. The Namibia Council and the Commissioner's work, on the other hand, was not as widely recognised because it was seen as being so close to SWAPO's position. This was spelled out by SWAPO, too.[331] The double role ceased to exist only in 1982 when Brajesh Mishra was nominated as the new Namibia Commissioner. The Council's work was strongly rejected by South

---

330. Interview with Glen Lindholm, 30.8.1995. He was the FINNIDA programme officer in Lusaka at the time, following Kari Karanko. Presently he is Finland's Ambassador to Nairobi, Kenya.

331. Foreign Ministry's Archives.

Africa. In actual fact, the Council's role in the political negotiations diminished.[332]

Finland had to review its policy carefully. Fortunately, from Finland's point of view, the UN remained logical in its policy and demanded a unilateral solution of the Namibian question. Finland stuck to that and continued its growing humanitarian assistance. In the end, the Namibian question was solved behind closed doors through a series of diplomatic efforts which took nearly another decade.

In its relations with SWAPO, Finland kept to the same line, backing it consistently. The powerful NGO alliance secured growing public support for SWAPO and for Finland's policy in assisting it. NGOs, too, had been quite ignorant concerning SWAPO's internal development. Furthermore, different opinions were presented. According to Ambassador Richard Müller in Dar es Salaam, Finland's policy toward the Namibian question ought to follow the line that the Frontline States had accepted. A negotiated settlement was critically important for them. To support this objective as actively as possible, Finland ought to follow the consistent Nordic line, which prioritised a peaceful settlement in all situations. He concluded that Finland's continuing one-sided commitment to support SWAPO would be politically and morally questioned if SWAPO did not accept the negotiated settlement of Group 5—as the Western powers which were leading the negotiations were called.[333]

As a matter of fact, Finland had not closed the door to other Namibian political groups. The representatives of SWAPO-Democrats indicated a wish to meet with the Finnish Government at the beginning of 1979. SWAPO-Democrats was formed after the 1976 crisis, when some of the activists who were expelled from SWAPO, formed a new organisation, led by Andreas Shipanga. Many of them were based in Sweden. The Foreign Ministry informed them that an appointment could be arranged at the officer level. Secretary General Ottilie Abrahams visited Finland on 31 January 1979 and met the head of section, Mr Sampovaara and Foreign Secretary, Mr Mäntyvaara. She explained the background to SWAPO's split and pointed out that Finland was giving all its Namibian aid to SWAPO. She wished that Finland would provide her organisation with help and give financial assistance and scholarships. Finland's representatives explained that Finland was channelling aid to SWAPO only. This policy was based on OAU decisions and on SWAPO's position at the UN, where it was recognised as the sole authentic representative.[334] No aid was eventually given to SWAPO-D.

Some time earlier, a number of members of SWANU had asked Finland for asylum. Referring to Finland's refugee quota as an official explanation, Finland

---

332. Heikkilä, 1997:109.

333. Letter R-194, Finnish Embassy in Dar es Salaam, Richard Müller, 8.5.1978. Foreign Ministry's Archives.

334. Memorandum, 5.2.1979, Foreign Ministry, Political Department, Hannu Mäntyvaara. Foreign Ministry's Archives.

dismissed the application. But actually, Finland did not want to spoil its relations with SWAPO, which were seen as being of primary importance. The issue never became a subject of public discussion. Only later, did Finland's strict policy regarding refugees raise concern among the human rights groups.

This relationship between Finland and SWAPO was not disturbed even by the small pieces of information which started to circulate concerning SWAPO's treatment of dissidents in the camps. According to this information, SWAPO had set up prison camps in Angola, where a growing number of its members were taken after being accused as spies. They were interrogated and false testimonies were forced from them. SWAPO's supporters, Finland among others, were aware of the rumours.

> It was something like 1986–87. We started to get information about the concentration camps and we started to be concerned over this, especially because many of the pastors who were within SWAPO were taken to prison by SWAPO and they were mishandled and killed.[335]

An international fact-finding mission was among the few measures organised because of the rumours. The worst stories were not confirmed—rather, the situation went more or less unnoticed. That was due, also, to the unprofessional manner, in which the critics of SWAPO were presenting their claims.[336] Their credibility was effectively denied by the powerful SWAPO leadership. The NGO alliance, concentrating all its efforts on securing growing financial assistance to Namibia, was suffering from an internal censorship. Many of its activists, had, after all, been in the camps and seen people disappearing. On the other hand, for most of its supporters, SWAPO's problems were completely unknown.

And again, the international community, among others Finland, regarded the continuation of the process toward independence to be more important, than the alleged violations of human rights. Not that the question was completely silenced, though. During the election campaign in 1989, the opposition parties took up the issue of detainees publicly. The Special Representative, Martti Ahtisaari, set up a Mission for Detainees group, consisting of nine members who were to familiarise themselves with the issue and make a report concerning the list of 1,100 prisoners compiled by various international organisations. After trips to SWAPO's camps in Zambia and Angola, the group produced its report. Controversies in the situation and bitterness led even to some juridical procedures, but the matter was never solved, because SWAPO did not

---

335. Interview with Kari Karanko, 25.8.1995.

336. See e.g. Thiro-Beukes et al., 1986. The relatives of the persons that had gone missing in exile set up a Parents' Committee, which tried to pressure SWAPO to reveal information on the whereabouts of their relatives and the existence of the prison camps. The efforts were in vain. The activists, who were officials of the Namibian Council of Churches (CCN), were later dismissed from their jobs. They blamed SWAPO, which was also directing the internal organisations in Namibia, among others CCN. See Leys and Saul, 1995.

agree to discuss the matter—referring, naturally, to the hundreds of detained and killed by South Africa. In short, SWAPO considered itself as being at war against South Africa, in which everybody had to choose his side. Those who hesitated were alleged to be spies, who were to be destroyed.[337] The problem was complicated by the fact that South Africa had not signed the Geneva convention on prisoners of war.[338]

Today, the truth has started to come out into the open. Up to two thousand members of SWAPO are said to have gone through the horrors of the prison camps. Many are still missing.[339] Although it is SWAPO's duty to solve the problem, the international community should accept part of the responsibility.

Martti Ahtisaari comments:

> The justification for that [supporting SWAPO unconditionally] was to concentrate the efforts vis-à-vis the occupying power. That was the fact which we had to deal with. But it obviously didn't make life any easier and the solution of the problem either. Because in the end, I think, the mere armed struggle would never have solved the problem; and if you go for a democratic solution, then you have to give everybody the chance to participate and agree conditions so that they would be starting on a fairly equal basis. ... It's even more remarkable that Namibia has become a sort of example of democratic society in the whole continent. ... I asked the Foreign Minister and we both agreed that if somebody would have asked us 10 years ago if this sort of development would be possible, I don't think anyone of us would have believed it. We would have expected much greater difficulties in building up a democratic society.[340]

Mr Ahtisaari was showing enormous patience in trying to draw things together during the negotiations. He was endeavouring to strike a balance between the different interests linked with the Namibian question. However, it was no longer only a question of one country's independence, but it carried a lot of weight in regard to the destiny of the whole region. The Finnish Government, regularly informed by Mr Ahtisaari, was backing his efforts. Even the Finnish President Koivisto himself approached President Kaunda of Zambia during the dramatic events of the transitional period in 1989, assuring the leader of the Frontline countries of Mr Ahtisaari's commitment to implementing the process

---

337. Heikkilä, 1997:157.

338. The report concluded that out of all the 1100 people reported as detainees, 484 were freed or repatriated, 71 were never even imprisoned, 115 were dead and 52 persons were impossible to identify because of missing information. In addition, it was impossible to find out the whereabouts of 315 people. SWAPO itself reported that it had released 215 prisoners (Heikkilä, 1997:157).

339. A recently (1995) released book, *The Wall of Silence*, tells the stories of some of the detainees, who were counselled by the German pastor Siegfried Groth. He had worked among Namibian refugees in Zambia since the 1970s. The Namibian Government has refuted his information as a blatant lie. In celebration of the 30 years of liberation war on 26 August 1996 the Government published a list of war heroes (Their Blood Waters Our Freedom), which included some of the detained and missing. The Government has consistently declined to have the issue of its detainees openly investigated.

340. Interview with Martti Ahtisaari, 29.1.1996.

resulting in an independent Namibia.³⁴¹ Despite all the difficulties, the Namibia process came to an end and the transition process was led by Special Representative Martti Ahtisaari—not without bloodshed, though. The Namibian ceasefire was broken just when this high UN official had arrived on the scene.

The traumatic event of SWAPO's troops violating the agreement on the process of transition to Namibian independence and entering Namibian territory, was solved by Martti Ahtisaari's decision to allow South African forces to stop SWAPO's soldiers. Mr Ahtisaari has not been willing to discuss this incident in closer detail, because it is more important that the process finally succeeded.

> I'm more happy that despite this disaster at the beginning we could carry out the exercise. ... I was in a much stronger position when I realised that they [the South African regime] didn't use the opportunity that SWAPO gave them. Because they could have taken the high road actually then and say, look, this is it, out we go, end of the process, UN out. But they didn't do it. And that then made me draw the conclusion that they are here to stay to the bitter end and see this whole process through. So one could say that this tragic death of these people served that purpose that it reinforced the process finally.³⁴²

Finnish troops participated in the UNTAG forces. Finland's direct support to SWAPO was terminated according to a non-partiality clause in 1989. The recently established SWAPO information office, financed by the Government, had to be shut down. Despite Finnish NGOs' protest for continuation of the official aid, SWAPO agreed with the decision. In actual fact Finnish support to SWAPO did not diminish at all, because NGO support could fill the gap—with considerable aid from the government. Nahas Angula admits:

> In the implementation, Finland was in the different position, because its national was the one implementing the programme here. And of course it was in the interest of Mr Ahtisaari to be seen to be impartial; and if Finland was seen to be partial, Ahtisaari's credibility could have been questioned by the other side. So that is understandable. But that is just that time of implementation.³⁴³

The NGOs continued their efforts, aiding SWAPO's repatriation and information work during the election campaign. The Finnish Namibian Friendship Society had become the co-ordinating NGO in Namibian affairs during the late 1980s. The society had since 1979 united Namibia's friends from missionaries to the leftist activists. A specially designed fund-raising campaign was started by the society. The students joined the campaign by collecting additional funds at the universities.³⁴⁴ The NGOs also organised a fact-finding mission to Namibia

---

341. Koivisto, 1995:105–106.
342. Interview with Martti Ahtisaari, 29.1.1996.
343. Interview with Nahas Angula, 22.8.1996.
344. Personal recollections of Iina Soiri and Pekka Peltola. Peltola was the chairperson of the Finnish-Namibian Friendship Society and Soiri the secretary for international affairs in HYY, responsible for solidarity, and fund-raising campaigns.

during the transition period, monitoring the registration of the voters, and many activists of the society served as election observers in 1989.

Finland's long standing relationship with SWAPO was then turned into normal cooperation between the two countries, and Namibia became one of the main recipients of Finnish aid. Namibia was actually adopted as a target country for development cooperation years back in 1976, but only now could the bilateral cooperation be started. Martti Ahtisaari's service for Namibia and in the UN in general earned him a lot of respect and popularity in Finland. In 1994 he was elected as president of Finland, standing as a surprise candidate of the Social Democratic party. He was later nominated as the first Honorary Citizen of Namibia.

After the Namibian settlement, things started to move faster in South Africa as well. Roelof 'Pik' Botha, then Foreign Minister of South Africa, notes the Nordic countries' role in acting as some kind of brokers in the negotiated settlement in the whole of Southern Africa. He reminds us of the importance of the events in the entire Namibian independence situation—including the withdrawal of Cuban troops from Angola—in relation to events in South Africa. They paved the way for what later happened there.

> Martti Ahtisaari is a Finn and he played a very, I would say, decisively important role. There is no question about it. I hope that history will accord him the credit that is due to him. I think of the years and years that he was waiting for a movement on the Namibian issue and how things went wrong, time and time again. But he displayed a reasonable attitude, and the two of us eventually got on very, very well together. We developed a personal relationship, which once again proved to me—as so many other events in my life—what can be achieved if we sometimes move from stern agendas and minutes, preconceived judgements and ideas, and just retain an open mind towards one another. It was mainly a result of that informal, yes, trust in each other's personal integrity.[345]

According to Mr Botha, Martti Ahtisaari's role was pivotal in that respect, also in comparison with that of the superpowers, which had later claimed the greatest credit in the process.[346] The South African developments will be dealt with in the next chapter.

---

345. Interview with Roelof 'Pik' Botha 12.9.1995 by Tor Sellström.

346. See e.g. Crocker, 1992. In his book, the former Assistant Secretary of State for African Affairs of the United States describes how the whole Namibian peace process was another American exercise. (That is implied in the title of the book "High Noon in Southern Africa. Making Peace in the Rough Neighbourhood".) All in all, Crocker recognises Ahtisaari's role as "an attempt which demands extreme skills from an international civil servant". A more balanced account is presented in Weiland & Braham (eds.), 1994.

5.12. Zimbabwe/Rhodesia and Finland

In the Rhodesian question, Finland had traditionally kept a low profile. Finland fulfilled the trade embargo obligations determined by the UN, and passed a law to forbid trade in 1967. There was not much to lose, because the trade relations were modest anyway. Finland regarded the Rhodesia/Zimbabwe question as an internal issue and did not want to protest—not even when some countries, among others Great Britain, openly broke the embargo. Finland's interests in relation to those countries were greater than its solidarity with the Zimbabwean people.

Another factor in the issue was that the complexities of the liberation struggle in Zimbabwe were not well understood in Finland. ZAPU and ZANU were known, but then all those alliances and factions did not really become clear in the eyes of the ordinary people or the foreign policy decision-makers. The situation was followed from the Embassy in Dar es Salaam, but their understanding of the events relied on secondary sources. ZAPU and ZANU did not develop a closer contact with the Embassy officers. ZANU was regarded as the more important and operative by the diplomatic community.

In the NGO sector, there were activists who promoted the Zimbabwean struggle. In its first fund-raising campaign, the International Solidarity Foundation gathered funds for Zimbabweans to buy hoes for in 1970.[347] The money was transferred through international partner organisations, and the recipient was simply the people of Zimbabwe, as stated during the campaign.

Among the NGO circles, in contrast to at the Foreign Ministry, ZAPU was the more popular movement in their understanding, because activists Börje Mattsson and Mikko Lohikoski had met its leader Joshua Nkomo several times. In the background was the fact that Mr Nkomo had a better relationship to Moscow and the socialist solidarity movement, with which the Africa Committee had a close connection. He was invited to Finland, too.[348] ZAPU had representation in the World Peace Council, whose headquarters were located in Helsinki. The Africa Committee—as a subcommittee of the Finnish member organisation of WPC, the Peace Committee—was influenced by its policies as well.

The NGOs were fully aware of the problems of mobilising for Zimbabwe.

---

347. *"Kehitysapua ihmiseltä ihmiselle"* (Development Aid from People to People). Kansainvälinen Solidaarisuussäätiö 20 vuotta (International Solidarity Foundation 20 years). Festivity publication by the Foundation in 1990.

348. "Of course, we had mostly contacts with ZAPU, Nkomo. Nkomo was here in Finland several times. I remember I brought him to sauna in Merihotelli, it was one of the most memorable experiences. We gave him a diploma, which must still hang on his wall somewhere, that he has been in 100 degrees, boiling degrees." Interview with Mikko Lohikoski, 22.12.1995.

And the legal status of the country was such that it made it more difficult to mobilise in Finland, which at that time very clearly justified its activity on the international arena. They were very careful to remind what were the legal grounds, because the question of non-interference was much stronger at that time.[349]

ZAPU had already asked for support from the Finnish Government in November 1972. The answer was always that Finland did not support groups with violent means. The Finnish government had not yet reached the decision of principle at that time and no aid to any liberation movement was authorised. Also ZANU approached the Embassy in Dar es Salaam asking for support. Both requests were repeated several times.[350] No funding was provided. The ANC (Rhodesia) also approached the Embassy in Lusaka, asking for assistance and planning a visit to Finland.[351] Nothing materialised. The 1973 working group on supporting of liberation movements had stated that Finland's assistance to Southern Rhodesia should be mainly in the form of refugee work. Support to the victims of apartheid was channelled through UN funds.

In April 1973 a border crisis between Zambia and Rhodesia occurred. Zambia, which was acting as host to the rival liberation movements, was left without access to the sea and railways when Rhodesia closed the border. The international community came to Zambia's help. Finland, which was giving development aid to Zambia, decided to put a cargo plane at the disposal of the Zambian Government for transport necessities. This air bridge formed by the Finnish plane was used by other international donors as well between Lusaka and Nairobi. The costs of the operation, 756,000 FIM, were paid from the humanitarian budget.[352] This is actually the only case where Finland got involved in any situation related to the Zimbabwean liberation struggle. In this case, its involvement was again indirect, targeted to a sovereign Zambian Government.

Some NGOs included ZAPU in their fund-raising campaigns and donated some material assistance to the movement. But the Zimbabwean struggle was left aside when other issues, which got more popular support—such as Namibia assistance and the South Africa boycott—absorbed the limited resources of the NGOs. But nearly always, when information campaigns were arranged, support to all the Southern African liberation movements was demanded and the regional struggle as a whole was emphasised.

Joshua Nkomo was again in Finland when an Africa Solidarity week was organised in March 1978.[353] He met Prime Minister Kalevi Sorsa and Foreign

---

349. Interview with Mikko Lohikoski, 22.12.1995.

350. Letter to the Government of Finland from ZANU, 8.5.197; letter from the Embassy in Dar es Salaam, Martti Ahtisaari, 25.3.1974. Foreign Ministry's Archives.

351. Letter from the Embassy in Lusaka, Martti Ahtisaari, 9.10.1975. Foreign Ministry's Archives.

352. *Suomi ja Kehitysyhteistyö* (1974) (Finland and Development Cooperation), Foreign Minstry, Department for Development Cooperation, p. 44–45.

353. SPR collection in the People's Archives.

Minister Paavo Väyrynen and explained the situation inside Zimbabwe whereby the international community had for years tried to organise a negotiated settlement between the different groups, who were getting more and more impatient.

Zimbabwe gained its independence in 1980. Finland had to experience something of the taste of bitter revenge during the celebration for independence which was attended by Finland's then Foreign Minister Pär Stenbäck. In his travel report he pointed out to TALKE, a standing parliamentary committee for economic relations with the developing countries, that Finland's reception lagged far behind the warm hospitality that the other Nordic countries received. This led to a more general conclusion that Finland's role was not so well known in Africa. As a result, TALKE decided that Finland had to raise her profile in Africa. Finland wanted to follow the example of Sweden, which, as TALKE believed, had gained substantial economic benefits due to its commitment to the liberation struggle. SWAPO and Namibia were identified as proper partners.[354] As we have seen, SWAPO, and to a lesser extent ANC, surely benefited from this indication of preferences on the part of the Zimbabwean Government, and perhaps from a sprinkling of vanity on the part of the Finnish Government.

The economic interest in Zimbabwe took precedence over the need for development assistance. At the beginning of the 1980s Finland granted some development credits to the country.[355] But development cooperation never played a significant role in its relations with Zimbabwe. The NGOs' less active promotion of support for independent Zimbabwe was certainly affected by the fact that ZANU was the winner of the independence elections.

---

354. Memorandum, TALKE, 1. Committee, minutes of the meeting 4/1980 and 5/1980. Foreign Ministry's Archives.

355. Foreign Ministry's Archives.

Chapter 6
South Africa, ANC and the Boycott Question

Side by side with the growing Finnish support for Namibian people, the NGOs had built up popular opinion against the South African regime and its apartheid policy. After the massacre in Soweto, the popular protest against South Africa intensified. Finland's double-faced policy toward South Africa became the object of several petitions and statements. The Africa Committee strengthened the boycott action by calling other NGOs to join the boycott movement. Important input came from the trade union movement.

In fact, after Niilo Wälläri's death, the sharpest criticism had already withered away in the 1960s. The brandy boycott was called off in 1969. The trade with South Africa had—to the disappointment of the Foreign Ministry— declined at the beginning of the 1970s. A commercial secretary was posted to the Pretoria legation, though concealed under the title of "secretary". The Foreign Ministry was cautious not to wake up the sleeping bear, public boycott action. A couple of Finnish companies had established minor manufacturing facilities in South Africa and Swaziland.[356] All of a sudden, in May 1976, there were reports in the German press that Finland planned to terminate economic relations with South Africa.[357] In an interview, President Kekkonen had said that Finland wanted to support the UN General Assembly recommendations aiming at isolating the apartheid regime. However, Finland had continuously repeated that it preferred mandatory sanctions set by the Security Council, according to the UN Charter. It was not aiming at any unilateral action.

The Foreign Ministry hurried to emphasise that no policy change was on its way. Instructions given by the political department to its diplomatic missions followed, stating that Finland was not considering termination of the economic relationship. Concerning the diplomatic relations, the question had not been raised at all, according to Mr Iloniemi. He instructed that the press reports should, however, be refuted carefully in order to keep freedom of action in this issue.[358]

This discussion shows that there were different opinions in the foreign policy decision-making circles. Finland's role in the Namibia question had been noted and Martti Ahtisaari's nomination as Commissioner was under specula-

---

356. Heino, 1992:40–42.
357. Telegram from Foreign Affairs to Cape Town, 20.5.1976, Jaakko Iloniemi. Foreign Ministry's Archives.
358. Ibid.

tion. According to sources close to the late President Kekkonen, he was quite radical in his standpoints towards Southern Africa. Although other matters kept him fully occupied, he occasionally displayed his will against the conservative Foreign Ministry officials. As described in the previous chapter, later the same year, Finland made a strong statement at the General Assembly, presented by the Centre Party Foreign Minister, Keijo Korhonen. The speech was altered several times, at Kekkonen's request, to contain more criticism toward Southern Africa.[359]

But in practice, as Heino also concludes, Finland's policy did not change to a great extent in the 1970s, although pressure came even from the parliamentary side.[360] The time was not ripe and Finland wanted to stick to its neutral position. A study by the Foreign Ministry on relations with South Africa, commissioned by an overwhelming majority in Parliament, did not present any reasons to change anything. Other options—terminating or lowering the status of the diplomatic relations, banning the export of capital to or urging companies not to invest in South Africa—were not adopted, because the Foreign Ministry was afraid that unilateral action by Finland would be seen as an indication that it did not believe in peaceful development or did not want to support it. Thus, Finland decided to abstain from all action and wait for the results of the international negotiations.[361]

6.1. Joint Nordic programme of action

Finland's reluctance to act unilaterally in the South African question made joint Nordic action more important. For the sake of strengthening its image of a neutral country, this suited Finland, because she wanted to be seen in the right company internationally. After Soweto, in 1976, the Foreign Ministers of all the Nordic countries decided at their meeting on a five-point programme concerning the South African issue. Most important was the objective of using all means available to establish an effective international sanctions policy within the UN framework. The Security Council adopted Resolution 418 for a mandatory arms embargo against South Africa in 1977. Accordingly, the Finnish government issued a decree prohibiting the export of all types of military equipment. Because no other obligatory sanctions were decided on within the UN framework, the Nordic Foreign Ministers adopted a joint Nordic Programme of Action against South Africa as a step towards unilateral Nordic sanctions.[362]

The Programme of Action—which recommended curtailing economic relations by stopping production in South Africa and discontinuing sports and

---

359. Interview with Juhani Suomi, 17.10.1996.
360. Heino, 1992:59.
361. Memo 11.10.1976, Relations between Finland and the Republic of South Africa, Foreign Ministry, Political Department, Jaakko Iloniemi. Foreign Ministry's Archives.
362. Heino, 1992:62.

culture relations as well as new visa regulations—had little effect in Finland. Finland already required visas from South African citizens, sports contacts had been to a large extent discontinued, and no Finnish manufacturing companies existed in South Africa. After that, sanctions were on the agenda every now and then, and Finland's policy did not change from the basic course set in 1976.[363]

6.2. Support for ANC and other anti-apartheid organisations

However reluctant Finland was to back the sanctions policy unilaterally, it was prepared to come into closer contact with ANC. In accordance with calls from the Security Council "to contribute generously for assistance to the victims of violence and repression, including educational assistance to student refugees from South Africa",[364] Finland concluded that there were no obstacles to starting to support ANC with humanitarian aid. Swedish official direct assistance to ANC had been a regular feature since 1973. Norway had already budgeted funds for the organisation. In 1977, Finland decided to start humanitarian assistance and agree on the details with ANC via the Finnish Embassy in Lusaka.[365] After the formal decision, the Foreign Ministry reserved 200,000 FIM to be allocated to ANC.[366]

An agreement with ANC was drawn up, and the money was transferred to its account in London. ANC was obliged to use it for humanitarian purposes only (for purchasing necessities, such as blankets, clothing and food etc.), and to report back to the Foreign Ministry on the use of funds. The official assistance to ANC grew significantly year by year, though never reaching Sweden's level.[367]

As a result, ANC was having difficulties in using up all the money in a given time, as Finland was strict about the justifications of how the money was available for use. ANC never challenged Finland's reservations, although it found Finland's position somewhat hypocritical, as Lindiwe Mabuza explains:

> All the cards were on the table. And although not everything would be specifically discussed there, there was no doubt that the Finnish authorities knew that when they are giving assistance to ANC, the assistance did not discriminate between those that were engaged in the military and those who were doing political work. Because if we were given food or art material for people in Angola, those were mainly soldiers. So there was no supply of weapons, but you and I know, that soldiers without food and soap and toothpaste can rise up in mutiny. So our movement, the leadership of the ANC, never made any attacks on the nature of the assistance, if on the face of it, it excluded military. We all knew better. There was under-

---

363. Ibid. p. 64
364. Security Council Resolution 31.10.1977. Foreign Ministry's Archives.
365. Decision by the Government's Foreign Affairs Committee 24.11.1977. Foreign Ministry's Archives.
366. Memo 27.1.1978, Foreign Ministry, Political Department. Foreign Ministry's Archives.
367. See Appendix 2.

standing too, that our military was essentially, first and foremost a political army. But individuals and some political parties actually gave contributions towards our military requirements.[368]

Martti Ahtisaari also points out the discussion centring around the nature of the aid.

> [In the beginning], basically no money was to be given, because of this whole discussion that always comes, that whether money would be directed towards purchase of arms, for instance. I think it is a simplistic discussion in a sense that if you get food, you don't need to use your money to buy the food. You can use it on something else. That's how it is.[369]

A proposal was made by the NGOs that part of the government assistance could be used in cooperation projects between Finnish NGOs and ANC. A large-scale *Taksvärkki* Campaign had been organised to collect funds for the liberation movements in 1978, ANC being one of the beneficiaries. It was agreed that a printing press would be donated, shipped and installed in its office in Luanda. An expert was needed to install the machine, which required additional funds. The *Taksvärkki* Committee then proposed, that government funds would be used to meet the additional costs. The settlement was accepted by all parties. Markku Vesikko[370] was sent to Luanda, thus beginning his long career of assisting ANC and SWAPO during the struggle.

Contrary to what happened in its SWAPO relations, ANC and Finland never started a joint coherent programme together, such as the scholarship programme. There were only a few ANC students in Finland invited by the NGOs, but scholarships were funded elsewhere by the Government of Finland. The majority of the assistance was given in kind, such as medical and other transport equipment for the camps in Tanzania and Angola. Negotiations with ANC were carried on by the Embassy in Lusaka and through occasional ANC visits to Finland. ANC had had an office with a full-time representative, Lindiwe Mabuza, in Stockholm since 1979.

> I was very apprehensive when I left from Lusaka to Stockholm. Here I was coming to a completely white world, to try and move the world more and more close to our positions. But I was helped by advice from the then ANC President, the late Oliver Tambo who said: "Don't worry, go there, you are going to be working amongst friends. That whole region has a very strong tradition of being against oppression and anti-apartheid is one of the main agendas of the region." And I found that to be so true in all the Scandinavian countries. In Finland I found that I really didn't have

---

368. Interview with Lindiwe Mabuza, 14.10.1996.
369. Interview with Martti Ahtisaari, 29.1.1996.
370. Markku Vesikko was staying in Angola until 1989, working for ANC and SWAPO in different Finnish projects. He then moved to Namibia, where he was working for the International Confederation of Free Trade Unions (ICFTU) in building and educating the Namibian Unions until the end of 1995.

to fight too much to convince people, of course there were those who supported the apartheid side.[371]

By 1985 the annual assistance had grown to over two million Finnish marks and a lot of previous years' allocations was still unused. In consequence, a proposal was made that the aid package should be negotiated annually between the Finnish Government and ANC, following the example of SWAPO. The first annual consultations were held on December 11–13, 1985. It was agreed that part of the assistance would still be used for purchasing of necessities (sugar, powdered milk, towels etc.); and for the remaining amount, ANC would provide requests and proposals in the following fields: construction, machines for agricultural development, and education. It was planned that a vocational training programme for teachers would be started. Finland was keen to promote its own manufacturing industry, as the list of goods in the document shows (Sisu trucks, sugar from Finland, etc.).[372]

In the consultations, the NGO aid to ANC was also always reviewed. NGO representatives were met with, and new programmes designed. Since *Taksvärkki* 1978, the number of NGOs in cooperation with ANC had increased substantially. Although many of the NGOs preferred assistance for Namibia and regarded South Africa more as an object of sanctions and political pressure work, ANC support was found to be important for many of them. That was not least because of Lindiwe Mabuza's personality and admirable talent for speaking for her organisation. She is, after all, a poet, far from the standard picture of a liberation fighter—and that again made an impact, like Janet Mondlane did in the 1970s.

Thanks to Ms Mabuza, many cultural organisations started training programmes or cultural activities in the camps, such as establishing a journal and a library. The Africa Committee was engaged in sending equipment and personnel to construct the vocational Training and Health Centre in Viana, Angola. The International Solidarity Foundation, for its part, funded personnel and equipment for a furniture factory in Mazimbu, Tanzania. The trade union movement joined in the assistance programmes as well. The Transport Workers Union (AKT) supported the SOMAFCO refugee camp; and the Central Trade Union Organisation (SAK) donated paper for the ANC printing works in Lusaka, formally to finance the printing of The Namibian Worker. SACTU and a number of other South African trade unions got some support from SAK and other trade union organisations in Finland during the early 1980s.

Many NGOs co-operated in the project work, although apart from the boycott organisation EELAK, there was no official co-ordination. Whereas there were nine NGOs in cooperation with ANC in 1984, with a total contribution of

---

371. Interview with Lindiwe Mabuza, 14.10.1996.
372. Summary Record, Annual Consultations between ANC and the Ministry of Foreign Affairs in Finland, December 13, 1985. Foreign Ministry's Archives.

approximately 400,000 FIM, the number of NGOs had increased to 13 by the year 1987, with projects worth 1 900,000 FIM altogether.[373]

Convincing proof of Lindiwe Mabuza's talent for getting Finns to support ANC was given when the Development Association of the Coalition (Conservative) Party decided to invite and provide funds for an ANC student to study in Finland. At the beginning of the 1980s, the Finnish Association of Adult Education, which was already supporting SWAPO programmes, wanted to support ANC students—because they were so many from Namibia and nobody from South Africa, as the chairperson Helena Kekkonen put it.[374] When the finances had been secured from FINNIDA, the two organisations both invited one student to study at Tampere University. Out of all the NGOs, the Conservative Party youth organisation was least likely to support ANC, because it had been the most vocal critic of the "policy of supporting the terrorists". Their scholarship programme thus showed that support to the liberation movements had become a widely accepted fact in Finnish society. The alliance in supporting the Southern African liberation struggle reached even the most conservative segments of the society. This was even more telling because many of the Conservative youth activists were still for a long time against any engagement in boycott activities. As Lindiwe Mabuza explains:

> We never assumed that it was impossible to move anybody in any society to see the light and to take strong position against apartheid. We never made that assumption. On the contrary, our assumption was that, we can make anybody change their position and their thinking about apartheid. And I think history has borne that out. The second thing is that when we were targeting groups in our countless campaigns—women's organisations, church groups, youth groups etc.—you presented a picture to them about their counterparts in South Africa. How was life in South Africa for young people, black and white? And the decision and choice was for them. The decision was for them to see what is wrong about apartheid. That led to decisions about counter-action, support to victims! We just created, painted pictures for them and the conclusion was for them to make! We always said, you isolate the policy, the regime, but you don't isolate the victims of the system. It was a much easier thing for the youth of any party, including conservative youth, who have more means, to come up and say we can work on a programme that actually helps you to prepare for the future. They had accepted the idea that ANC would be a future government and the future belongs to the youth. It was good thinking. It was politics but it was very humanistic, and it was exactly what we wanted. It was important that they broke away from conservatism and identified with our youth.[375]

At the beginning, ANC was the only South African organisation which got assistance from Finland, not counting the international funds for the victims of

---

373. Summary Records on the Annual Consultation on the Finnish Humanitarian Assistance to the African National Congress, Helsinki, December 10, 1986. Foreign Ministry's Archives.
374. Personal communication and archives of Helena Kekkonen.
375. Interview with Lindiwe Mabuza, 14.10.1996.

apartheid, such as the UN Trust Fund for South Africa, the Educational and Training Programme for Southern Africa, and the OAU Assistance Fund. They had all received annual contributions from Finland for many years. Furthermore, in 1979 Finland made a donation to the International University Exchange Fund, the one and only time. In 1983 PAC, the Pan-Africanist Congress approached Finland asking for assistance for its refugee camp in Tanzania. After a careful assessment, Finland decided to donate 20,000 FIM to the organisation. The justification was found from the OAU, which regarded PAC as a viable South African liberation movement.

By the mid-1980s, it had become clear that the public action against apartheid was greater than ever in South Africa. The trade unions had been organised, and different NGOs formed a mass democratic movement, the United Democratic Front. Their activities intensified side by side with the growing repression from the regime. The international community failed to find a solution to the situation. Mandatory economic sanctions were vetoed in the Security Council.

The Nordic countries had annually reviewed their policy against South Africa. When lobbying for mandatory international sanctions, they also started to support a larger number of democratic and non-racial NGOs and institutions inside South Africa. Finland's humanitarian assistance was allocated to different South African human rights organisations, universities and citizen associations. Political prisoners' and their families' legal and social aid was financed through IDAF and other organisations.

In 1985, when radical trade unions in South Africa formed COSATU, Finnish trade unions began to support this and several of its affiliated unions immediately. Up to 1995, the support amounted to 1.9 million FIM. Substantial assistance was given to the trade union movement, both directly and through the Trade Union Solidarity Centre (SASK), which was established in 1986. SASK also carried out some legal aid programmes.

> When SASK was launched, it had to start from the scraps. So we actually inherited the programmes that SAK had. Firstly, we actually had only the so-called old SAK programmes, and they were in Angola with the SWAPO and they were short-term humanitarian programmes. During the first year, we had nothing else but only SWAPO and the ANC and a small programme with the trade union centre in Mozambique. As a result, we started to grow and it became more logical to have trade union education programmes and not only short-term assistance programmes to liberation movements. It was clear financial assistance for their [trade unions'] existence. To support the organisation, the administration of the organisation, to support the salaries and everything. And then it was also so-called humanitarian assistance, from the Finnish humanitarian budget, which was for legal costs for victims of violence and detainees and families of detainees and

funeral assistance. That we got quite many years, from 1988 to 1993, from the Finnish Government.[376]

Contribution to the NGOs inside South Africa grew together with the ANC assistance until the beginning of the 1990s. This was done in full agreement with ANC. However, in South Africa the civil society was forming a wide anti-apartheid alliance committed to the abolishment of the regime. In contrast to SWAPO, which did not want the internal organisation to challenge its external leadership, the ANC was ready to accept a multifaceted, heterogeneous internal front as its partner in the struggle.

> Money was going to IDAF, and IDAF was supporting prisoners' programmes in South Africa. The programmes of the dependants of political prisoners, the lawyers' committees for the defence of those. All kinds of humanitarian work, including trade unions. And the money was going into a very critically significant job of mobilising our people. You know, that after the arrest of the major leaders like Nelson Mandela, Walter Sisulu, people went underground, people went out of the country, ANC was dislocated. In practice people were afraid to organise. We had to start almost from scratch, putting confidence back into people to re-engage in new ways. And we knew that the support had to be built step by step in order to build a formidable anti-apartheid resistance movement. And without FINNIDA going to these groups, assisting them, things would have been more difficult. FINNIDA would support what didn't immediately look like liberation struggle, support to the South African Council of Churches, support to FOSATU and later COSATU was support for the liberation of South Africa. It was for maintaining people, who were also working on a day-to-day basis to organise. Those people could be within a trade union movement, they could have been within the church groups, within women's organisations, within professions, within the lawyers or the medical organisations, but people that could be identified by ANC as the ones who would receive those monies that were agreed upon.[377]

Especially the Social Democratic Foreign Ministers Kalevi Sorsa followed by Pertti Paasio pressed for more and wider assistance to the internal organisation. In any case, ANC had always received more aid directly than it was able to handle. When ANC aid was discontinued in 1993, the South African NGOs had become important channels for supporting of human rights and democracy in South Africa during and after the transition to democracy.[378]

6.3. Pressure for sanctions and the trade ban law

In the 1980s, the NGOs' role in shaping Finland's Southern African policy became especially important. In fact, according to Heino, the South African

---

376. Interview 27.12.1995 with Mirjam Korhonen, a lawyer and the programme officer for SASK since its beginning. She was also active in EELÁK, and was its last chairperson 1991–1993.
377. Interview with Lindiwe Mabuza, 14.10.1996.
378. See Appendix 2.

question was the first Finnish foreign policy issue, in which NGOs had a significant say. As we have shown here, the NGO alliance and wide public opinion had already played an important part in the decision to start official direct aid to the liberation movements. And it was mainly the same organisations and institutions in Finland which joined forces against the South African apartheid policy. They built up public opinion into favouring trade unions' unilateral actions against the state. As a result, the NGOs—and especially the trade union movement—terminated Finland's trade with South Africa, as finally confirmed by law in 1987.

The process of change in Finland's foreign policy has been described thoroughly in Timo-Erkki Heino's book, so there is no need to go into all the details. However, it was an important side-product of Finland's commitment to involve itself by a variety of means toward ending colonialism in Africa, and to support the international community's policy toward ending apartheid. The description here follows his account closely, with the addition of information from archive sources not available to him. Risto Kuisma's [379] recent book *Tilinpäätös* (Closing the accounts) and his interview also supplement Heino's version. As Heino so appropriately describes it, the South Africa sanctions question was, first of all, a kind of a battle against the Finnish forest and paper industry.

Before going into the developments which led to sanctions, we have to say something about Finland's economic relations with South Africa. Several studies had concluded that Finland's trade and other economic relations with South Africa were of little importance.[380] However, although the trade itself was small in volume, it was the main interaction between the two countries. The function of the diplomatic representation was mainly related to trade.[381] As described earlier, Finland had had honorary consuls in South Africa since the 1920s. Diplomatic relations were only established in 1949, after the National Party, which had won the elections, wanted to establish its own foreign relations independently from the mother country Great Britain.[382] The trade was important before the Second World War, and especially in the 1930s, when the Finnish forest industry was looking for markets with new openings beyond Europe. After the Second World War, the political situation and Finland's participation in handling the question in the UN had had their impact on the trade

---

379. Risto Kuisma was a chairperson of the Transport Workers' Union. He later left the trade unions and is presently an independent MP. He was elected to Parliament in 1995 from the Social Democratic list, but formed in 1997 a one man parliamentary group of his own.

380. See for example Heino, 1978; and Väyrynen, 1977 and 1980.

381. Väyrynen, 1980:227.

382. Heino, 1978: 13–14. See also Uola (1974), who describes the relations between the two countries. He points out how South Africa assisted Finland in the Winter War. This fact was later, from time to time, used in the debate on South Africa. The promoters of the status quo against sanctions wanted to emphasise the good intentions of the South African regime and the need for reciprocity during hard times.

relations. Still, the 1950s and 1960s were most active years in building up the economic contacts, which were disturbed only by the brandy boycott at the end of the 1960s. Finland diversified its export from traditional forest products (like paper, pulp, machinery), increasing also the proportion of highly manufactured goods (electronics). Technology and know-how were imported, and Finnish experts were working in South Africa.[383] Finland's imports from South Africa consisted mainly of food—fruit, to a large extent. Continuing into the 1970s, the trade with South Africa decreased after the peak in 1974, despite continued promotion and the opening of the South African Embassy in Helsinki in 1967.[384]

Finland's trade with South Africa has constituted a minuscule 0.5 per cent of its total foreign trade.[385] The South African trade has thus never been of great importance to Finland. What is important, though, is that the terms of that trade were favourable to Finland, the exports being greater than the imports.[386] And in comparison with other developing countries South Africa was of some importance as regards trade, being among the most important developing-country partners.[387] A lot of Finnish exports have also gone to South Africa via other countries, which means that South Africa is an important consumer of Finnish products. With Namibia, Finland's trade was even more modest, consisting only of the importation of some leather and pelts.

One must conclude that in the framework of the national economy of Finland as a whole, the South African trade was of no importance. Those who had exported the most products to South Africa were Enso-Gutzeit Oy, Kymi Kymmene Oy and Oy Nokia AB.[388] The largest sector of industry which had benefited from the trade was the forestry companies.[389] These being the backbone of the Finnish industrial sector, it is quite understandable that the trade carried more weight than its actual quantity alone might indicate. The forest and paper industry has continuously come up with a justification of the South African trade linking it with employment. The industry has had no evidence to prove, though, that any more than 2,000–3,000 people could have been depen-

---

383. Väyrynen, 1980:219.

384. Heino, 1978:157–158.

385. Heino, 1978:158. Exports had varied between 0.2 % and 1%, and imports between 0.2–0.5% in the period 1946–1976. Finland's official statistics (SVT) 1 A. Foreign Trade. Presented in Väyrynen, 1980:211.

386. Väyrynen, 1980:212. According to Heino the imports from South Africa were between 5 % and 18% of the value of exports to it until 1940; thereafter the proportion increased to 45%, diminishing again to 30% by the 1970s. Heino, 1978:71.

387. According to Väyrynen only Iraq and Brazil among all the developing countries had reached the same or higher level. Väyrynen, 1980:215. Heino points out that in Africa, only Egypt had been an important export destination in Finland's trade. As to imports, Egypt, Algeria and Morocco, as well as Kenya and Zambia at a later stage had been significant countries from which Finland received imports. Heino, 1978:59 and 69.

388. Heino, 1978:159.

389. Väyrynen, 1980:217.

dent on this trade,[390] nor that the possible loss in employment after cutting South African trade could not be compensated for elsewhere.

As to Finnish investments in South Africa, their relevance was even more modest. Only the factory that Vaisala established in South Africa in 1962 (radiosondes for meteorological instrumentation) can be considered as one. On the other hand, Salora, a manufacturer of radios and televisions, established a TV factory in Swaziland, eventually aiming at South African markets.[391] The export companies in Finland had considered it more expedient to concentrate on exporting technology and machinery, but even that was in relatively small quantities. Banks or other financial institutions had no cooperation with South Africa except in one case, when the Nordic Bank (in which one shareholder was the Finnish bank KOP) granted a loan to the South African Government in 1976.[392]

With this background in mind, the struggle to cut off Finland's economic cooperation became a surprisingly difficult one. It did, however, carry implications which could be classified more as image and power factors than as factors of real economic importance. The Finnish forest and paper industry had always wanted to have its way in Finland's foreign trade, securing markets everywhere. That, in turn, had had its impact on foreign policy decision-making.

The trade being small in amount, but still a reality, the Nordic trade unions had taken action at the end of the 1970s and started to lobby their respective governments. Petitions were passed jointly to the Foreign Ministers' meetings, and negotiations with the political decision-makers were held.[393] For the unions, the joint Nordic Programme of Action was only partly satisfactory. During the five years from 1979 to 1984, relations with Southern Africa were discussed in the Finnish Parliament on 24 occasions, becoming almost a 'routine'. In the 1980s interest in breaking off diplomatic relations diminished, and most of the discussion focused on economic relations and specific economic transactions. No change occurred in Finland's policy.[394]

The NGOs' calls for boycott have been made with varying capacity and effect. In 1983, the different organisations joined forces and formed a pressure group, the 'Isolate South Africa Campaign' (EELAK). It was modelled according to a similar Swedish organisation, but its roots were in different campaigns organised by the Africa Committee and the early South Africa Committee as early as the 1960s. EELAK was an umbrella organisation co-ordinating the activities of different NGOs, including the trade unions and the Lutheran Church. Many of them were used to co-operating with each other in the

---

390. Heino, 1978:158.
391. Väyrynen, 1980:225–226.
392. Väyrynen, 1980:226.
393. Memo, 13.7.1977, Foreign Ministry, Political Department. Foreign Ministry's Archives.
394. Heino, 1992:77.

Namibia question as well as in ANC and SWAPO support.[395] But some new ones also joined in.

EELAK's first major campaign was to circulate a petition demanding the breaking off of economic relations with South Africa. The petition, signed by 26,000 Finns, was delivered to the Foreign Ministry in May 1985.

The turmoil in South Africa and the declaration of the state of emergency had aroused the outrage of the entire international community in 1985, and this was experienced in Finland, too. Political parties were mobilised and all the parties—with the exception of the Centre Party—proposed boycott action in regard to South Africa. In 1984, the relations with South Africa were discussed in Parliament 4 times; and in 1985 on as many as 14 occasions.

> Sanctions occupied a major part of our work here. You could divide it between that, because that was inclusive. You were dealing with churches, trade unions, you were dealing with professionals, school people, were dealing with all segments of civil society in pushing for the isolation of South Africa. But at the same time and almost equally you had to deal with the question of support to the liberation movement, to the various institutions we were trying to set up or run in Africa. Sanctions occupied more and more a central part because the campaign needed to be co-ordinated between the same formations like ISAK in Sweden and other Isolate South Africa organisations in the Nordic countries. And here, you had the Africa Committee starting and other organisations, that immediately joined in like the youth organisations of the various political parties. Like the youth organisations of the churches, they were always forward, in the forefront.[396]

Apartheid's reality and its brutal images were alien to Finland, and many were ready to say this. It was, after all, a moral and human rights question, no longer having anything to do with power politics.

> But by the time we completed in 1987, you had to count the organisations that were not part of that. So the mobilisation was almost total, starting from a small nucleus. The message was spread around. And you know, there is nothing like success to guarantee more success. And the more we succeeded with each given campaign, precisely because it was targeted, the more we won over other organisations. The greatest thing was when we got the youth of the conservative parties in all the countries, being a very essential part of this movement. In other words we succeeded in making nationals of Finland to be representatives of the ANC within whatever sector they operated from.[397]

In spite of growing pressure, the leaders of Finnish foreign policy continued to take a cautious and reserved stand on the South African issue. In April 1985, Foreign Minister Paavo Väyrynen,[398] one of the leading promoters of realist

---

395. EELAK's most vocal spokespersons were Helena Kekkonen, a well-known peace educationist, and Kimmo Kiljunen, Director of the Institute of Development Studies, among others.

396. Interview with Lindiwe Mabuza, 14.10.1996.

397. Ibid.

398. A Centre Party politician, who became a young MP already in 1970. He was the party chairman and became the Minister for Foreign Affairs several times. He always

foreign policy and closely connected with the business community, stated unequivocally that Finland would engage in economic sanctions only on a mandatory decision by the UN Security Council. The Government decided only to negotiate voluntary measures with the business community, with no significant effect. The paper companies were not at all willing to lose their markets in South Africa, the creation of which had taken decades.[399] The South African trade relations debate introduced again the question of morality in foreign policy. This time, it was the church which spoke out about it. The Archbishop of Finland, John Vikström, made his well-known speech at EELAK's public event accusing the Finnish Government of hypocrisy on the South African issue. The Foreign Ministry emphasised in its reply that measures were being planned by the Government. Nothing happened, though. The Foreign Ministry and the paper industry accused the church of not being as consistent in its foreign policy as the Foreign Ministry was.[400] The Ministry was not at all pleased by the church's growing involvement in foreign policy, because the church's concern attracted a lot of sympathy.

Frustrated, one trade union decided to act. In October 1985, the Transport Workers' Union (AKT) started a blockade of goods being shipped to and from South Africa. The boycott was started by one individual trade union, to be joined by others. Risto Kuisma tells how the decision was taken:

> In 1985, SAK established a working group to review the South African question. The group did not achieve anything, because there was no will. The representative of AKT was trying to push for the boycott, but it was not supported. We in the AKT decided to wait for SAK's decision, but the group was still sitting in the autumn with no results. The only decision was to urge members not to buy South African products. At the same time, in September, I was in a meeting in Norway, where we discussed with our sister trade unions that something should be done. The following day we had the AKT council meeting in Finland, and I said that now we have to decide something, otherwise the Norwegians will be ahead of us. And to my surprise, we made the decision to start a blockade, just like that.[401]

AKT was ready to take the total responsibility for the boycott. The chairperson's position in the union was powerful, because he had substantially improved the workers' position in the labour market. Workers in the transport sector were well organised and united under one federation, led by AKT's Risto Kuisma. The union, even though not that interested in international affairs in general, relied on the chairperson's judgement on the situation. The boycott action was dutifully implemented in the harbours, which had most experience in boycott

---

stayed firm on the Centre Party realist policy line, committed to the principles laid down by the late president Kekkonen. At the moment, he is a Member of the European Parliament.

399. Heino, 1992:78–80.
400. Heino, 1992:82–83.
401. Interview with Risto Kuisma, 11.12.1995.

actions, and especially when the other unions soon joined the boycott. For the Central Trade Union, SAK, the boycott came as a surprise.

> It was a meeting of the Social Democratic group of SAK, where I told them that your problems are soon over, when we start the blockade. They were completely shocked, couldn't believe it would be possible. But we had prepared the boycott for a long time, checked the legal aspects and all, so we had careful plans how to make it. Two weeks after they had a meeting and they joined the boycott by issuing a statement. They couldn't have done anything, because we stopped everything in the harbours.[402]

The Isolate South Africa Committee was also taken by surprise. The leading activists of EELAK had earlier contacted SAK to discuss possible boycott action, but the response was so depressing that they never contacted any individual trade unions. But their influence on Kuisma could be seen indirectly, in that the public discussion generated by EELAK and other NGOs had its effect on him and other members of AKT to make the boycott possible and effective. Mr Kuisma met the leaders of EELAK for the first time after the boycott decision, and was asked to join the board. Furthermore, AKT became an important sponsor of EELAK's activities.[403]

The forest industry, also taken by surprise—although not such a pleasant one—stated that the boycott was 'immoral', because it hurt most the people in the paper industry. But in fact, the Paper Workers' Union joined the boycott, and co-operated with the transport workers in carrying out the blockade.

The Government had mixed feelings about the boycott. The Social Democrats favoured the boycott, and President Koivisto stated that the measures taken by the Government and the trade union movement were along the same lines.[404] The Nordic trade unions joined the blockade, although it never had such a great effect in their countries, because the transport workers were not as effectively organised. In Sweden, the law prohibited 'sympathy' strikes and related action. But the Social Democratic government was influenced by the unions' pressure.

After the blockade, the development was rather rapid. A joint Nordic Programme of Action was renewed in 1985. The international community, which had become more favourable toward sanctions, had passed more effective resolutions on action against South Africa, though without a binding decision by the Security Council. In 1986, the US Congress decided on limited trade sanctions against South Africa. Laws prohibiting trade with South Africa went into effect in Denmark in December 1986, in Norway in March 1987, and were passed in Sweden in March 1987. Although Finnish trade with South Africa had already come to a halt in practice relatively soon after the blockade, the law was

---

402. Ibid.
403. Kuisma, 1994:293.
404. Heino, 1992:84.

passed only in May 1987, and came into effect on 1 July 1987. The Nordic trade embargo had become a reality.

AKT's unilateral action made it possible to change the course of Finland's foreign policy. Although few were against the boycott, apart from the business circles and the Centre party strongholds in the Foreign Ministry, nobody dared to take the initiative, finding it more comfortable to hide behind the legal excuses. When somebody finally did something, it was criticised but not seriously challenged.

> Many members were proud that it was their union that did it. There were a lot of criticisms, though, mainly saying that we were creating unemployment. The matter was debated, because many of the leading Finnish politicians were of the opinion that the Blacks were having it well in South Africa, and so on. It was not that kind of consensus like it is now, later. I was not pressured from the Government's side, I was never invited for a talk, for instance. Probably they thought that I have thought out this thing very carefully and that I have public support. We were challenged, however, with legal suits and everything, but nothing ever materialised. Only later on I learned that there was a lot of battle behind the scene.[405]

What made one trade union leader take a different course? Risto Kuisma himself elaborated his motives in his book. For him, it was a question of morality, first of all. The trade union movement, international in its essence, must take a stand that it finds morally right, even if the issue is far away. He dismissed the criticism of not taking action against all injustices in the world by citing André Brink: "There are two types of lunacy: firstly that you think you can do everything and secondly that you think that you cannot do anything." The search for justice, says Kuisma, has been his lifelong objective.[406] Still his actions were risky. Not protected against the criticism of using his position for his personal ambitions, Mr Kuisma had correctly assessed his followers attitudes. The boycott was discussed inside AKT as a whole at the next general meeting and it was decided to continue the boycott. According to Mr Kuisma, a big surprise for the political and trade circles was that the boycott was not a short protest action, but was meant to last until apartheid was dismantled.

ANC and the South African trade union movement were very deeply moved by the blockade. And so it happened that there was a delegation from the South African trade unions to participate at a SASK meeting just when the blockade came into effect.

> I did not know well these people from the liberation movement and South Africa, only met some a couple of times in the international trade union meetings. We were always told that they are communist, which was bad at that time for a Social Democrat. But once there was this old man from the trade union, perhaps a chairperson of SACTU [407], who said that he had for decades travelled around the world and

---

405. Interview with Risto Kuisma, 11.12.1995.
406. Kuisma, 1994:289, 415.
407. Stephen Dlamini was then the chairperson of SACTU. He visited Finland a few times during the years of struggle. However other sources reveal that the persons who

tried to implement the boycott, but now for the first time a union had finally done it. He was visiting SAK, and he was so honest and said that he had already nearly given up the hope.[408]

Börje Mattsson remembers how they went to see the action in the harbour:

> Africa Committee had two leading persons from ANC on that day. And I remember when I met them at the airport and I told them that today this boycott has been started. So they began just to shout, and I said we change all our programme, now we go to this union. And we had this meeting where Risto Kuisma was, and the general secretary of the union and some international secretary and then these men from ANC and me, and for the first time I have seen six or seven men just crying. We were everybody just crying in that meeting, and then we went to the harbour and looked for the shipment of the magazine published by the South African Government, that was imported by the South African Embassy and always spread in Finland. And now, for the first time, we went to this place where this paper came and then it was stopped by the union, and I took a picture, when these ANC representatives were standing on that pile of magazines. From now on this paper will never get spread in Finland. It was a wonderful moment.[409]

After the blockade, EELAK lobbied effectively for the sanctions law. Furthermore, it monitored the actions of the business sector, which tried to beat the blockade by transporting its products via other harbours. When the trade ban law came into effect, EELAK pushed for terminating the diplomatic relations. In this issue, the Government held on strictly to the status quo and the relations were continued. In addition, violations of the trade law were carefully monitored and reported to the authorities.[410] In practice, the public opinion was effectively behind the boycott policy; and, for instance, tourism to South Africa was not in fashion despite the South African Legation's and one tourist agency's marketing efforts. They were some individuals, though, who cooperated with the Legation, still situated in Helsinki, but they kept a low profile.[411]

---

visited Finland right after the start of the boycott were SACTU's and ANC's Mark Shope and Raymond Mokoena. They were very impressed by the boycott and paid a visit to Kuisma's office. *Auto- ja Kuljetusala*, (Car and Transport Sector, a union publication), 6.11.1985.

408. Interview with Risto Kuisma, 11.12.1995.

409. Interview with Börje Mattsson, 29.2.1996. According to other sources the ANC representatives Mark Shobe and Raymond Mokoena visited Risto Kuisma 22 October 1985. (see photographs). *Auto- ja Kuljetusala* (Car and Transport Sector), 6.11.1985.

410. EELAK was also producing books on South Africa in cooperation with professional publishers in Finland. An important one was Kiljunen & Lehtonen, 1990. Kimmo Kiljunen was at that time chairperson of EELAK and director of the Institute of Development Studies, he is now an MP for SDP. Satu Lehtonen was the first secretary of EELAK and an official in the Peace Education Institute. (See other publications in the list of sources.)

411. See, for example, Junnila, 1988.

6.4. Towards a democratic South Africa

In 1987, when ANC celebrated its 75th anniversary worldwide, an initiative was made for establishing its office in Helsinki. The same initiative included SWAPO's office as well. EELAK, with other NGOs, had organised a 'People's Parliament', a public event to mark the ANC anniversary. It was participated in by prominent ANC and SWAPO members, and generated further discussion on Finland's role in supporting the liberation struggle. A few NGOs promised to participate in funding the information offices, and lobbied government support. The Government decided to contribute to the establishing and running costs from its humanitarian budget. An information office was opened in 1988, headed by the ANC representative Mohammed Hussein.

> The work had become too much. And in any case we had always assumed when we came here, that it's much better to treat the countries of Scandinavia as individual countries, each with its own spirit of nationalism. And all nations want to be guided from their own territory and not from Sweden, as if they were satellites. So that once FINNIDA had agreed with the financing of an ANC office, which had been the only problem, then we were able to open one.[412]

The office in Helsinki made the implementation of the cooperation programme easier. The humanitarian support was increasing and new programmes were adopted. An NGO library project was turned into a governmental project and fully funded by the Government. The Finnish Library Association continued to implement the project, first in Mazimbu, Tanzania, and later in South Africa.

> Once one talks about the institutional assistance and organisational assistance, one can also overlook very important initiatives that were carried out by individuals. You had, for example, the Library Association, and Marjatta Lahti, who actually went to Mazimbu to start the library that the Centre Party youth of the Scandinavian countries had raised funds for. You had Finns who were individually committed to give up some of their comforts to go to some rural place in Tanzania to lend a helping hand. You had a decision by the Social Democratic party's international solidarity arm, to assist in establishing of a furniture factory in Mazimbu. And they got two people from Finland. We got the third one from Norway. The two from here were experts in a Finnish factory.[413] That entailed a lot of sacrifice in going to some strange corner of the world to deal with people, who knew nothing about carpentry. One of the most lasting and indelible impressions about some remarkable acts was the initiative by Helena Kekkonen and her husband Risto, to have a bus for a school in Mazimbu filled with all kinds of goods. Risto worked in a bus factory. He and Helena raised funds. The workers at the firm built the bus during their free time, without pay.[414]

---

412. Interview with Lindiwe Mabuza, 14.10.1996.
413. Leo Söderholm was one of the persons in question.
414. Interview with Lindiwe Mabuza, 14.10.1996.

Marjatta Lahti, a librarian, who was working in the Library Project in Mazimbu, tells about the atmosphere in the camps:

> Basically the ANC was very keen in promoting education and the libraries as such, they understood the importance of it. And the higher level were all for it and they tried to help in the best possible way. But of course in practice, as circumstances were so abnormal, that everything was difficult to run there. Not to talk about an outsider that comes there. Of course, they couldn't give as much guidance and orientation as we would have liked to have perhaps in the beginning. So it was very much up to us how we could adjust and find our ways how to deal with this project. And they were aware on a political level what Nordic countries had been doing, but of course when you live there then it doesn't matter so much any more where you come from. It's your own personality then that counts more.[415]

In the 1990s, after the release of Nelson Mandela and the unbanning of the ANC, the Finnish Government began to consider ANC as an ordinary party in a republic. On the initiative of Social Democratic Foreign Ministers—Kalevi Sorsa followed by Pertti Paasio—Finland had substantially extended its support to other organisations inside South Africa (see appendix 2). In the changing situation, Finland wanted to widen its contacts with the democratic non-racial forces inside South Africa. That had an effect in diminishing Finland's support to ANC.

In the end, many factors contributed to the collapse of Finland's aid to ANC. The general drastic decline in the development cooperation budget, the failure of ANC to use funds allocated earlier,[416] ANC's non-transparency in respect to its exile organisation,[417] and the Centre Party's long standing dislike of ANC, resulted in the discontinuation of most of Finland's projects in ANC camps. The pressure groups did not have the power behind them that they had earlier, because after the unbanning of ANC, things were considered as solved in South Africa. Trade interests were now legitimate. In 1993, the Centre Party Foreign Minister Paavo Väyrynen, who had had the 'honour' of silently and smoothly lifting the trade ban law in June 1991, indicated that Finland's aid to ANC had to be terminated at once. After a few postponements, the aid was terminated and the ANC office in Helsinki was soon closed.

---

415. Interview with Marjatta Lahti, 15.1.1996.

416. In the previous years when Finland's aid to ANC had sharply increased, the organisation had not been able to indicate how to use the funds. Thus there was a considerable amount of unallocated funds in FINNIDA's humanitarian budget earmarked for ANC. Those funds were easy to cancel when the overall development cooperation budget was drastically decreased.

417. Some NGO representatives who visited the camps presented some criticism over the administration of the exile organisation during ANC's Arusha Donors' Conference in 1991. They were also disappointed with the donors' aid to the camps. Discussion continued in Finland between solidarity groups and ANC representatives whether to continue supporting the refugee camps or to transform the activism inside South Africa. Personal communication with Outi Hakkarainen, then Secretary for Development Cooperation in SYL.

Chapter 7
Conclusion

This study has mainly been an account of how the liberation struggle in Southern Africa was understood and supported in Finland. It is an interesting part of Finland's foreign policy and NGO history, a curiosity in the large sphere of what are considered as the country's international relations. And yet because it moved the very foundations of the foreign policy doctrine, its importance is well beyond its actual size.

We have agreed with Heino's interpretation of Finnish foreign policy as a dynamic conflict between realists and idealists. We have tried to show that idealism, represented mainly by a number of non-governmental organisations, has in fact influenced the foreign policy of Finland. International politics is not completely determined by hard power play between state machines: softer human rights considerations do have real weight as such, not only as items of propaganda covering more sinister interests. The special characteristics of Finland, as a non-aligned welfare state and as part of the Nordic group of states, gave it resources and motivation to support liberation movements. One restriction grew from real and imagined trade interests connected with good relations with the forces that were continuing apartheid and other forms of colonisation. Furthermore, a close affiliation with those liberation movements which enjoyed Soviet support in the form of military hardware would have harmed Finland's precious neutral image in the eyes of the West. Finland's foreign policy during the Cold War was formed under a clear foreign policy doctrine. The country's main consideration was to balance between the East and the West and make its neutrality acceptable and useful everywhere, especially among its neighbours. This enhanced Finland's security and was very beneficial for its economy.

Some factors of Finland's foreign policy decision-making had been internal and non-material. Foreign policy was not only security, trade and guarding other direct interests. The young idealists wanted Finland to act on its own to support the progressive forces in international society, basing its policy on a broader definition of national interest. They wanted civil rights and international justice to form the basis of the foreign policy doctrine. And because they did not see through the bureaucratic jungle of foreign policy decision- making, they wanted to change its authoritarian and secretive apparatus.

This apparatus was responsive to the pressure brought by NGOs. Changes in policy did take place, especially after 1966 and again in 1973, in the very direction in which it was pushed. Initiatives had found response among the political leadership. Especially President Kekkonen and several social democratic politicians like Kalevi Sorsa and Väinö Leskinen were instrumental in bringing the pressure home to the Foreign Ministry. By and large, the officials in the Foreign Ministry were reluctant to accept—or else opposed—these changes, although there were a few exceptions. This changed slowly, when a new kind of recruitment policy opened the doors of the Ministry to young social democrats—but not to those still more to the left—in the early 1970s.

The paradox in Finland has been that although the Soviet Union was an important frame of reference, due to the imperatives of security, a major part of the foreign policy was actually intended to minimise the Soviet influence. Finland has always been, after all, a Western liberal democracy, with a capitalist economic system. A large majority of Finns have always wanted to belong to Western society. Leftists by ideology, the idealists of the 1960s were actually pursuing courses of action which could be seen as supportive of the Soviet line, although this was not at all the case with several organisations, as we have seen. Yet these too had to bear the 'communist' label stamped upon them by the political right.

The truth is, nevertheless, that a significant number of the activists who spoke on behalf of those movements were actually connected with organisations openly propagating Soviet foreign policy, like the World Peace Council. Apart from being openly nationalist, some liberation movements were ideologically linked to socialism and supported by the Soviet Union, its allies, or China. In the context of the Cold War, what might have been supportive for the one camp, was definitely against the other. Finland wanted to avoid this, fearing that it would be considered as a dependent Soviet satellite. This determined its relationship to revolutionary liberation movements for a long time. In addition, in the 1960s, many Finnish people were not at all concerned about the independence of the distant colonies. They preferred to look at the problems in the mother country.

The NGOs concerned with the situation in Africa pursued the cause, and managed to influence public opinion and turn it definitively against colonialism and apartheid. Ideological differences aside, they united NGOs representing large sectors of the society. Their attempts were joined by the Finnish Lutheran Church, which had carried out mission work in Ovamboland for over a hundred years. Being familiar with the living conditions of black people under the South African regime, the Namibian church and its Finnish servants, the missionaries, took a clear stand for independence, supporting SWAPO. Thus the occupation of Namibia, to a great extent, but also the struggle against Portuguese colonialism, were the common denominator which brought together trade unions and churches, radicals and conservatives, young and old, son and father. This broad alliance, which was further widened by the campaign against apartheid, managed to convince Finland's foreign policy decision-makers to include moral values as one of the justifications for foreign policy. A lot had to be changed, too, in Finland's decision-making apparatus and in the surrounding world. The period of détente, together with a new active political doctrine, gave President Kekkonen a chance for new openings in Finland's international activities.

After the decision of principle in 1973, which authorised Finnish humanitarian aid to be channelled to the liberation movements directly, the Finnish role rapidly became more active. Together with other Nordic countries, the open support for the movements legitimised their activities in the international arena, proving that the movements were not totally dependent on the support from the Eastern bloc. All in all, Finland supported five movements (PAIGC, FRELIMO, PAC, SWAPO and ANC), the latter two being the main beneficiaries.[418]

Finland's official support to SWAPO (including the Namibia programme, which in practice was channelled to SWAPO as well) over the years 1974–1989 was in total 74.5 million FIM. Finland's official humanitarian aid to ANC started in 1978, and totalling 39.4 million FIM, plus NGO support to ANC projects 6.7 million FIM. In addition to this, Finland supported the other democratic non-racial organisations and institutions in South Africa with 40.8 million FIM. After the support to ANC was discontinued in 1993, Finland was still channelling humanitarian aid inside South Africa to a value of 5.5 million FIM up until 1996, when bilateral development cooperation was started between the two countries. Furthermore, a lot of aid was given by the Finnish NGOs and the Lutheran church. From the first fund-raising campaign of *Taksvärkki* in 1969, the NGOs steadily increased their support to the movements. After 1974 their programmes were co-funded by FINNIDA, which always regarded the NGOs as important channels of aid to the liberation movements.

Over the years Finland's role in the Namibian negotiated settlement was a significant one. Since 1970, when Finland appealed to International Court of Justice to make a decision concerning the South African mandate in Namibia, Finland had acted as an important mediator in the conflict, which soon became subject to the international power game. Martti Ahtisaari led the process as United Nations representative, and showed enormous patience and skills over the years. Finland's policy of supporting the settlement under the leadership of the UN proved to be successful, and the transition to independence could be started in 1989. Finland also initiated several programmes to prepare Namibia for independence, both in the multilateral and the bilateral forums. After Namibian independence was achieved in 1990, Finland started bilateral development cooperation with Namibia, which soon became one of its main target countries.

Although Namibians are a small fraction of the peoples living in Southern Africa, their liberation struggle in a way spearheaded that in their big brother country—South Africa. From this angle the independence of Namibia contributed significantly to the democratisation of South Africa.

---

418. As the support to FNLA remains for the time being unclear, it is not included in this list.

A great deal has changed in international society—one important power bloc has vanished completely. Many of the changes in Finnish foreign policy have been directed by these general changes. But things have changed in Finland, too. Increased information and campaigning slowly changed public opinion, and in the 1980s a large majority of Finns supported liberation movements and development cooperation in general. Solidarity beyond the borders of one's own country became natural. Finland is presently run by a generation of politicians to whom international contacts have been natural from their youth onwards. This study has shown that many of them were 'idealists' to whom the liberation struggle represented a long-lasting commitment to development cooperation. It is clear that the very foundations of today's relations with developing countries were created via the experience of the liberation struggle in Africa and on other continents, too, not forgetting the Vietnam war. This study also shows that in a democratic country ordinary people can influence political decision-making even in the most closed and guarded area of all, foreign politics. It is not easy, and it takes a long time and many dedicated people, but it is possible.

This study is just a beginning. It provides documented interpretations for further analysis. Finland's relationship to liberation movements can be put in a larger context together with the other Nordic reports. However, this is a study on the liberation movements as seen from Finland's standpoint. The most important research must be done by the people of Angola, Mozambique, Namibia, South Africa, and Zimbabwe themselves. One clear idea behind this study was to provide a foundation for them to be able to write their own history of the events. We sincerely hope that we have succeeded in that respect.

List of Abbreviations

AAPSO	Afro-Asian People's Solidarity Organisation
AKT	*Auto- ja Kuljetustyöntekijöiden Liitto* (Transport Workers Union)
ANC	African National Congress
CCN	Council of Churches in Namibia
CND	Campaign for Nuclear Disarmament
COSATU	Congress of South African Trade Unions
CSCE	Conference on Security and Cooperation in Europe
EELAK	*Eristetään Etelä-Afrikka Kampanja* (Isolate South Africa Campaign)
ELOK	Evangelican Lutheran Church of Ovambo and Kavango
FCP	Finnish Communist Party (SKP)
FIDIDA	Finnish Disabled People's International Development Association
FIM	*Suomen markka* (Finnish Mark)
FINNIDA	Finnish Development Agency
FMS	Finnish Missionary Society
FNL	National Liberation Front of Vietnam
FNLA	*Frente Nacional de Libertação de Angola* (Angolan National Liberation Front)
FRELIMO	*Frente de Libertação de Moçambique* (Liberation Front of Mozambique)
FSS	*Finlands Svenska Skolungdomsförbund* (Finnish Swedish Pupils' Union)
HYY	*Helsingin Yliopiston Ylioppilaskunta* (Helsinki University Students' Union)
ICFTU	International Confederation of Free Trade Unions
IDAF	International Defence and Aid Fund
ISC	International Students' Conference
ISMUN	International Students' Movement for United Nations
IUS	International Union of Students
KAVAKU	*Kansainvälisten asioiden valmennuskurssi* (Training Course on International Affairs)
KEPA	*Kehitysyhteistyön Palvelukeskus* (Service Centre for Development Cooperation)
LWF	Lutheran World Federation
MI	Mozambique Institute
MPLA	*Movimento Popular de Libertação de Angola* (Angolan Popular Liberation Movement)
NNTUC	Nduuvu Nangolo Trade Union School
NUNW	National Union of Namibian Workers
OAU	Organisation of African Unity
PAC	Pan-Africanist Congress of Azania
PAIGC	*Partido Africano de Independência da Guiné e Cabo Verde* (African Party of Guinea and Cape Verde)
PLAN	People's Liberation Army of Namibia
RKP	*Ruotsalainen Kansanpuolue* (Swedish People's Party)
SACTU	South African Congress of Trade Unions
SADCC	Southern African Development and Cooperation Conference

SAK	*Suomen Ammattiliittojen Keskusjärjestö* (Central Organisation of Finnish Trade Unions)
SASK	*Suomen ammattiliittojen solidaarisuuskeskus* (Trade Union Solidarity Center)
SDP	*Sosialidemokraattinen Puolue* (Social Democratic Party of Finland)
SECO	*Sveriges elevers centralorganisation* (Swedish School Students' Union)
SIDA	Swedish International Development Authority
SKDL	*Suomen Kansan Demokraattinen Liitto* (Finnish People's Democratic Union)
SKP	*Suomen Kommunistinen Puolue* (Finnish Communist Party)
SOMAFCO	Salomon Mahlangu Freedom College
SRP	*Suomen Rauhanpuolustajat* (Finnish Peace Committee)
STL	*Suomen Teiniliitto* (Finland's Teen Union)
SWANU	South West African National Union
SWAPO	South West African People's Organisation
SYL	*Suomen Ylioppilaskuntien Liitto* (National Union of Finnish Students' Unions)
TALKE	*Taloudellisen kehitysmaasuhteiden neuvottelukunta* (Standing Parliamentary Committee for Economic Relations with the Developing Countries)
TSL	*Työväen Sivistysliitto* (Workers' Cultural Union of Finland)
UNESCO	United Nations Educational, Scientific and Cultural Organisation
UNIN	United Nations Institute for Namibia
UNITA	*União Nacional para a Independência Total de Angola* (Union for Total Independence of Angola)
UNSA	*Suomen opiskelijoiden YK-yhdistys* (Finnish Students' United Nations Association)
UNTA	*União Nacional dos Trabalhadores Angolanos* (Angolan National Workers' Union)
UNTAG	United Nations Transitional Assistance Group
WCC	World Council of Churches
WPC	World Peace Council
YKA	*Ylioppilaiden Kansainvälinen Apu* (Students' International Assistance)
YYA	*Ystävyys, yhteistyö- ja avunantosopimus* (Treaty of Friendship, Cooperation and Mutual Assistance between Finland and the Soviet Union)
ZANU	Zimbabwe African National Union
ZAPU	Zimbabwe African People's Union

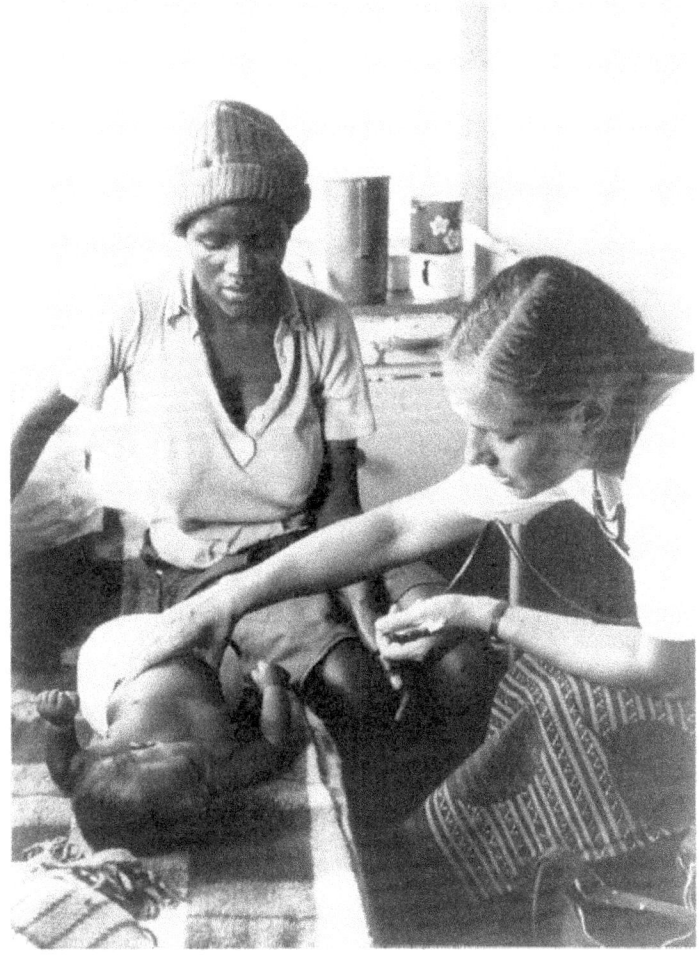

A Finnish medical doctor, Merja Saarinen, inspecting a Namibian baby in a tent at the SWAPO settlement in Kwanza Sul, Angola. Photo: Kansan Arkisto (left)

A representative of the World Peace Council, the South African Max Moabi, speaking at a workplace meeting in Finland. The interpreter is Hanna Virtanen. Photo: Kansan Arkisto (below)

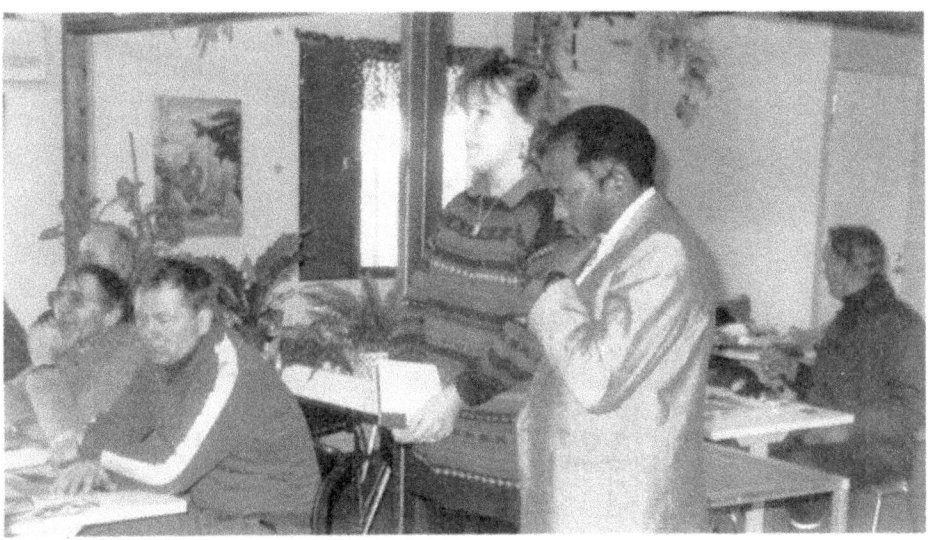

Markku Vesikko and Pertti Virtanen arguing with a foreman over the construction of the ANC camp in Viana, near Luanda, Angola, in 1985. Photo: Kansan Arkisto

Nelson Mandela visiting Finland on 22 May 1992. On the left, former Prime Minister and Foreign Minister Kalevi Sorsa. Photo: T. Koivisto

Finland and National Liberation in Southern Africa 163

ANC's representative to Finland, Mohammed Hussein

"Sign a petition to the city council" —campaigning against apartheid in front of the Old Student House in Helsinki. Photo: Anonym

Living in a tent with a baby in Kwanza Sul.
Photo: Pekka Peltola 1983
(left)

Building a hut in Kwanza Sul.
Photo: Pekka Peltola 1983
(below)

Labour students Nokokure Thobias, Selma Shiwana, Franna Kavari, Kayele Kambombo and Joe Nakatana, with Victor Nkandi (second from right), the director of all SWAPO camps, who later died in SWAPO's dungeons. Photo: Pekka Peltola 1983

Pekka Peltola (left) preparing form an open-air lecture on trade unionism at SWAPO's transit camp in Viana, Angola. Photo: Ilkka Tahvanainen 1979

The first official Finnish contribution to FRELIMO, a check of 100,000 FIM, was given to Samora Machel (second from left) and Marcelino dos Santos (first from right) by ambassador Martti Ahtisaari (second from right) and councillor Kimmo Pulkkinen at the FRELIMO office in Dar es Salaam on 10 October 1974. Photo: Kimmo Pulkkinen

ANC/SACTU representatives visiting the Finnish Transport Workers' Union (AKT) after the union had stopped all trade between Finland and South Africa in October 1985. From left: the host of the delegation, Börje Mattsson; Raymond Mokoena; the treasurer of AKT, Kaj Westman; Mark Shope; and the chairman of AKT, Risto Kuisma. Photo: Vesa Seppäläinen

Finland and National Liberation in Southern Africa 167

"In a brick house there lives a happy family". The end product of collective toil in Kwanza Sul. Brick construction.
Photo: Jukka Pääkkönen 1987

Life in Kwanza Sul.
Photo: Jukka Pääkkönen
(top left: Pekka Peltola)

The four editors are from left
Joe Nakatana, Joseph
Ashipala, Aron Seibeb and
Albertina Naukushu.

Wounded and captured SWAPO fighters in May 1989. Photo: Olle Eriksson

UN Special Representative Martti Ahtisaari meeting Finnish and Namibian church representatives in Oshakati, northern Namibia, during the crisis caused by SWAPO troops crossing over from Angola at the beginning of the independence process in April 1989. From left: Ulla Nenonen, Martti Ahtisaari, Matti Amadhila, Olle Eriksson. Photo: Olle Eriksson

Sam Nujoma and Solomon Mifima (right) with Lloyd Swantz at the Azania Front Church in Dar es Salaam around 1970.
Archive of Swantz

Helena Kekkonen, chairperson of EELAK, an organisation pushing for sanctions against South Africa's apartheid.
Photo: Risto Kekkonen

Kati Peltola and Tapio Leskinen lobbying minister of trade Jermu Laine (to the left) over the sanctions.
Photo: Risto Kekkonen

Kimmo Kiljunen and Helena Kekkonen trying to convince the chairman of SAK, Pertti Viinanen, over the necessity of a boycott.
Photo: Risto Kekkonen

SOURCES AND BIBLIOGRAPHY

Archive material

Archives of the Finnish Peace Committee, SRP/People's Archives
Archives of Finland's Teen Union, STL/National Archives
Archives of the Finnish Missionary Society/National Archives
Arquivo Histórico de Moçambique
Foreign Ministry's Archives
Personal archives of Helena Kekkonen
Personal archives of Pekka Peltola
Personal archives of Kimmo Pulkkinen
Personal archives of Mikko Pyhälä
Personal collection of Veikko Tupasela
SYL archives
University Library/Collection of press items on microfilm

Newspapers and Periodicals

Aikalainen
Auto-ja Kuljetusala
A Voz da Revolucão
Apu
Dagens Nyheter
Helsingin Sanomat
Kansan Uutiset
Nootti
Päivän Sanomat
Sosialidemokraatti
Studentbladet
Tilanne
Uusi Suomi
Ylioppilaslehti
Ylä-Vuoksi
Ydin

Unpublished sources

Humanitaarisen avun toimialaselvitys, 1985 (Evaluation of the Finnish Humanitarian Aid), Foreign Ministry.
Iloniemi, Jaakko, 1995, Suomen muuttunut kansainvälinen asema ja kehitysyhteistyö (Finland's altered international position and development aid) Selvitys ulkoasianministeriölle 13.3.1995 (Report to the Foreign Ministry).
Kumppanuutta rakentamassa (Building the partnership), Ulkoasiainministeriön ja Kirkon Ulkomaanavun yhteinen Namibian stipendiaattiohjelma vv. 1975–1993. Kirkon Ulkomaanapu, Helsinki, maaliskuu 1994 (The joint Namibia

Scholarship Programme of the Foreign Ministry and Finnchurchaid, 1975-1993. Finnchurchaid, Helsinki, March 1994).

Bibliography

A Trust Betrayed: Namibia, 1974, United Nations Publications.
Ahtisaari, Martti, 1994, "Namibiasta Bosniaan", in Kiljunen, Kimmo (ed), 1994, *Suomalaisia YK:ssa* (Finns in UN). Gummerus. Jyväskylä.
Autti, Pekka & Apunen, Osmo, 1965, *Yhdistyneet Kansakunnat 1945-65. Politiikan muotokuva* (United Nations 1945–65. Portrait of politics). Suomen Teiniliitto.
Blomberg, Jaakko & Joenniemi, Pertti, 1972, *Kaksiteräinen miekka* (Two-edged Sword). Tammi. Helsinki.
Bonsdorff von, Johan, 1986, *Kun Vanha vallattiin* (When the Old was occupied). Tammi. Helsinki.
Brotherus, Heikki, 1964, *Mitä Etelä-Afrikassa tapahtuu?* (What is happening in South Africa?). WSOY.
Crocker, Chester, 1992, *High Noon in Southern Africa. Making Peace in the Rough Neighborhood.* W.W. Norton & Co. New York.
Eirola, Martti, 1992, *The Ovambogefahr. The Ovamboland reservation in the making.* Societas Historica Finlandiae Septentrionalis. Rovaniemi.
Forsberg, Tuomas and Vaahtoranta, Tapani, 1993, *Johdatus Suomen ulkopolitiikkaan. Kylmästä sodasta uuteen maailmanjärjestykseen* (Introduction to Finnish foreign policy. From Cold War to a new world order). Gaudeamus. Tampere.
Front mot kärnvapen (Front against Nuclear Weapons), 1963. Helsinki.
Green, Reginald, Kiljunen, Kimmo and Kiljunen, Marja-Liisa, 1981, *Namibia. The Last Colony.* Longman. Essex. United Kingdom.
Groth, Siegfried, 1995, *Namibia. The Wall of Silence. The Dark Days of the Liberation Struggle.* Peter Hammer Verlag. Wuppertal. Germany.
Halinen, Sanna, 1988, *Namibian kysymys ja Suomi 1966–1974* (The Namibian question and Finland). Pro gradu tutkielma, Turun yliopisto, Politiikan tutkimuksen ja sosiologian laitos (Master's thesis, University of Turku, Department of political studies and sociology).
Hallman, Kristina, 1983, *Tottelisinko? Suomalaista Sadankomiteaa vuodesta 1963* (Should I obey? Finnish Committee of 100 since 1963). Vaasa.
Heikkilä, Hannu, 1997, *Martti Ahtisaari. Kansainvälinen tie presidentiksi* (International road for president). WSOY. Porvoo.
Heino, Timo-Erkki, 1978, *Suomen ja Etelä-Afrikan taloudelliset ja poliittiset suhteet 1920-luvulta nykyhetkeen* (The economic and the political relations between Finland and South Africa from the 1920s to the present). Poliittisen historian pro gradu-tutkielma. Helsingin Yliopisto. Maaliskuu 1978. (Master's thesis in political history. University of Helsinki. March 1978.)
Heino, Timo-Erkki, 1992, *Politics on Paper. Finland's South Africa Policy 1945–91.* Research Report No. 90. Nordiska Afrikainstitutet. Uppsala.
Hurskainen, Kai, 1988, *YK-aatteesta anti-imperialismiin. Opiskelijoiden YK-liikkeen kehitysvaiheita 1963–69* (From UN -ideology to anti-imperialism. Development phases of Students' UN Movement in 1963–69). Master's Thesis. University of Helsinki.

Ihamäki, Kirsti, 1985, *Leonard Auala, Mustan Namibian Paimen* (Black Namibia's shepherd). Suomen Lähetysseura (Finnish Missionary Society).
Jacobson, Max, 1983, *38. Kerros. Havaintoja ja muistiinpanoja vuosilta 1965–71.* (38th floor. Observations and Notes from the years 1965–71). Otava, Helsinki.
Junnila, Tuure, 1988, *Etelä-Afrikka—Ihmisoikeudet—Suomen Ulkopolitiikka* (South Africa—Human Rights—Finnish Foreign Policy).
Juva, Mikko, 1962, *Teollistunut Eurooppa ja teollistuva Afrikka* (Industrialised Europe and Industrialising Africa). Suomen Lähetysseura (Finnish Missionary Society)
Juva, Mikko, 1993, *Seurasin nuoruuteni näkyä* (I followed the vision of my youth). Otava, Helsinki.
Kansainvälisen Kehitysavun komitea (Committee for International Development Assistance). Helsinki 1963.
Kansalaisjärjestöjen kansainvälisen toiminnan komiteanmietintö (Committee report on the international activity of the NGOs). 1974:24. Helsinki.
Kauppila, Erkki, 1975, "Suomen ulkopolitiikka ja kansalliset vapautuspyrkimykset" (Finnish Foreign Policy and the National Liberation Efforts). *Ulkopolitiikka* (Foreign Policy) 1975:1.
Kehitysapua ihmiseltä ihmiselle. (Development aid from people to people) Kansainvälinen Solidaarisuussäätiö 20 vuotta (International Solidarity Foundation 20 years).
Kehitysmaat ja Suomi, 1973, (Developing countries and Finland), ed. Martti Ahtisaari, Olavi Saikku, Martti Kahiluoto, Unto Korhonen, Eeva-Kristina Forsman, Åke Wihtol. Poliittisen historian laitoksen julkaisuja C:8. (Department of Political History, Publication C:8).
Kehitysyhteistyökomitean mietintö (Report of the Committee on development cooperation). 1978:11. Helsinki
Kekkonen, Arja, Natri, Pasi & Väyrynen, Raimo, 1984, *Rauha ja oikeudenmukaisuus.YK:n neljä vuosikymmentä* (Peace and Justice. The four decades of UN). Tammi. Helsinki.
Kekkonen, Helena, 1993, *Rauhan Siltaa Rakentamassa* (Building the Bridge of Peace).
Kiljunen, Kimmo (ed.), 1975, *Rotusorron kahleissa* (In apartheid chains). Kansainvälinen Solidaarisuussäätiö (International Solidarity Foundation).
Kiljunen Kimmo and Kiljunen, Marja-Liisa (eds.), 1980, *Namibia—viimeinen siirtomaa* (Namibia—the last colony). Tammi. Helsinki.
Kiljunen, Kimmo & Lehtonen, Satu, 1986, *Etelä-Afrikan murhenäytelmä ja me.* (The South African tragedy and us).
Kiljunen, Kimmo & Lehtonen, Satu, 1990, *Mustavalkoinen Etelä-Afrikka. Apartheid, Suomi ja kansainvälinen eristäminen* (Black and White South Africa. Apartheid, Finland and international isolation). Kirjayhtymä. Helsinki.
Kiljunen, Kimmo (ed.), 1994, *Suomalaisia YK:ssa* (Finns in UN). Gummerus. Jyväskylä.
Koivisto, Mauno, 1995, *Historian tekijät. Kaksi kautta II* (History-makers. Two eras II). Juva.

Kolbe, Laura, 1993, *Sivistyneistön rooli: Helsingin Yliopiston Ylioppilaskunta 1944– 1959* (The role of the intelligentsia: Helsinki University Students' Union). Otava. Helsinki.
Kolbe, Laura, 1996, *Eliitti, traditio, murros: Helsingin Yliopiston Ylioppilaskunta 1960–1990* (Elite, tradition and change: Helsinki University Students' Union). Otava. Helsinki.
Korhonen, Keijo, 1989, *Mitalin toinen puoli. Johdatusta ulkopolitiikan epätodellisuuteen* (The other side of the medal. Introduction to the unreality of foreign policy). Otava. Helsinki.
Koskenniemi, Matti, 1994, *Kansainväliset pakotteet ja Suomi* (International sanctions and Finland). Lakimiesliiton Kustannus.
Kuisma, Risto, 1994, *Tilinpäätös* (Closing the accounts). Gummerus. Helsinki.
Kuparinen, Eero, 1991, *An African Alternative. Nordic Migration to South Africa 1815–1914.* Studia Historica 40. Migration Studies C 10. Institute of Migration. Gummerus. Jyväskylä.
Leys, Colin & Saul, John S., 1994, "Liberation without Democracy?" *Journal of Southern African Studies*, 20,1 (March 1994), pp. 123–147.
Leys, Colin and Saul, John S., (eds.) 1995, *Namibia's Liberation Struggle, Two-edged Sword.* James Currey, London. Ohio University Press, Athens.
Lipponen, Paavo, 1966a, "Nuoren polven ulkopolitiikka" (The foreign policy of the younger generation). *Ulkopolitiikka* (Foreign Policy) 1966/3.
Lipponen, Paavo, 1966b, "Suomen ulkopolitiikan tulevaisuuden näkymät" (The future prospects of Finland's foreign policy). *Ylioppilaslehti.* (Student Newspaper) 18, November 1966.
Lipponen, Paavo, 1985, "Lapualaisoopperasta nappulaliigaan eli kuinka radikalismi kesytettiin" (From the Lapua Opera to the Little League; or the taming of radicalism). *Kuvastin* 1985/3.
Mattsson, Börje & Lohikoski, Mikko, 1970, *Raportti Eteläisen Afrikan vapautusliikkeistä* (Report on the Liberation Movements in Southern Africa). SYL.
Mattsson, Börje, *Opinto-ohjelma eteläisestä Afrikasta* (Study material on Southern Africa). Tricont.
Mondlane, Eduardo, 1972, *Mosambikin taistelu* (The Struggle of Mozambique). Tricont.
Möttölä, Kari, 1984, "Suomen politiikka Yhdistyneissä kansakunnissa" (Finnish policy in the United Nations). In Arja Kekkonen et al., *Rauha ja oikeudenmukaisuus.YK:n neljä vuosikymmentä* (Peace and Justice. The four decades of UN) Tammi. Helsinki.
Möttölä, Kari, 1993, "Puolueettomuudesta sitoutumiseen. Turvallisuuspoliittisen perusratkaisun muutos kylmästä sodasta Euroopan murrokseen" (From neutrality to alignment. The change in the basic approach to security policy from Cold War to European upheaval). In Forsberg, Tuomas and Vaahtoranta,Tapani, *Johdatus Suomen ulkopolitiikkaan. Kylmästä sodasta uuteen maailmanjärjestykseen* (Introduction to Finnish foreign policy. From Cold War to a new world order). Gaudeamus. Tampere.
Namibia and the Nordic Countries, 1981, Nordiska Afrikainstitutet. Uppsala.
Pakaslahti, Johannes and Bonsdorff, Johan, 1970, *Valistuneet saalistajat. Kenelle hyöty kehitysavustamme?* (Enlightened Predators. Who benefits from our development aid?).

Peltola, Matti, 1958, *Suomen Lähetysseuran Afrikan työn historia* (The history of the Finnish Missionary Society's work in Africa). Kuopio.

Peltola, Pekka, 1995, *The Lost May Day. Namibian Workers' Struggle for Independence*. Finnish Anthropological Society and Nordic Africa Institute. Jyväskylä.

Saarela, Tapio, 1980, "Namibia Suomen ulkopolitiikassa" (Namibia in Finland's foreign policy). In Kiljunen, Kimmo and Kiljunen, Marja-Liisa, *Namibia— viimeinen siirtomaa* (Namibia—the last colony). Tammi. Helsinki.

Schubin, Vladimir, 1994, *Reflections on Relations between the Soviet Union/Russian Federation and South Africa in the 1980s and 1990s*. Centre for Southern African Studies, University of Western Cape.

Siitonen, Lauri, 1981, *Suomen kehitysyhteistyöpolitiikan tavoitteet ja perusteet* (The objectives and justifications of Finnish development cooperation policy). Pro gradu-tutkielma. Turun yliopisto, politiikan tutkimuksen ja sosiologian laitos (Master's thesis. University of Turku, Department of Political Studies and Sociology).

Sosialismi Tansaniassa 1, 2. (Socialism in Tanzania). Tricont.

Stokke, Olav and Widstrand, Carl (eds.), 1973, *Southern Africa. The UN-OAU Conference*. Part 1: Programme of Action & Conference Proceedings. Part 2: Papers and Documents. Scandinavian Institute of African Studies. Uppsala.

Sundbäck, Esa, 1991, *Suomen Ylioppilaskuntien Liitto ja suomalaisen opiskelijaliikkeen muutoksen vuodet 1968–1990* (The National Union of Finnish Students and the years of change in the Finnish student movement). SYL.

Suomi ja Kehitysyhteistyö, 1974, (Finland and Development Cooperation) Ulkoasiainministeriö, kehitysyhteistyöosasto (Foreign Ministry Department for Development Cooperation).

Suominen, Tapani, (forthcoming), *Ehkä teloitamme jonkun? Opiskelijaradikalismi ja vallankumousfiktio 1960- ja 1970-luvun Suomessa, Norjassa ja Länsi-Saksassa* (Perhaps we execute someone? Student Radicalism and Revolution Fiction in 1960s and 1970s Finland, Norway and West Germany). Tammi.

Thiro-Beukes, Erica and Beukes, Attie and Beukes, Hewat S.J., 1986, *Namibia. A Struggle Betrayed*. Rehoboth. Acasia Drukkery.

Toveri Musta. Työväki, pääoma ja rotuerottelu Etelä-Afrikassa (Comrade Black. Working class, capital and racial segregation in South Africa.). SAK, second edition 1984.

Tuomi, Helena, (ed.), 1976, *Suomi ja Kolmas Maailma* (Finland and the Third World).

Tuomioja, Erkki, 1969, *Valkoisen vallan Afrikka* (The Africa of White Power). Tammi. Helsinki.

ULA (Foreign political statements and documents). Foreign Ministry 1959

Ulkoasiainministeriön julkaisuja. Yhdistyneiden kansakuntien yleiskokouksen kolmas erityisistunto sekä kuudestoista istuntokausi ja sen jatkoistunto (Publications of the Ministry for Foreign Affairs. The 3rd Special Session of the United Nations General Assembly, and the sixteenth session and its resumed session). Helsinki. 1962.

The United Nations Council for Namibia, 1987, *A Summary of Twenty Years of Effort by the Council for Namibia on Behalf of Namibian Independence*. United Nations.

Uola, Mikko, 1974, *Suomi ja Etelä-Afrikka. Kanssakäyminen ja käsitykset toisesta osapuolesta 1800-luvulta apartheid-kysymyksen kärjistymiseen* (Finland and South Africa. Interaction and opinions about each other from the 1800s until the apartheid question came to a head). Alea-kirja. Tampere.

Viemerö, Rauno, 1975, "Suomen Eteläisen Afrikan politiikka YK:ssa" (Finland's Southern African policy in the UN). In Kiljunen, Kimmo, (ed.), 1975, *Rotusorron kahleissa* (In the chains of racial oppression). Kansainvälinen Solidaarisuussäätiö (International Solidarity Foundation).

Voipio, Rauha, 1980, "Sopimustyö ambolaisen silmin" (Contract work in the eyes of an Ovambo). In Kiljunen, Kimmo and Kiljunen, Marja-Liisa, *Namibia —viimeinen siirtomaa* (Namibia—the last colony). Tammi. Helsinki.

Väisälä, Marja, 1980, "Suomalainen lähetystyö" (Finnish missionary work). In Kiljunen, Kimmo and Kiljunen, Marja-Liisa, *Namibia—viimeinen siirtomaa* (Namibia—the last colony). Tammi. Helsinki.

Väyrynen, Raimo, 1977, "Suomi ja Etelä-Afrikan taloussuhteet" (Finland and South African economic relations). *RKL:n tutkimustiedotteita* No 8. (Institute of Peace and Conflict Studies. Research Bulletin No. 8)

Väyrynen, Raimo, 1980, "Suomen taloussuhteet Etelä-Afrikkaan ja Namibiaan" (Finland's economic relations with South Africa and Namibia). In Kiljunen, Kimmo and Kiljunen, Marja-Liisa, *Namibia—viimeinen siirtomaa* (Namibia— the last colony). Tammi. Helsinki.

Weiland, Heribert and Braham, Matthew (eds.), 1994, *The Namibia Peace Process: Implications and Lessons for the Future.* International Peace Academy. Arnold Bergstraesser Institute. Freiburg.

Walläri, Niilo, 1967, *Antoisia vuosia. Muistelmia toiminnasta ammattiyhdistysliikkeessä* (Rewarding years. Memories of the activities in the trade union movement). Helsinki.

Appendix I

Finland's Direct Support to SWAPO and Namibia[1] (1000 FIM)

	SWAPO	Type of support	Other	Total
1974	100	Assistance in kind		100
1975	400	UM/KUA[2]		400
1976	400	UM/KUA		400
1977	505[3]	UM/KUA	60[4]	565
1978	550	UM/KUA		550
1979	300	Health project	69[5]	369
1980	600	Health project		600
1981	900	Lusaka representative[6]		900
1982	1,000	Nyango camp[7]		1,000
1983	1,700	Kwanza Zul	3,800[8]	5,500
1984	2,000	Assistance in kind	4,500[9]	6,500
1985	2,350	Assistance in kind	6,500[10]	8,850
1986	3,600		6,874	10,474
1987	1,000		11,000[11]	12,000
1988			12,297[12]	12,297
1989			14,000[13]	14,000
Total	15,405		59,100	74,505

1. Does not include donations to: UN Trust Fund for Namibia, Namibia Institute (e.g. 1984: 2,000, 1985: 2,000), Namibia Nationhood Programme (1984: 2,500, 1985: 3,000 + Finnish expert since 1976). NGO aid is not systematically listed, either.

2. UM/KUA: the scholarship programme, financed by the Foreign Ministry and administered by Finnchurchaid.

3. 500 to the UM/KUA scholarship programme, 5 to furnish SWAPO's office in Dar es Salaam.

4. Support to the UN Secretary General's programme in Zimbabwe and Namibia.

5. Funding the transport costs for equipment collected by the *Taksvärkki-78* Campaign.

6. Food, support for the kindergarten and agriculture, agreed on with SWAPO.

7. Financial aid to a student dormitory in the Nyango refugee camp.

8. Namibia Education, Health, Nutrition and Research Programme established. Consisted of UM/KUA, Education Material Programme, Education Extension Unit, Research (e.g. History Project), and Nurses' Training Programme.

9. Namibia Programme: 280 Otava/Primary Textbook Project, 1360 Nurses' Training Programme in Jyväskylä.

10. Namibia Programme.

11. Namibia Programme: 1,094 UM/KUA Scholarship Programme, 2400 Otava/Primary Textbooks project, 584 Nurses' Training Programme, 1,035 Teacher Training for Visually Handicapped, 2,120 Technical Training, 1,018 Skills Development, 700 Health development, 303 SWAPO Farm, 500 Namibia Extension Unit, 155 assistance in kind.

12. Namibia Programme: 3,350 assistance in kind, 2,395 Tampere/Civil Engineering course, 2,140 Otava/Primary Textbook project, 1,340 Kongo/Practical Subjects' Teaching Project, 770 UM/KUA, 708 Teacher Training for Visually Handicapped, 538 Nurses' Training Programme, 500 Namibia Extension Unit, 353 Information Office/Helsinki, 103 Audiometrician Training Programme, 100 travel expenses.

13. Namibia Programme: 3,465 health materials, 1,623 UM/KUA, 2,498 Otava, 2,988 Tampere /Civil Engineering Course, 3,425 Kongo/Practical Subjects' Teaching Project.

Appendix 2

Humanitarian Assistance to ANC and Other Organisations in South Africa (1000 FIM)

	ANC	NGOs[14]	WUS	Others	Total
1978	200				200
1979	300			120[15]	420
1980	400				400
1981	600				600
1982	746				746
1983	1,325			200[16]	1,525
1984	1,500				1,500
1985	3,200	400			3,600
1986	2,400	1,500			3,900
1987	3,500	1,900	550	1,500[17]	7,450
1988	5,304	1,700	550	4,100[18]	11,654
1989	5,000	1,200	683	1,500[19]	8,383
1990	10,133		720	5,180[20]	16,033
1991	11,383		850	14,340[21]	26,575
1992	-6,533[22]		190	6,802[23]	459
1993	8[24]		170	3,580[25]	3,758
TOTAL	39,468	6,700	3,713	37,122	87,203

14. Finnish NGOs in cooperation with ANC. Statistics not available for every year. Project cooperation started at the beginning of the 1980s and increased towards the end of the decade.

15. International University Exchange Fund.

16. Panafricanist Congress (PAC).

17. International Committee of the Red Cross (ICRC).

18. IDAF-London 1,200, contribution for anti-apartheid activities in South Africa (several receivers)1,400, ICRC 1,500.

19. IDAF anti-apartheid 1,500.

20. Africa Cultural Centre 80, Africa Educational Trust 200, COSATU 400, Grassroots Education Trust 150, Human Rights Commission (HRC) 80, IDASA 300, Kagiso Trust 100, Lawyers for Human Rights 80, Luthuli Culture and Welfare 400, Promat Colleges 190, SAHWET/SASK 200, Scotaville Publishers 200, IDAF 1500, Repatriation Programme 500, SACC 250, University of Witwatersrand 300, University of Cape Town (UCT) 150, University of Western Cape (UWC) 100.

21. Africa Education Trust 200, African European Institute 210, COSATU 250, GET 200, Get Ahead Foundation 400, HRC 200, ICFTU 180, IDAF 700, IDASA 300, LHR 1050, Luthuli Memorial Trust 400, NCCR/exiles 2000, Promat 2500, SACC 250, Sacred Heart College 100, Scotaville Publishers 200, Southern African NGOs 100, UCT 1,650, UWC 1,350, University of Witwatersrand (Wits) 2,100.

22. New money not allocated, but in fact reservations from previous years untied to a total value of 6,969.

23. COSATU 100, GET 160, Get Ahead Foundation 250, HRC 170, IDASA 250, LHR 550, Promat 1300, SACC 100, Sacred Heart College 90, Scotaville Publishers 150, Southern African NGOs 96, Wits 1,100, UCT 850, UWC 700, AEI 600, EDT 336.

24. Old reservations cancelled to total value of 18.

25. LPI 210, COPIC/SADC/Conference on Democracy and Human Rights 50, GET 100, HRC 100, IDASA 100, Matla Trust 100, Sacred Heart 100, LHR 370, UWC 500, UCT 560, Promat 600, Wits 600.

Aid to Human Rights and Democratisation. Republic of South Africa

	ANC	NGOs	WUS	Others	Total
1994			150	2 910[26]	3 060
1995			70	2 440[27]	2 510
TOTAL			220	5 350	5 570

Appendix 3

Currency conversion table

	1 USD =	1 FIM =
1965	3,223 FIM	0,310 USD
1970	4,180 FIM	0,239 USD
1975	3,679 FIM	0,271 USD
1980	3,730 FIM	0,268 USD
1985	6,206 FIM	0,161 USD
1990	3,831 FIM	0,261 USD
1995	4,365 FIM	0,229 USD

26. Aid to Republic of South Africa: Grassroots Education Trust 100, HRC 100, LHR 400, IDASA 100, Sacred Heart 100, UCT 410, UWC 500, Promat 600, Wits 600.
27. Support for Democracy and Human Rights: UWC 430, Wits 500, Sacred Heart College 70, UCT 350, Promat 550, Grassroots Education Trust 80, HRC 80, LHR 300, IDASA 80.

Appendix 4

Persons interviewed

Officials
The President of the Republic of Finland Martti Ahtisaari
Mr David Johansson
Ambassador Matti Kahiluoto
Mr Kari Karanko
Ambassador Tauno Kääriä
Ambassador Glen Lindholm
Mr Leo Olasvirta
Ambassador Kimmo Pulkkinen
Ambassador Mikko Pyhälä
Ambassador Ilkka Ristimäki
Mr Keijo Ruokoranta
Dr Juhani Suomi
Mr Veikko Tupasela

Activists
Ms Tuija Halmari
Mr Yrjö Höysniemi
Archbishop Mikko Juva
Ms Mirjam Korhonen
MP Risto Kuisma
Ms Marjatta Lahti
Mr Mikko Lohikoski
Mr Börje Mattsson
Dr Marja-Liisa and Dr Lloyd Swantz

In Southern Africa
Minister Nahas Angula, Namibia
Mr Roelof 'Pik' Botha, South Africa (Interview by Tor Sellström)
Minister Hidipo Hamutenya, Namibia
Minister Nickey Iyambo, Namibia
Ambassador Lindiwe Mabuza, South Africa
Mr Abdul Minty, South Africa
Ms Janet Mondlane, Mozambique

Appendix 5. Interviews

Interview with the President of the Republic of Finland, Martti Ahtisaari 29.1.1996

Pekka Peltola: First of all, we would like to discuss your article "From Namibia to Bosnia", where you mentioned six factors which influenced in the early 1970s the Finnish foreign policy in the question of development policies. These were the leftist student organisations, liberal Finnish Swedish thinking, Christian values, as well as the Nordic frame of reference and the role of the UN for the fifth and the sixth the commercial interests. In that connection you didn't discuss their relative weight, however. Could you elaborate this now?

Martti Ahtisaari: I would say that, perhaps the first three or first four are by far the most important ones. That means the interest of the political and particularly the youth movements and solidarity groups in Finland. And traditionally the Swedish People's Party or the Swedish speakers had a lot of interest perhaps for development cooperation more than actually in assisting the liberation movements but there was absolutely no opposition from that side. And then basically the Missionary Society and some active members within the Missionary Society. Particularly those who had had direct involvement either in Tanzania or in Namibia by having been in direct contact with the members of the liberation movements.

A Nordic frame of reference was helpful, it gave the opportunity for those who argued in favour, because there was a lot of opposition here as well to entering into a too close relationship with the liberation movements. Therefore it was strictly limited to humanitarian assistance or technical assistance to the liberation movements and to those recognised by the UN, which was based on the recognition of the OAU. I would say the other arguments were less important. Commercial interest hardly played any role, except in South Africa and to some extent in Namibia, because potentially Namibia was supposed to be a rich country.

Iina Soiri: The UN had passed plenty of resolutions concerning apartheid and colonialism.

MA: Yes, that helped because the question was actually how to cross that bridge from supporting the UN programmes to having direct dealings with the liberation movements.

PP: It was also the time of the Cold War, which set the frame of all foreign policy throughout the period until the late 1980s, and Finland was certainly a part of that frame of reference. What was the impact of this setting on Finnish policies towards the liberation movements in Southern Africa?

MA: If you look at the groups that were involved, they either had a Pan-European frame of reference which you can always find in solidarity movements. I mean those people who had actually been active in different Western European countries, not only Eastern Europe, where it was more or less organised and perhaps which didn't have the same sort of natural basis for the solidarity that one could see in Western Europe. The church's role was important. Let's take United States for instance, where I have met over the years people who had been longer involved with the question of Namibia than I had been and who basically were Lutherans who either through the Lutheran World Federation (LWF) or World Council of

Churches (WCC) had been active and had received African people in the States. I should give you one book by a friend of mine who is one of the real activists who can tell you more stories about those times than many others. Those were people who were active also on questions of race relations much earlier than they actually became a popular issue in USA. I think that softened basically the attempt of Finland, to counter-argue in our internal debate the bias, that the idea of supporting the liberation movements was purely and initially coming from the parties that were from the left of the political spectrum.

PP: In our interviews we have noticed quite a strong current of a kind of value free realism especially among the civil servants. Did it bring any problems in regard to this, in your opinion?

MA: No, only that it was perhaps not seen as the most important issue on the agenda of Finnish foreign policy, clearly. But then you have to remember that in the 1960s and 1970s a lot of people joined the foreign service as well, who actually had been active prior to joining the foreign service. Let's take our present Ambassador in Beijing, Ilkka Ristimäki as an example. I belong to the same category myself, and there were others, so that basically helped, plus the interest of the political parties because we really had a positive support for that. So basically no money was to be given, because of this whole discussion that always comes, whether money would be directed towards purchase of arms, for instance. I think it is a simplistic discussion in a sense that if you get food you don't need to use your money to buy the food, and you can use it on something else. That's how it is.

PP: So, Mr President, you were the Ambassador to Tanzania from 1973 to 1976. I have a picture here about how the first cheque of money was given to FRELIMO, to Samora Machel.

MA: This, I'm sure, is Marcelino do Santos.

IS: And this is Kimmo Pulkkinen, who told us about the discussion, that was held between the Foreign Ministry and the Embassy because you were handing over a cheque.

PP: It was in 1973 when a decisive turn took place in the Ministry of Foreign Affairs when the support to the liberation movements became possible.

MA: That was a debate, as I have tried to describe to you, where we were under pressure because there was a lot of activity going on in Dar es Salaam. For instance the student union, central student union was active with the printing press. It was one of these years.

IS: 1969–70.

MA: Yes, it was prior to my going there, so actually it was the NGOs who actually had the first contacts with the liberation movements and they were pressing government as well. I think had there not been that political pressure I don't think that the government would have moved.

PP: Did you somehow get some additional information from Dar es Salaam which helped to mould the government's position?

MA: I don't think so, I think it was like with many other things that I don't want it to sound more positive than it was, in a sense because we were the latest in coming to the field. All the Nordic Countries were involved and those who were anxious in developing relations used that as an argument. In that sense the policies of the Nordic governments played an important role because there was hardly any issue, whether you talk about money for development purposes or humanitarian assistance for liberation movements, where you couldn't use the Nordic Countries. Sweden particularly acted as an example that was already going on. And therefore it was a combination of these things. I joined the foreign office 1965 and we had a period there of nearly 10 years before we could get something concrete going.

PP: Finland has always been materially a very low profile compared with Sweden, Norway and even Denmark. What kind of influence did it have on our role when we were together with our Nordic friends?

MA: The Nordism as such served a purpose, for us because we were the smallest shareholder in the Nordic activities but we were obviously one of the Nordic countries. And that was used as a carrot in the internal debate in trying to raise the development cooperation funds which then included these humanitarian funds as well. It has had an important effect because if you wanted to be one part of the Nordic group you couldn't deviate from their policies unduly, so that for us who wanted to get this thing going it served the most useful purpose. But I would not underestimate the role of the NGOs, both the political ones and those in the labour movement as well. It was a very active time. Little money was used, but there was much more activity. A sad reflection is that perhaps when there is more money there is less activity.

IS: The foreign policy doctrine in Finland was at the time realism.

MA: It has always been that, and it will never change. You will see the same trend throughout the Finnish foreign policy, so I don't think one could have argued that that was a deviation that line when that move to support liberation movements was made. And there is no question that it was criticised at the time. There were those who didn't want even to hear about it. But it happened and in a long term we became rather active then in the UN context, and very many people were active.

IS: Would you then say it was kind of a new branch in Finnish foreign policy ?

MA: The whole development aid and the relations with the third world was a new thing and liberation movement policy was the most politicised part of those contacts.

PP: What you think about the argument that the activism in development questions was balancing somehow our close relationship to the Soviet Union?

MA: No, I don't think it has anything to do with that, because those who were opposed to it could very well argue that we went along with the trend that was rather common in the Soviet Union and Eastern and Central Europe, with all the solidarity movements which were government run at that time. So, as a matter of fact, those who wanted to oppose said that. It was just a contrary argument that you heard very often. But it was balanced by the fact that all the Nordic governments were doing it, the Dutch were doing it, even there were other NGOs in Europe who were involved in supporting the liberation movements. The LWF and the Council of Churches were becoming extremely active on these issues and they covered a vast group of people and it was very difficult to say that they had any sinister motives.

PP: We had a very pleasant and long discussion with Archbishop Juva just recently.

MA: He is fascinating and he did a remarkable job in changing the attitudes of the church.

PP: He was quite alone for some time.

MA: Yes, exactly, I realised it, that's why I regard him very highly for those years, he is a good friend of mine still for which I'm very happy. But you have to realise that we lived during the Cold War years in a rather simplistic political climate. And the fact that, this sort of humanitarian activity which was commonly shared by the churches, for instance, was regarded as something coming from the left of the political spectrum, was an attitude less nuanced than it should have been at the time.

PP: How important was SWAPO in your activities during your time in Dar es Salaam in and around 1976?

MA: When I was the student union secretary general here for development activities, YKA, we used the World University Service as a channel. From there we got ideas where the money could mostly go. It was the embryonic phase; we received the first Namibians here, Nickey Iyambo was among those and so the first contacts were there. But again I would say that the church had much broader bases of contact with members of SWAPO because quite a number of people in exile were SWAPO members, though not all. So when I moved to Dar es Salaam as an Ambassador where they were placed and had representative there we met regularly in the context of the liberation movement. And they attended the social functions as well.

PP: When you were asked to follow Sean MacBride in 1976 it was actually the time of the so-called the Shipanga affair inside SWAPO. Did you know about it and what was attitude of the Finnish government to it?

MA: No, actually those who faced it, more concretely were people like Kari Karanko who was on the spot in Lusaka. Because if you are active like he is, well whether you have been less active, somehow you couldn't actually avoid that sort of issue. So we were aware of what was going on, but I don't think it had any major impact on our policy. It was simply an indication that there were difficulties in perhaps catering for different views in the organisation. The liberation struggle, as I have very often said, it is not the most democratic phase in the life of an organisation, because you are bound to have very authoritarian ways of running the organisation. Whatever you say, I mean it is hard a fact of life that democracy is not very high on the list. And that's why it's even more remarkable that Namibia has become a sort of example of democratic society in the whole continent. I asked the Foreign Minister and we both agreed that if somebody would have asked us 10 years ago if this sort of development would be possible, I don't think anyone of us would have believed it. We would have expected much greater difficulties in building up a democratic society.

IS: But was there any pressure that the Nordic Countries should play any role in defending human rights?

MA: No, I don't think so. I think that the difficulty comes that when you are too close to the recognised power, it's very very difficult to actually show and take a sort of distance and then very easily you say that this is an internal matter. I have no recollection I think it would be better to talk to Kari Karanko, did you already?

PP: Yes, we have discussed it.

MA: Whether he remembers anything, whether there were any instructions given to him?

IS: Yes, there were, he was told not to interfere.

MA: Yes. Because I would think that that would be the case. I would again say that perhaps some individual members of the Missionary Society showed much more courage in dealing with SWAPO than many of us who had an official position. Mikko Ihamäki is a good example of that. This thing has changed over the years. But at that particular moment when we still were basically sort of beginners in this, I don't think that we questioned them the way we perhaps should have at that particular moment. It was very difficult though to say who was right or whether the thing was justified or not. And I wonder about the other Nordic countries, how did they do? Somebody you should interview perhaps is Anders Bjurner. He is now the under secretary for political affairs in Stockholm. He was the number two in Lusaka at the same time. And another person would be Ann-Mari Demmer, who is in UNHCR in Geneva. She was the UNHCR representative in Lusaka. She was the head, and the number two was a Dane, who I think is now the representative for UNHCR. But these people could actually give you more inside information, because UNHCR was perhaps more involved in the internal things than anybody else was, because they had to be, because of their mandate to deal with them.

PP: Then you mention in your article the difficult problem was the fact that the international community only accepted one or maximum two liberation movements to represent the people of the country. For instance like SWAPO got the sole representation of the Namibian people. And in South Africa two were selected, the ANC and PAC.

MA: No I don't think it was the most democratic way of going about it but I think the justification for that was to concentrate the efforts vis-à-vis the occupying power. That was the fact which we had to deal with. But it obviously didn't make life any easier and the solution of the problem either. Because in the end, I think, the mere armed struggle would never have solved the problem; and if you go for a democratic solution, then you have to give everybody the chance to participate and agree conditions so that they would be starting on a fairly equal basis.

PP: Of course it didn't help the cooperation of ANC and PAC either when they were both accepted but instead they still competed all the time to quite an extent or do you think they cooperated well, if at all?

MA: No, I don't think they did. But there was the time in UN when the others could also come and petition. Take from the opposition politicians, if you take Kauara for instance, he appealed, appeared in front of the committees, the Herero chiefs who were not SWAPO members appeared and appealed on behalf of Namibia. So earlier on it was possible for them to do that. But then basically they were eliminated from that political opportunity and that of course diminished plurality and complicated matters. So only those remained who were prepared basically to accept if not that SWAPO was the sole and authentic, but at least that they were a central political body, that somebody had to play a central role. It was agreed by only those who were involved in the activities of the Council for Namibia. That's why it didn't became a normally elected UN entity. It was those who shared that basic assumption politically.

PP: Then there is a difficult area we want to step into, that is, I think, when the most dramatic days of your assignment to Namibia began on the first of April 1989, when SWAPO troops emerged inside Namibia despite agreements which were supposed to prevent it. And there are lot of questions which haven't been discussed because of the sensitivity of the issue, but we ask some questions. First of all, do you think it was possible that soldiers, PLAN soldiers did not know that SWAPO did not have a right according to the agreements to have bases inside Namibia?

MA: How far the information would have gone, I think is anybody's guess, because I can't expect that every PLAN soldier ...

PP: Yes, well, that's another thing but I mean those who sent them.

MA: But I still believe the leadership must have known what was discussed because those matters were discussed at length.

PP: Am I right when I say that after 1978 a couple of years the main issue, actually the main discussion was exactly this.

MA: Yes, because we tried, because I believed firmly that it was a sensible idea. Because everyone knew, everyone recognised, even South Africa military agreed, that you had SWAPO fighters inside but no bases. That's not what stage the guerrilla warfare had actually reached. So I thought it would have been easier to put them under lock and key, literally speaking. Perhaps some of the internal parties also felt that would give SWAPO an added advantage in the elections that SWAPO could claim that they actually had the bases there. So, the only explanation that I can think of was that it was an attempt to get troops inside in order to justify the claim that there was a bigger number of people inside. And actually, at least some sort of claim for the bases inside.

PP: According to the agreements, Cubans and Angolans were supposed to prevent any incursion below the 16th parallel.

MA: Yes.

PP: Why didn't they do it? Was it monitored at all?

MA: It might not have been. I think both Cubans and Angolans were furious about it. I think in Chester Crocker's book there is a good explanation, as well about how things went on. I know that from the little I heard from the reactions of the Angolans and Cubans that they assumed that SWAPO should have known. And I don't think that we could have settled the issue with that fastness if there was not that sort of thinking behind it. But I must confess that I have not discussed this issue at all because I thought that it would not be necessary. You will always argue that it would be nice to know the details, but I'm happier that despite this disaster at the beginning we could carry out the exercise.

PP: Did you believe before the incursion happened that South Africa would go ahead with the peace plan if something like this would happen?

MA: I was very worried actually at that particular moment because they had all the reasons to stop it. If they wanted to have an excuse, they had it. But when they didn't use it then I was in a much stronger position when I realised that they didn't use that opportunity that SWAPO gave them. Because they could have taken the high road actually then and say look this is it, out we go, end of the process, UN out. But they didn't do it. And that then made me draw the conclusion that they are here to stay to the bitter end and see this whole process through. So one could say that this tragic death of these people served that purpose that it reinforced the process finally. That was my conclusion and that of my senior colleagues as well. And that reinforced our hand in dealings with the South Africans.

Anyway I couldn't do anything else because of the agreement. We knew that the South Africans were going to leave the bases and what we tried to do was to limit that they should not take their full forces and bring reinforcements, because they could have done it. And it would have ended in a worse massacre.

PP: Did you know many days before that SWAPO was coming?

MA: No, I arrived on the 31st, so I got information immediately on my arrival.

IS: And what was done to prevent it? Was there nothing done to prevent it?

MA: No, I sent immediately a group of people, actually three of my senior aides, I sent Danio Bande, the Kenyan, Brigadier Cedric Tornberg and then a Nigerian staff member to interview the prisoners and I think it was fairly obvious that they had crossed the border.

PP: I was lucky to get hold of Olle Eriksson who happened to be in Oniipa. He was hiding a wounded SWAPO PLAN under his bed and the government troops were around looking for those wounded people. Olle told me right away that they came from Angola. That was extremely important information to me because I was confronted by the press here as chairman of the Namibia Society.

MA: The sad thing is that when you are in a position like I was to implement an agreement, you had to be as tough with your friends as your foes because at that time you could hardly say that the South Africans were my friends. But you had to deal with it and basically you had to give them credit that they behaved correctly, they were on the first of April all in their bases as the agreement demanded.

PP: So then you appreciate quite a lot the contribution the Frontline States gave in the liberation process. Do you think that the cooperation still has an influence on what happened there?

MA: I don't think so. Because first of all what was important is that people who stayed in Angola and Zambia particularly, they could see what was happening in these countries. I think that had a big impact on the future attitudes of the political elite of SWAPO. Then the Frontline States served a useful purpose for SWAPO mainly, but also for the whole process I would say. Because one could say that sometimes they were uncritically supporting SWAPO's views but that was important. It was a sign of solidarity and I think one has to understand it in that perspective. And I think it was useful that they also looked critically on what we were doing. So we had to justify to ourselves in debates with them as well that what we were doing was something that we believed ourselves, because there were a lot of visitors, as you know. All sorts of brilliant ideas were put to us. If nothing else, our patience grew when you had to go through basically the same things 20 times over. But it was important because it gave us an opportunity to explain and intelligent people then see whether you are right or not. They didn't agree on all issues, they said no, you are wrong, but afterwards they established their embassies. It may be like the Finnish Ambassador in Stockholm has a special status, in that sense I would say that their influence is there but I would not over emphasise that because I think, it is very important for a country to take control of its own affairs and then it needs to distance itself a little bit from those who have actually been supporting it. I don't know what your experience is but you know the situation better than I do.

And if you go further, let's say how Nujoma reacted to the Nigerian developments when I was on a state visit, in a very statesmanlike manner, taking distance from it. It's sad that this is happening in Africa. I don't think he as a head of a liberation movement would have said those things. But there is a good sign that you are defending the line you have actually accepted as a basis for your own society.

PP: This might be a detail, but anyway, when we are discussing Southern Africa there are a few countries where we have lively cooperation. But with Zimbabwe or Southern Rhodesia we didn't have much to do before 1980 and maybe since then a little bit more but it's understandable. But you personally had quite a lot to do with Angolans when you were in Tanzania. And still we have almost nothing going on with Angola.

MA: For the simple reason that if we can have any impact we can't spread our resources too thinly. I think now particularly when the resources have been cut it's more sensible that you work where you are. And in Angola it has been very difficult because you are not secure in moving around, it's not a safe place to do practically anything sensible. So I visited there a lot, and I have always had very candid discussions with Angolans. As Crocker describes it in his book about my visits to Angola. But I'm thankful that because of my contacts we have a good relationship in the same way I have with Samora's successor, Chissano on the other side.

PP: Then you mention positively that president Nujoma distances himself from Nigeria. But still one can see in many Southern African countries a little bit of a concentration of power and also personalisation of power. Does it worry you?

MA: It always worries me, because my message here is that for God's sake, like in our own society as well let's not look for authoritarian leaders here, but let's start thinking with our own brains for a change. And the whole education should cater for that. That's why my message to those who were active in human rights issues and civic liberties before independence is that they have to continue now as well. Because you have to build up that tolerance of the political leadership to accept that you are being criticised.

IS: So do you see that there should be support for the civil society in those countries? Should that be our role now ?

MA: Well at least sometimes I wonder how can you help as an outsider? It's a very delicate issue, could you use your money for instance to build up a press? What would your role be there? It was understandable that you donated the printing press to FRELIMO, but how can you help in a democratic fashion and ensure that you all of a sudden are not associated with somebody whose motives are questionable. You have to have a continued dialogue with political leadership, that's why the contacts are absolutely vital.

I think it is an issue, in the same line of questioning, is whether SWAPO when they now have the majority will change the constitution to have a life president. I think these are issues they have to debate. And I think they are fully aware of the consequences of that sort of move. It's not looked upon kindly by the outside world. It's true that even we have had a nearly life presidency here in our history but then we changed the laws. So one should be a little bit careful in criticising but they agreed that it's two terms only. One should not build a sort of feeling that one is irreplaceable. And if a president in any country starts thinking that he or she is irreplaceable then he or she should be changed.

IS: But if the people in that country think that way? I, for example, interviewed a lot of women two years ago who said that if there was no Nujoma as a president we don't want a president at all.

MA: I would not respect their views, with all due respect. Sometimes I think you have to let people understand that democracy means also that you are not building up such a power base that offers you an opportunity to misuse that power.

PP: One last question, which is only interesting but not maybe vital. You learned a lot certainly during your years in Africa, and in Namibia and with Africans. But with that learning could you see any similarities when you went to Bosnia, in the Yugoslavian situation?

MA: My admiration for Namibians grew tremendously because, despite the fact that with a little bit of assistance from South Africa there was an attempt to place the Namibians against each other, it was still possible for them to find each other, others as Namibians, so fast after the elections in the constitutional process, in 72 days. I organised one or two dinners where they would sit and drink together and talk, and after that they didn't need the *mzungu* there anymore. They realised they were schoolmates and that it was much more important for them to agree on the basis of a democratic society that it would serve the purpose for each and every one whether they were in opposition. I think it will take ages, if ever, to reach that in the Balkans. So why is it so, I ask myself. I very often speak about the sort of Christian gentlemen and gentle ladies of Namibia or Africa. And that preparedness to forgive rather horrifying things that went on, even if they were not necessarily going on between one Namibian and another but were inspired by South Africans, but they can even talk to South Africans.

When I went as State Secretary to northern Namibia I asked my black colleague how did you get along with Carl von Hindsberg? Extremely well, he said. I just came with my wife from a visit to them in South Africa. That to me is a great thing. It gives me a belief that despite the old differences you can find the right people like Carl and you can achieve a damn lot. And they together very smoothly ran Walvis Bay's transfer to Namibia.

PP: It went very well indeed.

MA: And it shows that it is possible. There is much more cruelty we Europeans seem to be capable of.

I was very pleased to see teenagers here in Finland from different ethnic groupings—Serbs, Croats, Muslims—talking to each other and see that there is a ray of hope. But how do you get rid of those who actually are the culprits of this and how to prevent that they will ever come to positions of power?

PP: So, thank you very much Mr President.

Interview with Mikko Juva, former archbishop of Finland, 24.11.1995

Pekka Peltola: Archbishop Mikko Juva, would you please describe in which capacities you have been in touch with the liberation of Southern Africa?

Mikko Juva: My first contacts with the liberation movement were already in 1961. That was the time when Africa was awake, Sharpeville and Congo aroused some turmoil in the board of directors of the Finnish Mission Society (FMS). I was at that time the chairman of its board and I told my board that now in this situation we cannot rely only upon the reports of our missionaries whose reports might be biased. Is it not time that the board itself sends a few representatives to visit South West Africa and analyse the situation there. So it was decided, and I, the president, and Reverend Vallisaari, the secretary, went to South West Africa and spent seven weeks there. Our host was at that time moderator Alpo Hukka and second clergyman in the leadership of the newly established Ambo-Kavango church, Leonard Auala, who then later became its first bishop.

And there I was told that the new political movement SWAPO had caused unrest among the missionaries. For instance a group of these people went to meet one of our missionaries armed and threatened him but no actual violence occurred. And they had certain demands which they after that presented to Reverend Hukka in written form. The Finnish mission was accused of many things. Some accusations were understandable, some just due to, let's say, inadequate education of the Africans.

Now when I came to Africa the general feeling among the missionaries was that this was just a turmoil caused by some outside propaganda and as you can read from these papers they are not able to distinguish between essentials and non-essentials. But I told them that you might be right, that they are not yet ready to take their destiny into their own hands, but the future lies inevitably among those Africans who want their countries to be liberated. So please take seriously this movement and do not judge them according to the present standard and status of their work. And I think this presentation of the board director for the mission side had some impact and we worked out certain guidelines. One was that as a foreign organisation FMS does not take active part in the politics of the country. Secondly, that we should follow very keenly what happens among the people of the country. And as soon as they have a leadership, which can be taken seriously so we must have negotiations and contact with them.

I did not question the judgement of Alpo Hukka because he knew much better the people and the situation, but I very definitely advised him not to let the rough language of these letters be the only determining factor. And so I tried to have contact with SWAPO people but they apparently were afraid. I think that they judged that the FMS was not to be trusted at this moment and I do think that they were right because in Ovamboland I met some local SWAPO people, not the leadership but some local people and naturally not being very politically sophisticated I asked them questions, that I know that you people leave the schools in Ovamboland and join the dissidents outside Namibia and how can you do that. Now they of course reminded us that this is a very serious question and I later understood that these secret contact lines are not revealed to someone you don't know. And so my contacts during that journey were very superficial.

PP: I have been wondering, because it was very early you took that stand to understand the liberation movement. You were several years in front of everybody else.

MJ: That is true and the reason was that at that time I was elected to the executive committee of World Student Christian Federation (WSCF). And there we met Asian and African students among American and European students and their leaders. And we heard about liberation movements in Asia, which already had some success—Indonesia was I think independent at that time—and they had taken part in guerrilla war against colonial powers. So I had already made up my mind that first of all, these nations have the same right for liberation as we Finns have had. And secondly, that in this fight for liberation they will take as their allies anyone who can help them.

And even if my attitude towards Communism in Finland was that of an opponent—coming from my family background and my experience in the recent war—I had some understanding that even if I did not change my opinion that Communism would not be helpful for Finland, it might really help these new emerging nations. And in this respect I followed the general trend in WSCF. In certain countries, at a certain stage in this pre-capitalist society, socialism may be the fastest way for national development and independence. With this attitude I went to South West Africa. And of course I was not bound by the bias of some of the missionaries, who just took the Bible and said there is the beast of the apocalypse and what SWAPO say isn't it just described in the last book of the Bible as being part of the work of devil?

PP: That time when you were there, there were only very few SWAPO people abroad, mainly only president Nujoma and very few others and inside Ovamboland there was Toivo ya Toivo who was the main organiser. Did you find a single person among the Finnish missionaries who shared your attitude?

MJ: I think Mr Hartikainen. Mikko Ihamäki was at that time in South Africa doing his linguistic studies.

Iina Soiri: How common was the support for SWAPO at that time in Ovamboland? Would you say that you met several people who were SWAPO people ?

MJ: I really can't answer that question. It was serious enough that the South African administrator came to Ovamboland and called all the Chiefs and Kings to a meeting. I've mentioned that episode in my book. He told that there are certain snakes that have come to this country. And it was very dramatic sitting there in the shade together with the white people and seeing black people sitting in the sun, mostly silent. It almost could be seen that the black establishment, that is the kings and the chiefs and their servants were loyal to the South African administrator.

But among the youth and especially among the small group of them who could study in schools—the lower high school and teachers' college and theological college, which were the existing schools there—people were very active and intellectually awake. Their Finnish teachers had discussions with them about history and about society. I think I have mentioned it in my book that probably the first lecture on Communism, which was ever held by a white person in Ovamboland was given by me to the students in the theological seminary. That's of course elementary wisdom that if you know you are going to meet another ideological opponent so describe what it is, so that this or that can later challenge Communism. And I tried to give a fair picture of Communism, its goals and its aims and then of course the usual criticism from Christian theology. But the young people especially those who were studying, did at least know that something was going on.

IS: But how openly did the students of theology and people who work for the congregations express their support for the liberation? When I read the book about Leonard Auala "Mustan Namibian Paimen" he seemed to have been very reluctant in the beginning.

MJ: He was very reluctant. I met Auala in Finland, he was the first member of Ambo-Kavango church, who was allowed to travel to Finland. I later on heard that the local administrator had taken him for a ride saying that now you go out and now you are representing South West Africa and be careful, that you do not say anything detrimental. And that was I think 1959, so two years before I went to Ovambo.

I had a discussion with him and I told him here in Finland in safety and openly, that Finland has been for centuries under foreign rule, first Swedes and then the Russians, but when the time was ripe and we had had higher education and the historical situation arrived when we could declare our independence, we did it. And I'm quite sure that sometime in the future your country will achieve the same. And now everybody who is working to educate people of South West Africa—Namibia was not mentioned because there was no Namibia, I spoke about Ovambos—they are all working, of course, mainly for the kingdom of God but also the future free South West Africa. So it was in such general ideologist terms I spoke to him, but Auala's reaction was horrified. And I understood it a few years later, when I learned what instructions Auala had received. And he must have thought that now this man, this good Finnish man, chairman of the board is saying something he doesn't understand and doesn't know what demands this puts on me. I can't speak, I can't answer, I must be silent. So I only noticed a very hard stress and we didn't discuss it that time any more.

That was my first contact with Namibian liberation and definitely I didn't foresee any rebellion. I would be horrified if I would be interpreted in that way. But it was just that I as a student of history knew something about how nations develop and I thought it wise to tell Auala that he should not be afraid to think of the future liberation. Nobody suggested that the time is now but that it was coming.

PP: And it's very clear that Auala was a courageous man, because he was really the one who started the open confrontation with the government officially.

MJ: That is true, but you see it was 9 years later. And during those years we elected Auala to the Executive Committee of Lutheran World Federation (LWF), the second representative from Africa. At that time there were two from Africa in our Executive Committee. Every year he travelled from Namibia to some place in Europe, in Asia and in Africa and he learned all the time. He didn't speak very much but he was very alert. And he came to a situation where an African was equal to all Europeans and learned how we discuss things, he learned that white people are not like Gods, not baases as the reality was in South West Africa and South Africa. And without that experience I don't think he would have had that courage to stand up. Auala did not invent the idea of an open letter, I think it probably came from the radical students but anyhow he was willing to accept that responsibility and that was a tremendous shock to Vorster.

PP: But then you had these ideas already in 1959 that the future of South Africa sometime is to be free.

MJ: Yes, but of course that was not very much, but it grew from my general understanding of history. The second starting point was, of course, my discussions in the Student's Christian movement.

PP: But then of course you did get into a conflict inside the Missionary Society for a few coming years. But you won the confrontation.

MJ: Yes, that was actually when I was not any more in the WSCF but in the LWF. I was the Chairman of the Commission on Theology. As a commission chairman I took part in the Executive Committee meetings, so I met Auala and all Executive Committee members every year. And there the question of racism came up, partly from the American scene, but mainly from the last remaining colonies in Africa. And our black member churches in South Africa and Namibia/SWA raised the question and asked from us that the LWF must say something to our white member churches. So I was in the midst of that discussion when I found that the FMS board was in this context thinking very backwardly. So I thought that now it's time that at least we in Finland take a very clear stand. But what they do in Ovamboland, they must decide themselves. We can't from Finland give them concrete orders, but we can support with a clear stand. And I then suggested that we condemn directly and clearly apartheid—the very words were that racial segregation is sin and that it must be condemned.

But some people in the board said that segregation is not sin, it might be in a certain historical situation the best way to prevent friction and fighting. But then they said that we rather like separate but equal. But I said that's not enough in this situation because that's exactly what the apartheid defendants say. But I lost and then I said I resign, I can't be Chairman of the Board which accepts separate and equal.

Then the director, Olavi Vuorela, who supported my stand immediately contacted Martti Simojoki who had just become Archbishop. Simojoki was a member of the board not present in the discussion. And so Simojoki together with Vuorela worked out a formula, which helped everybody save his face but which in practice condemned segregation in the form apartheid applied it. So I won and after that I said I can withdraw my resignation and continue.

PP: You had conflict even inside the Missionary Society. But how about the reaction of the Finnish government? Kekkonen was already then president and it was only about 10 years later when the Finnish government took a positive stand in favour of liberation movements.

MJ: You see, my stand strictly speaking was not a stand to assist liberation movements. It was just a stand to assist the African church. So it was church politics but not international power politics what I said. So I don't think I contacted the Foreign Ministry and they did not contact me. I think they thought that it is something which is up to the churches, they can take a stand, they have a different basis for their decisions and we do not mix with theological positions as long as they do not interfere with us. And this condemnation of apartheid was nothing new, many other churches had done that, so that didn't cause any friction.

IS: It was done by Finland actually in the UN also.

MJ: Yes, I think so, that it was more or less the general opinion, general enlightened opinion in Western Countries provided this stand did not affect economic or political interests.

PP: In the early 1960s one could say that you together with Olavi Vuorela were more or less friendly with SWAPO, and so you helped Nujoma personally also. How did that happen?

MJ: Yes, Nujoma came to Finland. I don't know which year it was, but Vuorela proposed the matter saying let's take him as our guest. Vuorela was so cautious, thinking that we cannot pay his trip from the Mission money collected by good people for mission work. So we collected a few thousand marks—I paid some and Vuorela paid some. I don't know who else was there but we just paid his tickets to Finland and back. And we had discussions with him. When Alpo Hukka in Ovamboland heard about that he wrote an exceptionally sharp letter—he was a courageous man too by criticising his superiors—claiming that "you have made a wrong decision". And his main argument was that we in the mission here are making a very clear stand that we do not approve and support SWAPO, who meanwhile had started guerrilla warfare.

And that was the difference between my stand then and later on. I really thought then that if the mission in Ovamboland is cautious, it's their situation and they have the right to be cautious. But we in Finland, we are in no danger and if we take Nujoma that maybe helps his political situation a little bit. Because I don't remember exactly what I thought, but I can now argue that in the long run independence was inevitable and if we during the struggle refused to have anything to do with them we were wrong. I do remember that I said very clearly that armed struggle is something we as a mission organisation can have nothing to do with but otherwise, the educational work and so on we fully accept. But I think we helped Nujoma to have contact with our Foreign Ministry and in that way we gave him this kind of personal assistance. But we did not speak for him but we helped him to speak for himself.

PP: Then you also mentioned that it was important when Emil Appolus from SWAPO came to Finland. By the way he came together with Anders Shipanga and I met them, when I was working in radio. I also remember and can confirm what you say that it was kind of a breakthrough. He condemned the Finnish church comparing it with the Anglican church inside Ovamboland for being passive and giving only comfort to the apartheid regime, which Anglicans did not do anymore. So I remember the church defending itself that it was not so but maybe it was only you and some others who did so. Most of the missionaries might still have had other attitudes. But the change took place sometime around 1965–66, do you think so?

MJ: At that time I was busy in politics, I was a Chairman of a political party. But I was somewhat hurt about his accusation because maybe he was right but my understanding of our missionaries was somewhat different. Ihamäki was there already and Hartikainen was there and I had some correspondence with them, so I thought Appolus was unfair. For that reason I sent a letter to the editors of Sosialidemokraatti, I can't recall the details of that discussion. But even if I opposed Appolus, so it was in the spirit that our missionaries must be on the side of those who work against apartheid. And in that sense I sided with Appolus. And that caused some discussion in Finnish papers. Perhaps my condemnation of Appolus' unfairness was not so serious as my approval of the right of SWAPO people to speak for themselves.

PP: I remember very well the discussion that it was important, as you stated also. Maybe it was easier to accept those who had been passive, maybe it was easier to accept now when they were criticised. You were defending them but still saying that people are supporting and must support the struggle of the Ovambos.

MJ: These were just the years when the attitude of the leadership of our missionaries was changing from being passive to giving active support. I think that was the time of change inside the missionary corps but also the time of change in the Ambo-Kavango church and we could not follow that change so well here in Finland. But later on I think it became clear it was just these years when Hukka had left— Hukka was a man of God, an excellent man but he didn't understand that times were changing—and Ihamäki was a man of the future.

IS: So the change came rather when new people took over?

MJ: Yes, that's right. But Hartikainen was the first missionary who became a member of SWAPO. And he came back to Finland and went back to Ovamboland again.

PP: Yes, you mention it here. He says that he is in contact with Toivo ya Toivo.

MJ: Oh yes, and he was unhappy about the controversy between me and Appolus and tried to take an immediate stand that Appolus went too far.

PP: Every now and then this conflict appears or there is at least some argument on the role of the church and SWAPO. I remember even in the 1980s when Toivo ya Toivo was back from jail, he came over to Finland and gave an interview to the press and said something critical about the role of the Finnish church which even was at that time quite unfair. Then maybe also the papers, evening papers, maybe overdid it as well. Then we had discussions on that with the SWAPO people who were here in Finland.

MJ: You probably know that the legal defence of Toivo ya Toivo was paid by LWF. And so that was at that time the second organisation, where I was a part, which took a much clearer stand for SWAPO than did FMS.

PP: I know Toivo ya Toivo rather well and he has actually no hard feelings against the church at all. I know it for sure. He was actually trained not only by Finnish missionaries but at Odibo, by missionaries as well.

IS: Perhaps this criticism is part of the ideological rhetoric of a liberation movement.

PP: Yes, it could have been that he had been reading the speech and there is a sentence which the Finnish papers picked up and made a big thing although it isn't. Now we have gone through your role which has been very important in the early 60s. I was really surprised how avantgarde you were at that time. Then in the 1970s it was more widespread among people, not only in Finland because of your influence, but also internationally. And you spent so many years with the LWF. There you had different struggles.

MJ: Yes. That was the question of giving economic support to liberation movements. I was asked by Kotimaa, what I was saying when the World Council of Churches (WCC) had started a special fund to combat racism which intended to give economic support to all those movements who fought racism. And I said, to put it very simply, racism is sin and sin must be opposed, those who oppose the sin must be supported. That was interpreted that I would advocate armed struggle against racism, which I actually didn't. So I got some criticism particularly in German press.

But I was in line with the work of the World Service of LWF, which very definitely took as a guideline that the only reason to give help is that people need help and political, religious and social differences have nothing to do with the fact where we go. And so for instance in Mozambique where there were liberated areas we sent help because the only possibility to help them was through their organisation. We were very keen that we would not give them money to buy weapons, but of course we knew that if you support a certain movement, who is fighting they can use their money for weapons if they don't have to use it for books. Bruno Muetzelfeldt who was leader of all these operations was not naive.

PP: We must return to international affairs and your activities in the LWF and its influence. You told in your book that you also visited the Natal area and saw something.

MJ: Yes, that was 1971 or 1972 after the LWF assembly in Evian, where we made certain decisions concerning communion fellowship in South Africa and South West Africa. The white churches did not invite the members of black Lutheran churches to holy communion and the clergy in both countries was in principle willing but they could not get their laity to this kind of closer fellowship with the blacks. And so we sent a delegation headed by myself and our General Secretary André Appel and in Southern Africa we divided ourselves in two different groups. I together with Calle Hellberg went to Natal and Johannesburg and André Appel went to Cape Town and Namibia. And we discussed with the people and visited the churches and preached both in black and white churches and saw the enormous difference in equipment and in living standard and so on. But could not really change anything. The pastors said that they were willing and in the conferences where the Federation of Lutheran churches met— and the conferences were dominated by of course the clergy—they lived in the same place, and in the church they had mutual communion but this custom did not spread anymore.

So we just went back and reported to LWF that there was not very much to be done. But we suggested stronger steps towards the white churches. What meant more to the LWF was that the German Church refused to send pastors to these churches in Africa, who did not comply to the anti-apartheid stand of LWF. So they had problems in recruiting clergymen. And in some places the pastor and the congregation had clashes, but by and large no major changes happened. Then in the next assembly after Evian LWF went one step further and that was in Dar es Salaam.

IS: Holding the conference in Dar es Salaam had caused some discussion inside LWF, whether it should be held there.

MJ: Oh yes, that was prior to the assembly. But this was not due to the racism controversy but due to East-West controversy, because Tanzania took help from China and LWF had churches in Hong Kong and Taiwan and these churches were not allowed to get visas to Tanzania. So some of the members of the preparation committee said that we just can't have a conference in a country, which does not allow all member churches to participate. Us having behind us the controversy, which moved, just on these grounds, the assembly from Porto Allegre, Brazil, to Evian, I strongly advocated not to move the conference this time because that would practically mean that Third World countries would have no possibility to get Assemblies and that would badly influence the image of LWF in all developing countries. So we had our meeting in Dar es Salaam.

PP: According to your book, you had differences of opinion inside LWF between the hard-line anti-imperialist line and softer pro-liberation line.

MJ: That's right. The same movement towards the left which was very strong in all universities was felt also in churches and particularly among younger clergy and younger academic teachers. And I tried to keep balance in a sense that the Federation could not go further than the member churches go. But I don't think that controversy influenced our attitude towards liberation movements because we continued our established policy to send help where the help was needed, not to take part in any military assistance and to press the apartheid regimes wherever they were in power. So in all these points the Federation as a whole had the same line.

IS: But coming back to Finland, how strong do you see the pressure or the opinion of the church in influencing Finnish policy towards liberation movements?

MJ: Now the major part of the 1970s I was in university, so I did not take part in policy making of the Church, except that I was a member of the Church Assembly and also a member of the Foreign Council of the Church of Finland. But the Council was led by Martti Simojoki and the Finnchurchaid was led in practice by Ahti Auranen. And Ahti Auranen was very strongly against giving any support to any movement, which had some connection to armed liberation struggle. So at the time when I was a member of the Foreign Council and when I was, as Archbishop, Chairman of the Foreign Council of the Church of Finland, I all the time met very strong resistance from Ahti Auranen and after him Pentti Viita who both wanted to keep a very clear line, that the money collected by the Finnchurchaid could not be used for anti-apartheid struggle.

Now I deliberately kept that struggle away from publicity, I did not write anything about it. I thought it's an internal matter of the church and particularly when I was Chairman and Archbishop so I didn't think it is good that the Chairman publicly criticises those, who are serving under him. That would be disastrous. So that was one of the matters I as an Archbishop had to deal with; the groups in the church who knew their rights and kept their position, which opposed that of the Archbishop. So that to the very end the Finnchurchaid did not give any support to the WCC anti-racism fund. Then in the 1980s they voted for one small amount to be given to an Australian project, which gave support to some aboriginal project to give publicity to their oppressed situation.

That was considered to be a non-violent project of the antiracist struggle. But otherwise I can't recall anything of significance during my time as Archbishop.

IS: Do you see that the opinion the church had held before had a certain impact on official foreign policy?

MJ: I don't think it had had because so late as in the middle of the 1980s when John Vikström criticised some action taken by the government concerning refugees, if I remember correctly, minister Väyrynen publicly wondered how an Archbishop appointed by the President can criticise the decisions made by the government. This controversy then developed further and in the early 1990s there was a major controversy between the government and the church involving even president Koivisto when in a press conference Archbishop Vikström answered the question whether he considered apartheid to be a sin that yes, racism was a sin. And Koivisto said ironically that if this was a sin it would be good to know how this sin could then be practised. And I got angry at being the Chairman of the Committee, who had written a proposal for churches' attitude towards refugees and made very many suggestions. When Vikström approved our proposals I criticised publicly Koivisto with rather hard words.

Whether that has influenced the attitude of the government I do not know. I think, I do not think that any foreign minister at the moment would repeat what Väyrynen said. I think that the church has through these actions gained the right to have its own theologically argued opinion concerning controversial points. And the church has the same right to criticise government as for instance the unions.

IS: Then are you willing to assess why the government supported the liberation movements and the apartheid struggle?

MJ: I would say that no doubt that the public opinion has influenced the government and in this public opinion the church has played a certain role. So I wouldn't say that the church separately has done so much but as the church, which traditionally is conservative—at least is supposed to be conservative—and in a certain sense represents traditions has helped the government to change its attitude when also a conservative and traditionalist institution like the church is for modernisation of that attitude.

PP: Yes, I've already mentioned in another interview the fact that in the early 1980s when the trade union movement also began to do something concrete in Southern Africa, we immediately joined hands with the Church through Mikko Ihamäki and decided to work, not formally but actually, in liaison and in cooperation and feeling that if we work together the public opinion will maybe follow. At least in such a way that it's not wise to attack both these large organisations which have such a following.

MJ: I was such a short time as Archbishop, that I did not have time to really see whether any changes happened. But my idea was very strong, that the major folk movements in the country—that is the socialist movement and the church—if they joined hands that would have tremendous effect on public opinion. And in the long run also in the policy of the government. And when I compare the relations between leftist organisations and church organisations in the middle of the 1970s and now, it would be worthwhile to make an objective and thorough investigation how the personal relations between leading people in the church organisations and in the leftist organisations have developed, what kind of friendships have been born and strengthened around 1980 and how the public statements from both sides have changed. I think that really is one of the turning points in our internal history.

PP: Whenever we saw that we could work hand in hand especially in the Namibian question, we knew it created such a broad basis that nobody really dared to at least openly attack that cooperation. And so we had free hands and our educational effort was not hampered by local opposition who would defend apartheid or anything. And it also influenced the actions of the government, which of course was already in favour of supporting and was already supporting.

MJ: I think you are just on the right track and rather than ask, how the church has had impact on the government actions, you should ask how the new cooperation on a very broad basis between people from the church in a very large meaning and people from leftist organisations have worked together in the same organisations.

Take the Finnish-Namibia Society, take the Espoo-Namibia Project and I think there are many like this. And that Finnchurchaid and the Unions they have common committees, so it's something, which is completely new. This thing did not happen around 1970 but in 1980 it was an established fact.

So about what you say that the government had difficulties, now you must remember that Finnish society is organised differently in the right half and in the leftist half. In the left everything is—if not strictly political—then at least has political connections. It's difficult to find a leading spokesman on the left half of our society who is not attached to one or another political, union, cultural leftist organisation. But in the right half it's quite different. There the politicians are a group in themselves. There are cultural organisations, social organisations, Christian organisations, the opinion leaders on the bourgeois side of the society are much less political than on the left. Now that does not mean that the right would be unpolitical, they are not unpolitical. But their organisation is different and when in this major question opinion builders on the left and right met each other, so the church has had in this development a good and important role. So it's quite right to say that.

PP: It's been a great thing, I agree.

IS: Yes, but the reason to cooperate; were there various objectives for cooperation? I mean, Namibia cooperation was one reason why trade unions and the church joined hands. But was it more like a general trend, I mean when you were talking about these refugees and racism, the struggle against racism or are we only talking cooperation in this respect?

MJ: Of course I know the development from our side, but one thing which must be remembered first, was the new interest in developing countries, the notion that this world is not dominated by East-West conflict which was the traditional thing that influenced all Finnish opinion prior to the Second World War and very much after that too. And in churches awareness of that the future of our world depends on how we in industrial countries treat the developing countries. That's the important question, not the East-West conflict.

That's what I spoke of then in 1962 and this opened eyes that we have allies, and possible allies with those who here in Finland emotionally are in this East-West conflict on the eastern side. But that's not decisive. The question is where we stand in the North-South controversy, and the similarity of our evaluation has been the underlying thing which led us together. So that means that when I speak about friends and enemies, I don't speak about those that we should fight enemies, but enemies are those who oppose what we think is right. And the strongest opposition—which I would call it without any value judgement—to the Christian view of North-South conflict were people in our midst, they were the conservative bourgeois, the allies were on the left. And this was something which the international contacts, this new insight, gave to us and after that it was natural to find allies on the left.

Interview with Janet Mondlane, former Director of the Mozambique Institute in Dar es Salaam, 18.7.1996, Maputo, Mozambique

Iina Soiri: Can you tell me something about yourself and the Mozambique Institute and your connection to the Nordic countries?

Janet Mondlane: First we had a grant from the Ford Foundation to educate refugees from Mozambique. The American Embassy had its Ambassador in Portugal and the Portuguese made a direct complaint to the American government, that this American foundation was making a grant to this rebel movement, these terrorists. It made a lot of noise, in the State Department of the United States and in the Ford Foundation and finally the Ford Foundation dropped our support.

IS: Which year did you start the Institute?

JM: That was 1963. We already had a lot of Mozambican refugees then, I don't know how many. Actually, we have it in those documents, that I spoke to you about, how many refugees there were. Because we did a lot of work in terms of publicity to get funds for the Institute. After, when I found out that Ford Foundation had dropped it, I went to the World Council of Churches and did get a grant from them. But I think on that same trip, or certainly after, I went to Sweden. I may have a report about that, somewhere, certainly it must be in the FRELIMO archives, but the FRELIMO archives are all mixed up. Anyway, the first real contact in Sweden was with the Secondary Students' Union, the School Union. They were going to have a work day as they always did.

IS: Operation Day's Work.

JM: Exactly, and marvel of marvels, they adopted the Mozambique Institute. And I think probably that's how Finland began to get involved in this as there was an alliance among those Secondary School students. It turned out that all the Secondary School Unions finally adopted the Mozambique Institute as their Day of Work. Maybe not Denmark, because sometimes they were a little bit out of the picture, but Norway, Sweden and Finland, but that would have to be checked. I went to Finland many times linked with the Day's Work. They did it every third year, it wasn't every year. Finland with Erkki Liikanen, and his group. He was very active. I don't remember whether he was the president of the Union at that time but he certainly was very influential, had many inroads in government. And I remember he was the one that organised the appointments for me in the government with parliamentarians and so on. And I suspect that's where all this began. And the Secondary School Students were very active. I was so impressed with the students, how mature they were. In Sweden when I was speaking to Pierre Schori at that time about the secondary schools, how they were organised along political lines. And there were conflicts among the various lines, just like political parties. And maybe these young students grew mature politically very rapidly. They really understood what was going on there, at least in their own countries. I have a feeling that Operation Day's Work may be the first real contact that Finland had with Africa. I have a suspicion that the first contact—except when you are talking about Pretoria—was through the Mozambique Institute. Because then these Secondary School students went on and they became important figures in their own country. And they were very active in the Secondary Schools Student Union. They were likely to succeed when they went out.

IS: When I went through the Foreign Ministry's (FM) archives, I found out that there had been a FRELIMO delegation to Finland as guests of the Social Democratic Party—Erkki Liikanen was a member of that party—at the end of November 1970. One of them was Joaquim Chissano. This is the first record that I found in the FM about meeting somebody officially from FRELIMO.

JM: I think I should explain what the Mozambique Institute (MI) was. I have to go back to explain how the Nordic governments got involved with FRELIMO. That was via the Mozambique Institute. The MI was founded separately from FRELIMO. It was not legally a part of FRELIMO. We had our own legal constitution. We had our own Board of Trustees. I was the Director. And we can say yes, the MI served FRELIMO as much as that it helped to educate refugees. Also the fact that the director of the MI was the wife of the president of FRELIMO always counts for something. But if one really tracks down to see how it developed, one could see that of course there was a very strong link with FRELIMO, but really we developed separately. That was the excuse the Nordic countries used to say that they were not involved with a terrorist organisation. They were involved with a refugee school, people who were working with refugees and then later on with the social services because MI didn't stay as a school, it expanded tremendously and even went to the liberated areas of Mozambique. And we were organising the social services of FRELIMO without saying we were FRELIMO. So when the MI went to Sweden and Norway and Finland and Denmark it was going as a separate branch of FRELIMO.

IS: Which was very wise.

JM: Actually it was very wise. I didn't even realise how wise it was until long after the fact. But the Nordic countries held on to that legal difference and ran with it. But what they were really doing was working sideways with FRELIMO. And the development of FRELIMO as a liberation movement meant that it was involved not only in war but in development of a new idea, a new concept for a future Mozambique. That was very important for the Nordic countries and I hope that the Nordic countries today realise what a contribution they made in that sense. It was a tremendous contribution. And they were the only ones that made it. So although you can have the first official encounter recorded in 1970, most of it rested with me in the 1960s because I was sort of the go-between. I had many contacts in Finland, but they were probably unofficial. I remember going to the parliament building talking to parliamentarians, talking with members of government.

I think I saw the Foreign Minister as well. But it was very informal. And my job was to mobilise and dynamise these Nordic governments to understand what this struggle meant for the independence of Mozambique. That was really my job. FRELIMO didn't get into it until later on. I began in Sweden in 1965, and worked very hard for almost up to independence, really up to independence.

IS: Were you ever staying in Sweden?

JM: I was staying in Dar es Salaam. But I made frequent trips to the Nordic countries.

IS: But apart from the fund raising of the students and the contribution they made for the MI, did you get any official state aid from Finland?

JM: No

IS: Never?

JM: Official state aid, no. At that time Finland, as you well know, Finland was very traumatised and neurotic by the fact that it had this border with Soviet Union. And it seemed to determine a lot of Finnish policy. At least this is, what I was told at the time. At the same time they were walking the tight-rope with their Western allies. But really I sympathise with Finland and I think it made the political life a bit difficult. I felt there was a lot of resentment about the Soviet Union—about what had to be done and what positions could be taken. But one must say that if they had to work with or please or be careful with the Soviet Union, the liberation movement wouldn't have disturbed that at all because the Soviet Union was involved with liberation movements. Like at that time with the whole Eastern bloc. But it was very difficult for the so-called Western bloc to be allied or seem to be talking with these revolutionary movements. But I do not remember any direct aid coming from the Finnish government to the Institute.

IS: In 1972 a number of Finnish NGOs filed a petition to pressure the Finnish Government to give direct aid to the liberation movements. They were speaking first of all of the liberation movements in Portuguese colonies: FRELIMO, MPLA and PAIGC. And to their own surprise—I talked to these activists—they managed to get the signatures of all the political parties and all main NGOs in Finland. The petition was handed to the Foreign Minister. The Foreign Ministry had been very reluctant to even give support to the student conference which was discussing anticolonialism. They didn't even want to fund it because they said that if we fund it we support violent activities. So then after this petition they set up a working group whose main idea was to find ways how Finland could give some money to the movements, because all the other Nordic countries were already supporting the movements directly, that means, not only through the liberation committee in Dar es Salaam, the OAU and UN, but directly. So in 1973 they finally decided that, OK we can give support to FRELIMO, MPLA and PAIGC as humanitarian aid, strictly humanitarian aid. And no cash. Some materials for example. But it took a lot of bureaucratic hassle before they got this thing off the ground. Then in 1974 the Dar es Salaam Embassy reported to the Foreign Ministry after the coup in Portugal that we haven't given anything to FRELIMO—all the other Nordic countries gave—so we have to do something and very fast. Give something to FRELIMO in order to be recorded as a supporter of FRELIMO. To secure the relations, because we never know what's going to happen. So they managed to give a cheque. It had been a long process before the Foreign Ministry agreed. Thanks to that there exists even a picture of that occasion when Mr Ahtisaari, ambassador to Tanzania at that time, and counsellor Kimmo Pulkkinen were handing a cheque to Samora Machel and Marcelino dos Santos. And that was the first and only financial contribution to FRELIMO.

JM: It was just under the line...!

IS: And thereafter Mozambique gained its independence and the relations between Finland and Mozambique were established according to the normal diplomatic manner.

JM: That is the history of the official government aid, I see.

IS: All through these years the students and the NGOs funded the liberated areas. And that is what I don't know anything about yet, which you maybe can shed some light on.

JM: And that's very important. I think I must get you the documents of the MI, so you can photocopy them. The most important thing that Finland did, was to give the printing press to the MI. The person who came down with it was Kid Ahlfors, we called him Kid. He was a Finnish fellow. He taught people how to use the press and if I am not mistaken, the man I got to work with Kid is still here in Maputo. He is a Tanzanian and his name is Paul Silveira. He and that machine are still running.

IS: And the machine belongs to whom now?

JM: It belongs to the National Press, Impresa Nacional. And it must be in that building that they have down there, almost at the 25 de Setembro, its on Vladimir Lenin, just at the bottom. His name is Paul Silveira. He must be a pretty old guy by this time. But very nice. An extraordinarily nice, quiet and capable person. He worked with Kid. And then there were others who worked with him. There was a fellow by the name Simango, can't remember his first name for the moment. Anyway there were a group of them. And the whole thing was transferred down here to Lourenço Marques when it came independent. That printing press did a lot of things. The evolution of that printing press, the justification I made, was to make textbooks. That was the justification. And we made the first textbooks of FRELIMO really, for FRELIMO schools. So those Finnish students were really involved in the first educational programmes of an independent Mozambique. And some of those text books certainly still exist, they are still around somewhere.

IS: Apart from this printing press did they give material aid or did it cost all the money which was collected? And was it a Finnish printing press?

JM: I think it was bought in Finland and shipped to Dar es Salaam. And we could make a very good finished product. It had eight or sixteen colours. There were a lot of technical discussions. But it made a very good finished product. And it was really impressive. And certainly we were the first liberation movement with a printing press, if we can say it was a liberation movement's printing press. In fact it put out a lot more than just MI text books. It was the printing press that printed the magazine "Mozambique Revolution", which was an international magazine. FRELIMO really did very well on the international arena. Better than after independence. Because there were a group of people including Jorge Rebelo. He worked at the MI. He had his office at the MI. He was the information officer of FRELIMO. I can even remember where it was. It was a small office right on the courtyard, just outside and when we walked outside of his office into the alley there was the printing press. So Finland, those secondary students—that's why I have admiration for those students— worked on it and they stuck it out and they also provided different kinds of paper. They never just dropped it, but they just kept going with that and produced fantastic things.

IS: I found out from the archives of the Africa Committee that they used to collect money and that they had donations from the Finnish paper industry. That paper was then packed and shipped to Dar es Salaam together with some clothes and sports things, footballs and things like that. Later on this system whereby state the was also funding NGOs started, but this support to MI was so early that all the money they collected was from students or their parents. So it was private money, there was never any state money. They were all pure donations because the students ran from company to company asking for things.

JM: I remember I had to go speak to schools, representatives of schools, I had to go to public meetings organised by them. The idea of these students was that this is what we are doing today, but it will have a very longterm effect not only on the attitudes of the students as they grow, but on their parents because the students and their parents are so linked with ideas. If students are working hard on a project, of course their parents are going to get involved. If not physically involved at least they are going to get intellectually involved. So I think it made a big impact on the Finnish political and social scene.

IS: But how were you received? I mean that if somebody in Finland is expecting a person from MI, he won't expect a person like you. Are you an American citizen?

JM: At that time I still was.

IS: Just talking about these images, must have been a surprise for them to find you, a white woman.

JM: From US. It's very interesting, because what I had to handle in terms of that was non-existent. Now, what they had to handle in Finland or in the Nordic countries I don't know. The only time I remember—and I am not sure if it was after my husband was killed—as I was making a speech in a big hall. It wasn't Finland, I have a feeling it was in Norway or Sweden. A Portuguese got up and criticised me for what I was doing. How could I possibly represent the Mozambican people because I wasn't Mozambican and

I wasn't this and I wasn't that. So but that's the only time I can remember. I am sure it was because I was the wife of the president and I just didn't dispute that.

IS: The first representative of the liberation movement who was officially invited to Finland and had an official reception was Amílcar Cabral.

JM: I would imagine.

IS: And the story tells that people were astonished because they were waiting for a guerrilla, you know, a little bit backward, a real fighter, even blood on his hands and then they received a civilised and highly intellectual person. What I mean is that these images are very important. We are talking about 1960s Finland, where one never really saw a black person. There were no black people in Finland.

JM: Yes, Finland was very isolated.

IS: And the image of Africa was non-existent. People didn't really know. The only ones that we had were some SWAPO students or Namibian students throughout these years. So for many, even for students who read about things, and who are more aware, it was a new thing and then for many politicians who are of an older generation for them to meet a black person who is intellectual was a very enlightening encounter. His visit really made an impact after which they said OK, these people are good, and they know what they are talking about and so these liberation movements are not just hopeless guerrillas fighting for fun but they want to do something and they are right in what they do. And that made an impact on the political front. And also, of course, the students who long ago allied with the MI and also met other people and spoke about this.

JM: And they had worked on it, they had really worked on it. And they really knew. I am trying to think if they made any visits to Dar es Salaam, they must have. But you see they finally had Kid Ahlfors there so he was counselling and there was a lot of feedback there. But we had a lot of communication with Finland. There was really a lot going back and forth.

IS: Can you tell about any other organisation which supported you?

JM: In Finland? I think they probably developed. But I can't tell you right now. I just cannot remember what organisations they were. Whatever they would have been, they certainly would have worked through the union, or with the union at least. I don't know if there were church groups. The World Council of Churches or the Programme to Combat Racism also worked with us.

IS. What about the Lutheran World Federation?

JM: Yes, LWF. No, it could be that the LWF received funds, because it was safer that way. Churches didn't want to get mixed up.

IS: They did get money from Finland, from Finnish churches.

JM: I am sure they did and of course we talked about that. I talked about that with the Lutherans that this was a way to support us. Because I was telling this while in Finland, to the Nordic countries that they should really make use of it. If you could get the Finnish Lutheran Church archives, and find out how much LWF gave. They gave a lot of money, they did give us a lot.

IS: Well, the purpose of our study is not only to try to discover the impacts of our aid or our support to these movements and people in these countries. It is also to find out the impact in our society. Because it goes both ways. And these things you are telling now are very important, because the relationship with MI somehow enlarged the world view of Finnish citizens. Especially because—like you mentioned yourself—of the Soviet Union, our contacts with the outside world and our foreign politics actually were very strictly limited to certain ways. Only certain individuals were allowed to have contacts. Certainly it was not like Eastern Europe, of course not, we were much freer. But anyhow about foreign policy, our old president used to say, that it is not a thing for an ordinary citizen, it is too complicated. That was the saying. So but really with students' contacts and this type of solidarity work there was a new world opening up for Finns. And then in the 1970s there were a lot of—apart from contacts to Africa—others, e.g. Chile came and Vietnam. The Vietnam war at that time as well painted the map much wider for Finland, and the development cooperation could grow on that foundation.

JM: It grew on that foundation, yes it did. That's why I always say, the MI was really the first, say, liberation movement entity which was in the Nordic countries. And from that then the liberation movement didn't seem so strange, didn't seem foreign. And maybe it was a good idea that here comes this white American, because sometimes even after independence when I was a member of government delegations they would forget who I am. And I remember speaking with—I was in a delegation for development—we were in Italy and I was next to the Minister for Foreign Affairs and Development and he started telling me all the things wrong with black people. Because, of course, he didn't think. As one gets going one forgets what I am really doing and what my links are. So probably it was an advantage in a society like Finland which was extraordinary insular at that time. And I remember Erkki Liikanen explaining to me the complications of the foreign policy. It was something that I could understand and take into account, because I came from a society with a much wider way of looking of the world, I wasn't confined to the Mozambican viewpoint. So it was easier to cultivate the Nordic countries. After a while I began taking Mozambicans with me, at least one Mozambican with me, to integrate him into the business. This was before independence, when a black person didn't seem so strange any more.

IS: From the records I found that you have been to Finland in an official delegation in 1980 as National Director of International Cooperation with Joaquim Marcos?

JM: That was such a tiring trip.

IS: You went to many countries?

JM: I think eight. I was exhausted, that was the first time I have ever been thoroughly exhausted. Didn't they have an international women's conference in Finland during that time?

IS: There was one, yes.

JM: I went to that with Josina Machel. I was there. And the Palestinian women. That was my first contact with the Palestinian women. I couldn't believe it. It was very interesting. I also went to a lot of solidarity meetings in Europe, to which Finnish people went. And there was always that problem in the Nordic countries, well maybe not as much as in Germany. Germany had terrible problems, with such internal conflicts in these student unions. Of course based on political parties. Germany was very conservative. Some of them were very conservative and some of them were very much on the left.

IS: But that is a character of European politics. It is because of this East-West division. I think in Finland even we had very strong communist, well communist as well, but leftist fractions. Our communist party was established in the beginning of the century and the social democratic party as well and they were always like cat and dog. Even if they were both on the left, but they had such ideological differences that sometimes it felt very ridiculous. But it was in the 1970's, when the student radicalism which started in the 1960s, was swallowed by the political parties. First many of those student activists were not aligned, they just absorbed leftist ideas, but they were not members of the parties. So then later on they found out that, because there was this new openness in political parties, so they became members of the political parties just like Erkki Liikanen himself, who eventually became an MP at the age of 21.

JM: I know, he was the youngest

IS: So I mean suddenly all the power was in his hands. Because there was a kind of generation change in the beginning of the seventies. So like everywhere else, the Foreign Ministry absorbed most of the radicals in the beginning of the 1970s. In that way those who were very critical towards Finnish foreign policy, became officials themselves. Because that was the policy of our late president Kekkonen, he wanted to use this kind of integration tactics. He met himself many of the student leaders, very radical ones, who one day were protesting outside the presidential palace and next day having tea with the president. It was his tactics, his strategy. So, and then they were absorbed into the political parties, they became either politicians or they became officials. And this development cooperation or this solidarity work, humanitarian aid was a kind of subject they were allowed to deal with. So Kekkonen never touched it, but he said OK, it's not a problem, it's not as long as you keep our policy, don't bring a conflict in the decisions, you can deal with it. You give humanitarian aid to FRELIMO. You give that to SWAPO, ANC, that's fine. It was a kind of way of integrating them and keeping them busy with this task.

JM: Better join them.

IS: He was very clever in that sense.

JM: But of course the result was that is also changed the government. Of course. You cannot expect to isolate them. What I felt and have always felt until recently. Certainly in the 60s and the 70s the Nordic countries as a whole—well I always put Denmark a little apart.

IS: Because it was a EU and NATO member.

JM: But the Nordic countries were happily naive about what was really going on in the world. How essentially horrible the world was. Because if you are working in the revolution, in the revolutionary movement, all the things that go on and all the things that happened to us were horrible. I also started out as a very innocent, idealistic teenager and so on. Also naive, I must say. One learns a lot. I felt that the Nordic people were in that category they hadn't gone out to the world yet. So one would appeal to that. And say: "You know there is something horrible going on in the world, you have to do something to change it!" And they kind of woke up and blinked their eyes and said: "You are right". But that changed, that has changed now. Through communication, media and so on. And unhappy things have happened in the Nordic countries. But at that time that was the typical picture of what I had in dealing with the Nordic people. People that I would meet. It was probably a selected group, self-identified group, but they were open to these ideas and just really observing that these things were going on in the world. It finally hit them, later on.

IS: Was your appeal more emotional than rational? If you saw them being naive at the same time when people were being killed. And to think of the way the Portuguese government was treating people. So was it an emotional appeal?

JM: No, it was combined. One had to talk about the situation as I used to do. The situation in Mozambique, the situation in the struggle. What we were trying to do to solve it. Of course it appeals to the emotions of the people even if they hadn't thought of it before. But for one to get over the emotional effect, you have to appeal to them also intellectually, otherwise it doesn't stick. That's where the secondary school students were good, because although they were caught up in a sense of an emotional side, they were also very intelligent. Those that I dealt with. And I admired them a lot. I felt they were so mature for their age.

IS: It was a special generation and that's what we are hearing all along. I mean I was a student in the 1980s and I was always told about those in the 1960s. But I just heard from someone who is a student now that they are no longer told stories about the 1960s but they are told about the 1980s. Because we were the ones who started anti-apartheid and started this developmental, solidarity and environmental movement as a new combination, what then became the Green movement. So now they say nothing is happening. But maybe in the year 2000 then they will have thought about other things, it starts again.

JM: Sure, these ideas come back again. They've only got energy every twenty years. I really am convinced that the MI was the forerunner of the relationship between especially Mozambique, but Southern Africa too. And for the Southern African governments and the Nordic governments I think the really root was MI. We did a lot of publicity.

IS: And then like in Finland's case, we had this missionary relationship to Namibia. And we had a student, a Namibian student, Nickey Iyambo, who is now a minister. So he was in Finland. But he didn't have any resources, no backing. SWAPO didn't exist, well it did exist but it had got no network, so he was doing a lot on his own scholarship and he was a roommate of Erkki Liikanen. So that was also what made Erkki aware, surely, because he was staying in the same room with one liberation movement activist! Later on SWAPO came into the picture because of the Martti Ahtisaari connection and everything. I was surprised, because I was so young when Mozambique got independence, so I don't have any recollections myself and I sort of thought it all started with SWAPO but it is not the case! The solidarity started with Portuguese colonies and FRELIMO, that was the focal point.

JM: My son has told me that I must write a story on the MI because it was a great success story in the Nordic countries and it was really laying the foundation for the future relationships between the Nordic countries and Mozambique and other Southern African governments as well. But I have been too busy, maybe I will do it one day.

Interview with Minister Nickey Iyambo, 20.8.1996, Windhoek, Namibia

Nickey Iyambo: I came to Finland in the last days of November 1964. And my reason for going to Finland was actually to study. That was reason number one. Two, I also had a responsibility given to me by SWAPO of Namibia to mobilise and inform the people in the Nordic countries in general and Finland in particular about life in Namibia, particularly the political life when it comes to the position of the black majority in this country. That was because of colonialism that was in place in Namibia. Before going to Finland I lived for a brief period in the United Republic of Tanzania, where I was working as a broadcaster through Radio Freedom spreading the news to the people of Southern Africa and Namibia in particular.

I was born in the northern part of Namibia, it is where I grew up as a boy looking after my father's animals: cattle, goats, donkeys and the like. Like any other African boy I had to do that until I was about 9 or 10 before I could actually be allowed or permitted to go for schooling. I went through my primary school in the northern part of Namibia, and part of my secondary school and then I had a great interest in teaching. I went to a teacher's seminar and after the teacher's seminar I migrated to Windhoek. Before I left the northern part of Namibia I was thrown in to the political life of Namibia through people like Andimba Toivo ya Toivo, and Sam Nujoma. They were people that we heard those days so much. My contact particularly with Toivo ya Toivo was so rewarding, so educating particularly to us as young boys of those days.

I left the northern part of Namibia in 1959 at the very end, came to Windhoek, lived in Windhoek. Soon after I arrived in Windhoek I was caught up in the mobilisation of the black people as far as their political rights were concerned. It was during those years that we had to mobilise and rally on the call to the UN to come and end the mandate of the then apartheid South Africa which occupied our country. In Windhoek I quickly went up and gained respect from my people and I was elected as SWAPO's first secretary, branch secretary actually, in the then newly created location for the blacks, where blacks had to live, called Katutura. That location is still around. It is actually the place where majority of the black people lived until today, here in Windhoek. Being a branch secretary of an organisation which was working against the social and political order of the day was indeed very difficult. The white rulers of those years could not imagine that in this country the black aspiration would go so far as wanting to change the socio economic and political circumstances that prevailed in the country. Because of my opposition to the then social order, I and many others were very often at the loggerheads with the political establishment of those days. To the extent that we had to be arrested, we had to be beaten up by the police. But of course we had to mobilise our people.

So by the beginning of 1963 I attempted to leave Namibia to go into exile because many of my peers had by that time left Namibia, went abroad, first particularly to Tanganyika which became the United Republic of Tanzania later on. Others got scholarships from Tanzania and went to study abroad to continents such as America, Europe and of course the rest were spread throughout a few independent African states those days. But I was arrested in the North-Eastern part of Namibia as I attempted to escape and I was in prison for three months. I went to court accused of wanting to escape from the country. That issue I purposely denied since my objectives were to go abroad to study and indeed to join others in the struggle for freedom of this country. At the trial I was sentenced to six months imprisonment.

It was a very difficult time. Very often I was beaten up in prison and I was interrogated. I was asked about the United Nations. I was asked about what I and others were trying to do, and why we were against the establishment of those days. We were informed that it was not possible for black people to rule themselves. And when I referred to black people in countries such as Ghana, Tanzania, Nigeria, Liberia, who ruled themselves, I was often informed that those are different black people. It was only that we did not know them, but they were different. So we were informed that, that for us in this part of the world, our place was to be servants. Fetch water, chop wood, and work as kitchen boys for the white people. And we should forget that the day could come when we could rule ourselves.

It was painful to be told like that. It was degrading, it was despising, it was unacceptable. Yet the force, the brutality that was vented on those who turned out to organise against the establishment those days was so harsh that there was nothing you could do but simply be around, like it or not. And of course we happened to have been born in this country.

So when I was released I stayed in the country for about four months and very early in March 1964, I together with another two of my colleagues—unfortunately they are all now late colleagues because of the struggle, because of the war of liberation, they are no longer with us—left Namibia, escaped and went into exile. We got a political asylum in Tanzania because we were belonging to SWAPO—which was actually a positive measure those days, because there were a number of African liberation movements in Tanzania all housed in Dar es Salaam. We were all looking for political recognition from the Organisation of African Unity, which was formed in May 1963. After a brief time staying in United Republic of Tanzania I then went to Finland for the purpose I stated earlier which was to study and after studying to come back to join my colleagues in Africa to continue the mobilisation of the international community on behalf of my country Namibia and of course against South Africa.

Iina Soiri: Why was particularly Finland selected ? Was it a scholarship given by Finland or was it the importance which SWAPO placed on Nordic countries? Or what was this special reason why you—of all the countries—went exactly to Finland?

NI: The international community those days was really yearning to learn about problems on this planet. And as you know the Second World War had just ended in 1945 and time went by when the European states were busy with their reconstruction. But after, I must say, the successful programme of the Marshall Plan in Europe, the fire for solidarity grew in Europe and in America to assist people that were fighting against oppression. And this solidarity was also amplified by the number of students' movements. There was an organisation called the World University Service which was spearheaded by students. Students of that organisation thought it to be their duty to mobilise resources and assist their peers from developing countries, so in my case I was given a scholarship by WUS. It is to that organisation that Finnish students also belonged and that organisation had an office also in Finland. And when I was given a scholarship by that organisation I was informed that the place for me to study would be Finland and I should go and undertake political science. That is how I went to Finland.

Of course I was delighted because the name of Finland was not strange to me as a Namibian who was born and grew up in the northern part of Namibia which is the part of Namibia where Finnish missionaries were very active since 1870. And in fact, the primary schools I went to were schools organised and belonging to the Finnish Missionaries in collaboration with the local people of the northern part of Namibia. While in Finland I met many

Finnish people, and some of them were to be almost my life long friends, should I say. And among them I include the current president of Finland, his excellency Martti Ahtisaari and many more others who quickly became my acquaintances and made my stay in Finland a happy one.

IS: So one of your tasks, in addition to studying, was to mobilise support. What kind of support did SWAPO expect or wish to get from Finland especially and the Nordic countries in general?

NI: When I went to the Nordic countries and Finland in particular, I had a clear vision of what I wanted to achieve. And the messages that I wanted to convey to the people in the Nordic Countries were as clear as daylight in my mind. I knew that the Nordic Countries had no colonialist pattern, in other words they never colonised any country in Africa. And so because of that I knew they were not very well acquainted, vested with the problem of colonialism. And therefore I was convinced that they might be ignorant as far as the problem of apartheid was concerned. Yet I knew too, that I would most probably not find it difficult in the end, to impart the information about the difficulties in Southern Africa in countries such as Angola, Zimbabwe, Mozambique, South Africa and Namibia. I knew that there would be an economic assistance possibility that we could get from the Nordic countries. But I thought before embarking on that economic and other social assistance the first task has to be the mobilisation.

Because in the first place people did not know where the country was—something about *Ambomaa*, a little bit. But not really much in terms of the social and political difficulties the country was undergoing, because the duty of the missionaries was obviously to spread the good message of conviction and Christianity. It was not very clear to them whether they also had to look into social difficulties of the country, particularly the political arrangement. They thought that was part of the local politics and they were from a far land and they should not really spend considerable energy on political issues, but rather consider spreading the Gospel of faith.

The mobilisation started with the student movements, because these were my peers. It was easier. They were the people I associated with. They were people I sat with. They were the people I drank tea or coffee with. They were the people, that we went around skiing together and so on and so forth. So it was therefore just natural that they were very close to me and therefore easy to talk to. Also they wanted to find a new role that they could play in their countries in terms of first increasing their horizon of knowledge so that they could no longer limit their knowledge and activities to Finnish or European affairs only. It was the time of expanding their knowledge beyond Europe. And I was a resource to tap for concrete information and experience. Also to gain from the personal concrete stories that I was able to tell of what I had gone through myself.

Slowly but surely we expanded the horizon from the student organisation to the mass organisations of Finnish society, particularly the trade unions and indeed the political organisations. And in those days it was the political organisations of the left of the political spectrum that were more forthcoming than those of the right political spectrum. Now after that it was the time to expand this to the academics. And soon we found Africa and African affairs discussed in seminars, seminar papers prepared, and that people even introduced some texts where African history, Africa politics, African sociological perspectives and information were discussed. And because of that, I realised quickly that indeed sooner or later we would get to involve governments of those countries as well.

By the time we talked to governments we then had assistance of the citizens of those countries, students in particular, members of political parties of the left political spectrum and soon thereafter academics. They were not many people, that came up in the beginning. But soon thereafter a few African research papers were produced. That is how the interest was developed. We found after that there was also a whole yearning of interest particularly in Asian problem, because those were also the years of the Vietnamese war. And therefore the link was shown that the problems in Asia—when it came to the Vietnamese war and others—could not be divorced from colonial problems that were reigning in Africa.

So because of that, many scholarships were granted to African students. I was perhaps the third or fourth African student in Finland those days. And soon thereafter the number increased which also made the stay more pleasant because I could discuss and relate my African experience to other Africans, those who were not from Namibia. And quickly too they came to my assistance to help to mobilise the Finnish people in particular and the Nordic population in general. So we find that working through these student organisations was followed by the fact that organisations such as Africa Committee of Finland was created and so many other associations trying to help Africa. I remember Africa Group of Sweden was created. And so we were invited to so many seminars, to so many conferences, to so many meetings in the Nordic Countries to mobilise the population.

I think by the late 1960s FRELIMO, a liberation movement of Mozambique, was already gaining momentum and upper hand in the fight for liberation of Mozambique. As a consequence FRELIMO got attention in the Nordic Countries as a viable organisation that needed to be supported materially, financially and much more morally. And of course we were working together with most of the African students who were given scholarships to study. And quickly thereafter we found that appointments and meetings did take place between African students and Nordic politicians although at the lower level those days.

IS: Did you have a colleague in any other Nordic country?

NI: I was alone from 1964 until 71. I was operating from Helsinki, covering all the Nordic countries. But in 1972 I was joined by another SWAPO member who was stationed in Stockholm. And when he came it got naturally much easier for me to organise from Finland. May I say more of less I concentrated then on being in Finland only. But that situation was planned, because in 1969 I finished my political science, which I was doing in Finland, came back to Africa. But in 1971 I went back to Finland again, for the second time I went for the purpose of studying medicine. It turned out that doing medicine was not the same as doing political science. I was more busy with the studies than with the political activities as it was compulsory to be in the lectures. And that was actually partly the main reason that SWAPO had to recruit another candidate for the Nordic countries.

IS: Who was this colleague of yours?

NI: That time it was somebody called Paul Helmut who stayed there until 1974 or so. Then he was replaced by another colleague, Ben Amathila, who today is Namibia's Minister of Information and Broadcasting.

All in all, I must say that the concrete official contact both in Finland and in Sweden as well as the rest of the Nordic Countries—that means the position for us to be heard and to be listened to by the Nordic governments—started with the assistance of those countries' student movements. In Finland the Africa Committee and in Sweden the Africa Group of Sweden. So much then, that soon thereafter our leaders, in our case, my president, his excellency, doctor Sam Nujoma also came to visit Finland frequently in those years to meet Finnish politicians. And slowly we got even financial assistance from Finland. The first financial assistance from Finland we got was from the Social Democratic Party. As well the SKDL of Finland was always ready to give a hand in local arrangements. And later on we got some financial assistance also through the trade unions.

And so we went on, to the end of 1976 when contacts between us as members of the liberation movement and the Finnish government improved considerably, because by that time we had the Finnish government's kind of direct involvement with Namibia through the UN because at that time Martti Ahtisaari—who is an old friend of mine—was appointed to be the UN High Commissioner for Namibia. He left his post in Tanzania, where he was the Finnish Ambassador, in early 1977 and ever since our contact with the Finnish authorities really increased. A number of students were sent to Finland to study, Finland proposed a number of measures that were aimed at improving the education and social preparedness of Namibians through the UN Institute for Namibia in Lusaka to which Finland also contributed financially. Finland also did serve as a member of the Senate of that institute.

I must say, that the contact between Finland and Namibia through the arrival of the missionaries turned into a positive enterprise of contacts between the Namibians, who were struggling and fighting for the independence and the 1970s politicians of Finland to the extent that today Namibia and Finland enjoy an excellent relationship.

IS: This was actually a good evaluation of the relationship. But if you still would compare Finland to the other nations, can you see that Finland had a special role to play in the international community concerning the Namibian issue?

NI: I think Finland did what she could. What we were told those days was that Finland also had a very delicate political situation of its own. Being a country sandwiched between East and West means that although Finland has been for a long time a Western country, it had the then Soviet Union as a neighbour under a different political system than Finland's. It was cleverly balancing its own position between the East and West, Finland of course being a western country.

So I think because of its policy of neutrality there was sometimes, should I say, a disinterest as far as remote issues were concerned, in this case Namibia. It was a question whether Finland had something to gain, if it takes an active participation and side in African politics. Because those countries that did colonise Africa, of course had all the monopoly of information that was spread all over the world. You had a trade between Finland and South Africa. And Finland unfortunately had to balance between what it was getting in trade with South Africa and to compare it with the simple word and statement of Nickey Iyambo, who was a student of Finland. And who could not actually visualise, conceptualise, that it was sooner or later to be us, those that were oppressed, to gain the upper hand.

But Finland in my view did not lose much time to grasp the wind of change that was sweeping across Africa. Although I have to say much of the acceptance was not really brought by us from Africa talking to Finnish people, but an achievement by Finnish students to a large measure. They were really quite an asset for us. Otherwise the historical isolation of Finland made it difficult in those days for Finland to see beyond Europe, unfortunately. Particularly in regard to African issues, which came gradually and slowly with time. Indeed, one would have wished to have a Finnish active participation in positive politics because Finland was a neutral country. But I think if you ask a Finn he will have a different view.

IS: Concerning Moscow, did you have a colleague in Soviet Union?

NI: Oh yes, they were many.

IS: Did you exchange views politically?

NI: Oh yes, we did, we did. There was actually a large number of contacts among the Namibian students wherever we were. Those that were in the Soviet Union or in the rest of the socialist countries, those that were in America, those that were in a number of African countries, yes indeed, there were a lot of contacts.

Interview with Minister Nickey Iyambo, 20.8.1996, Windhoek, Namibia

Nickey Iyambo: I came to Finland in the last days of November 1964. And my reason for going to Finland was actually to study. That was reason number one. Two, I also had a responsibility given to me by SWAPO of Namibia to mobilise and inform the people in the Nordic countries in general and Finland in particular about life in Namibia, particularly the political life when it comes to the position of the black majority in this country. That was because of colonialism that was in place in Namibia. Before going to Finland I lived for a brief period in the United Republic of Tanzania, where I was working as a broadcaster through Radio Freedom spreading the news to the people of Southern Africa and Namibia in particular.

I was born in the northern part of Namibia, it is where I grew up as a boy looking after my father's animals: cattle, goats, donkeys and the like. Like any other African boy I had to do that until I was about 9 or 10 before I could actually be allowed or permitted to go for schooling. I went through my primary school in the northern part of Namibia, and part of my secondary school and then I had a great interest in teaching. I went to a teacher's seminar and after the teacher's seminar I migrated to Windhoek. Before I left the northern part of Namibia I was thrown in to the political life of Namibia through people like Andimba Toivo ya Toivo, and Sam Nujoma. They were people that we heard those days so much. My contact particularly with Toivo ya Toivo was so rewarding, so educating particularly to us as young boys of those days.

I left the northern part of Namibia in 1959 at the very end, came to Windhoek, lived in Windhoek. Soon after I arrived in Windhoek I was caught up in the mobilisation of the black people as far as their political rights were concerned. It was during those years that we had to mobilise and rally on the call to the UN to come and end the mandate of the then apartheid South Africa which occupied our country. In Windhoek I quickly went up and gained respect from my people and I was elected as SWAPO's first secretary, branch secretary actually, in the then newly created location for the blacks, where blacks had to live, called Katutura. That location is still around. It is actually the place where majority of the black people lived until today, here in Windhoek. Being a branch secretary of an organisation which was working against the social and political order of the day was indeed very difficult. The white rulers of those years could not imagine that in this country the black aspiration would go so far as wanting to change the socio economic and political circumstances that prevailed in the country. Because of my opposition to the then social order, I and many others were very often at the loggerheads with the political establishment of those days. To the extent that we had to be arrested, we had to be beaten up by the police. But of course we had to mobilise our people.

So by the beginning of 1963 I attempted to leave Namibia to go into exile because many of my peers had by that time left Namibia, went abroad, first particularly to Tanganyika which became the United Republic of Tanzania later on. Others got scholarships from Tanzania and went to study abroad to continents such as America, Europe and of course the rest were spread throughout a few independent African states those days. But I was arrested in the North-Eastern part of Namibia as I attempted to escape and I was in prison for three months. I went to court accused of wanting to escape from the country. That issue I purposely denied since my objectives were to go abroad to study and indeed to join others in the struggle for freedom of this country. At

education from the socialist countries we can ask arms. When it came to the west, we knew the question of requesting arms that was out, but we could ask for scholarships and financial assistance. So we then said if that continues, we get scholarships and arms from the socialist countries, scholarships and financial assistance and other political support from both of them wherever possible depending now what is the issue at stake. We were really comfortable with that.

I think the positions that were drawn there we realised them too, that countries had to take their positions and it is very difficult when you are sovereign. Sometimes people think it's easy, but it's not. There are state matters that we have to deal with, that are very concrete, very evident, that even if you want to, you can't do otherwise. So I think those issues made us understand that obviously even if we might like to get so many things from our friends, there is a limit. We understood that.

Of course we condemned, we did condemn any relationship that there were between the West and our colonisers, we did condemn when those relationships were economic relationships, or military relationships or perhaps financial relationships in terms of trade. Those were condemned by us, but they did not go so far that, for instance, as cutting off the contact with them. There were always ways and means of continuing talking to these people.

IS: So about the scholarship programme which was started in 1976 by the Finnish government and administered by the church. Did the idea come from SWAPO? Was it SWAPO who put it to the government?

NI: I have to be honest with you, I don't know whether it was SWAPO who requested, or it was Finland that requested it. I really have to look into the research papers to see what went on, but let me put it this way, that the idea of establishing the UN Institute for Namibia to educate Namibia and to prepare Namibians for the future administration of their country really came from Finland, because it was proposed in the UN and all of the UN organs then agreed to it. So I can't now remember the additional preparation apart from financing the Institute and Finland taking part in that institute as far as the senate is concerned. Perhaps that prompted Finland to discuss the possibility of taking up more young Namibians to study in Finland in 1976. But sufficient in any case is to say that scholarships were funded by the Finnish government, and money was given to the missions to administer these scholarships.

IS: I discussed this with Mr Karanko when I did an interview. And then also with Mr Yrjö Höysniemi from the church.

NI: What did they say?

IS: They said that there had been discussions with some SWAPO representatives and it came up as a common idea, because at that time SWAPO was very much requesting the scholarships, partly because the church had already given scholarships. And now SWAPO wanted to have a full programme, which would be financed by the state. And by that time in 1973 the Finnish government decided that they could give humanitarian aid for liberation movements, starting with FRELIMO. So then it was kind of a good idea, a good way to use this humanitarian aid. But then Mr Karanko himself said that, because the government, or the Foreign Ministry didn't want to get involved in administering the programme, they asked the church, the church's foreign aid to do it for them. Because they already had some experience about this. And also because this old missionary was very familiar with the young Namibians, and could assist. So he himself came to Lusaka to select the students.

NI: I would agree with that assessment. Most probably during that time the contact between Finland and Namibians really got increased because even the missionaries that were then in Namibia were getting involved. I remember the late Mikko Ihamäki, who was also asked to leave Namibia—actually who went to Finland and was not allowed to come back—was in fact the one who came to Zambia that time to fetch the first large group of Namibians. There was a positive evolution taking place, the increased contacts between us, members of the liberation movement, and realisation from the Finnish government that it had to increase its participation in humanitarian endeavours Therefore it made the proposal of the UN Institute for Namibia. And at the same time the SWAPO members were getting more attention in the decision of the Finnish government, which was now willing to be directly involved in increasing humanitarian assistance for Namibia in terms of scholarships. Again the Finnish missionaries—when it comes to Namibia culturally or socially—knew it better than anybody else in Finland those days. I think that provided a platform.

IS: And many people said later on that because of Mikko Ihamäki's participation in selecting the first group it was very successful. He even knew many of the families where the young students came from, so he could know what kind of a basic education they had gone through. And then later on he was no longer there to assist, and then also the student groups were specialised, which means they were no longer this general group. But the students started different courses like this Wärtsilä group for technical education and then the nurses and so on. The scholarship programme changed character.

NI: Yes it did to a certain extent, definitely. I agree with your assessment.

IS: There are so many things to discuss, but I am sure that we have covered most of the things. I really thank you for this interview.

www.ingramcontent.com/pod-product-compliance
Lightning Source LLC
Chambersburg PA
CBHW080603170426
43196CB00017B/2884